OPERATIONS RESEARCH SOCIETY
OF AMERICA

Publications in Operations Research

Number 19

PUBLICATIONS IN OPERATIONS RESEARCH

Operations Research Society of America

Editor for Publications in Operations Research

DAVID B. HERTZ

* Out-of-print

THE IMPLEMENTATION OF OPERATIONS RESEARCH

JAN H. B. M. HUYSMANS

WILEY-INTERSCIENCE

A DIVISION OF JOHN WILEY & SONS

New York · London · Sydney · Toronto

Library of Congress Catalog Card Number: 76-120730

ISBN   0-471-42594-X

Printed in the United States of America

10 9 8 7 6 5 4 3 2 1

PREFACE

Twenty-five years after it was recognized as the science of management, there is little doubt that operations research (OR) has earned its place in industry. However, even though individual success stories have helped to gain general acceptance for the "magic new management tool," many operational and organizational barriers still have to be overcome before OR's full potential as an aid to business decision making will be realized. Therefore, the OR practitioner who is concerned about the implementation of his recommendations must not only command the tools of OR analysis, but must also be able to make effective use of the findings of other disciplines, particularly those of the behavioral sciences.

This book describes an approach to OR implementation that focuses on the need to consider the interdependence between social, psychological, and technical aspects of the system under study during all phases of an OR project—from the moment of identifying management's problem and formulating it in OR terms to the point of implementing the recommendations made on the basis of the analysis. It proposes a unified approach in which these aspects are considered *jointly* during an OR study, as opposed to the traditional *sequential* approach which pays attention to behavioral and nontechnical factors affecting implementation only *after* a technical OR solution to management's problem has been found.

We built our approach on the basic OR philosophy of agreeing on objectives, identifying alternative actions by which they can be reached and then determining the kinds and amounts of inputs required to perform each action. Inputs with limited availability constrain the degree to which objectives can be attained. When an OR analyst disregards an input during his analysis and subsequent recommendation to management, he in fact assumes that the input is or can easily be made available to the extent needed. But if his assumption is incorrect, the neglected—but constraining—input will cause problems the moment implementation of the research results is attempted. The input becomes an "implementation constraint" that must be made ineffective if implementation is to result.

The above description applies to *all* types of inputs, including behavioral ones, required to perform a given action. Thus, only when the OR practitioner considers all inputs *jointly*, can he decide (a) what factors can be ignored in the analysis and preparation of recommendations and (b) what action should be taken to prevent these factors from developing into effective implementation constraints.

After defining the problem of OR implementation and illustrating the significant differences in attitude toward this problem that exist within the OR profession, we identify in Chapter 1 as potential implementation constraints some nontechnical factors that an OR practitioner often disregards, but that are part of the total problem he is dealing with. To this end we restate and evaluate some of the more important findings on effecting change in individuals and groups reported in social sciences' literature in terms familiar to the operations researcher. Our survey shows that, even on the theoretical level, the social sciences and the area of technical OR analysis have been too strictly separated. Chapter I closes with the formal statement of a specific implementation problem that we consider in the remainder of this book.

A framework for a theory of implementation built around the approach described in the preceding paragraphs is presented in Chapter 2. Here we focus on the OR analyst and outline alternative strategies he might use to achieve the improvements he has proposed for a given system. To demonstrate our approach we selected the difference in cognitive style—or ways of reasoning—between manager and operations researcher as a potential implementation constraint. A review of a number of successful *and* unsuccessful OR studies led us to this choice, as we explain in Chapter 2.

The hypotheses of this study concern the effectiveness of alternative OR implementation strategies, given the cognitive styles of operations researcher and manager existing in a particular situation. These hypotheses were tested in a laboratory experiment that took the format of a management game. The management problem we formulated in this experiment was such that a particularly strong OR solution to it (at least from a technical point of view) could be derived. Thus, we emphasized the fact that OR implementation is not merely a question of strengthening the tools of OR analysis. Computer-programmed "managers" and a teletype communication system were introduced to ensure that experimental control would be sufficient to demonstrate significance of the experimental results statistically. At the same time, we increased the relevance of these results to implementation problems outside the experiment by imposing human filters between the computer-programmed "managers" and the experimental subject who was made "President" of the firm. Thus, we ensured adequate experimental control without unduly restricting the richness of the experimental environment. These features and other details of the experimental design are described in Chapter 3.

The analysis of experimental results in Chapter 4 shows that (a) effectiveness of the cognitive-style constraint could be anticipated so that the OR specialist in the experiment was able to design his research and implementation strategy in accordance with his findings in this respect, and (b) a significant improvement in implementation could be attained by properly adjusting these strategies. We conclude this chapter with a discussion of validation and present our view on the extent to which our experimental findings can be extended to real-life situations.

In Chapter 5 we compare and relate our experimental findings to some well-known theories and experimental work in the social sciences. In this chapter we return to our general approach to the problem of OR implementation, which, in a sense asks for a revival of the interdisciplinary approach in applying OR. However, bringing the various disciplines together has proven to be a major difficulty in itself. We hope that this book will contribute to a more effective exchange of information between disciplines and will open new roads to accomplishing this objective.

JAN H. B. M. HUYSMANS

Amsterdam, The Netherlands
March 1970

ACKNOWLEDGEMENTS

In addition to the general acknowledgement of indebtedness that I owe to a great many people who have assisted me in various ways while I was writing this book, I would like specifically to thank the following: Professor C. West Churchman for wakening my interest in the problems of implementing operations research recommendations and for providing invaluable guidance during the years that this book was originally written as a doctoral dissertation; Dr. Philburn Ratoosh for his encouragement and comments; and Mrs. Hilda Carmichael, Dr. Erik R. Metz, and Dr. Edward Berman for their assistance in carrying out the experiments reported here. Finally, I would like to thank Dr. David B. Hertz, the editor of this series, for his encouragement during the final preparation of this work.

I am indebted to the following authors and journals for permitting me to quote their publications: R. L. Ackoff and John Wiley & Sons, Inc.; C. West Churchman and Prentice-Hall, Inc.; Cyril C. Hermann and John F. Magee and the Harvard Business Review; Preston P. le Breton and Holt, Rinehart and Winston, Inc.; Alfred J. Marrow and John R. P. French, Jr. and the Journal of Social Issues; Philip M. Morse and the Department of Operations Research, Case Institute of Technology; James G. Miller and John S. Roy and Behavioral Science; Harold F. Smiddy and Management Science; and William I. Spencer and the First National City Bank.

Finally, I thank the editorial and technical support staffs of McKinsey & Company Inc. for their aid in preparing the final drafts of this book. My greatest personal thanks go to my wife Andrée, who not only actively participated in preparing this work but also had the patience to accept the many evenings and weekends devoted to it.

CONTENTS

THE IMPLEMENTATION OF
OPERATIONS RESEARCH

Chapter 1

IMPLEMENTING OPERATIONS RESEARCH: DEFINITIONS AND SCOPE OF THE PROBLEM

1.1. THE IMPLEMENTATION OF OPERATIONS RESEARCH: A PROBLEM?

Opening a study on the implementation of operations research (OR) with this question may seem somewhat academic; however, if the paucity of literature[1] on the subject is any indication, it is by no means clear that its answer is affirmative to everyone. Moreover, a clear statement of the problem area of this study is certainly desirable, given the confusion that exists about the meaning of the term "implementation"—a confusion that is understandable, since even those who explicitly profess concern about OR implementation disagree about the meaning of this term (see, e.g., Stillson [2]).

It therefore seems prudent to start out with a provisional working definition of OR implementation. We will say that an operations research recommendation is implemented if the manager or managers affected by the recommendation adopt the research results in essence and continue to use them as long as the conditions underlying the research apply.

Implementation is obviously a matter of degree. Some modifications of an OR proposal should not be construed as its rejection; they are usually necessary. On the other hand, it should not be a foregone conclusion that implementation has been achieved if the manager's decisions turn out to be the same or very close to the ones proposed by the opera-

---

[1] For example, Batchelor [1] in his annotated bibliography of OR literature does not mention "implementation" in the subject index. The search for literature under related headings, such as "use of" and "management" led to astonishingly few references.

1

tions researcher. This is why the last part of our definition emphasizes adoption "as long as the conditions underlying the research apply." In other words, our definition requires at least some managerial understanding of the research underlying the OR recommendations. Assuming rational management, our definition thus reserves the term implementation for "good" operations research, introduction of which will further management's objectives and lead to a net improvement in the organization's operations. Poor research recommendations can be used, but cannot be implemented.

We can best clarify the objectives and the scope of the present study by delineating its boundaries:

1. Our interest does not focus on the introduction of the OR function as such by a client system. Awareness of OR's existence—although not always known by this name—is fairly widespread. Industrial surveys seem to indicate that the actual introduction of OR activity has been lagging,[2] but these results should not be overemphasized. Traditionally OR has been conducted under many different organizational arrangements—ranging from a centralized staff function to a highly decentralized line-connected function—and under many different names such as operations research, systems analysis, quantitative methods, or computer services. As a consequence OR activity is often not recognized as such.

A series of studies concentrating on the introduction and acceptance of OR in industry has been conducted by Rubinstein, et al. (see, e.g., [5]). These studies highlight the relationship between OR effectiveness, the degree of acceptance of the OR activity, and the variables that determine this degree of acceptance.

The scope of our study is more limited. We will focus on the behavioral characteristics that determine if and how a specific OR proposal will be accepted by management. We will take it as given that the OR function as such has already established itself in the organization. Obviously, successfully introducing an OR function and successfully implementing a specific OR proposal are interdependent. The results of our study should therefore be qualified for and integrated with the findings in a larger framework such as Rubinstein's.

2. Neither are we at this point interested in the shortcomings of OR in

---

[2] For example, a survey held in 1958 by the American Management Association [3] showed that of 631 U.S. companies included in the survey, 57% used OR to some extent; a survey held in 1965 by Oldaker [4] showed that only 39% of 84 surveyed American companies was actively engaged in OR. However, differences in defining the population from which the sample was taken and in defining OR itself preclude a meaningful comparison of these results.

its technical aspects. The extension of methodology and techniques that will allow the operations researcher to cope with more and more complicated problem situations is being studied extensively and forms the main content of the professional OR journals at this time. We will restrict ourselves to the case in which the technical OR function has produced results, for it is only when the research can technically be called "successful" that implementation—as defined above—may arise as a problem.

We can finally return to the question raised at the beginning of this chapter. By now, one might think, the problem of OR implementation— if it exists at all—has been reduced to insignificance owing to the restrictions that we imposed on our subject matter. Some survey results should convert the doubting reader. Schumacher and Smith in their 1965 industrial survey selected 65 companies from *Fortune*'s top 500: 49 of these companies reported having OR activities, but "only 2 companies reported no major problem in the implementation of the OR program." [6]. Even more to the point, an in-depth survey of 25 corporations and five government agencies by McKinsey & Co. in 1962 reports the following findings:

> In conducting this survey, we found that the problems and difficulties in OR programs more than offset the successes—at least thus far . . . . Many companies interviewed had failed to bring their OR projects to successful implementation: *while there is a number of instances of technical success*—an analytical model has been developed—in many cases, OR has not yet had a real impact on how companies plan and make decisions. [7] [Italics are ours.]

The last statement gains still more in significance when one realizes that the McKinsey survey was heavily biased toward oil companies— recognized leaders in the use of OR—and toward companies "which seemed good prospects for OR success stories." [7].

That we are dealing with more than a temporary problem, typical of any new revolutionary change, is supported by a quote from Smiddy's keynote address to the Institute of Management Sciences in 1964:

> 'Precision planning' in competitive business situations is for the birds in my opinion—no matter how scientific the techniques marshalled or how competent the planners are in planning methodologies—if only because the "unknown" in the other fellow's planning can so easily be a more influencing force on actual progress than all the factors so patiently tabulated and calculated in methods-dominated approaches.[8]

We are not yet in a position to evaluate the many proposed remedies to overcome the difficulties in implementing OR. But comments like the one quoted above should make it clear that relatively simple solutions, such as educating management in quantitative techniques in order to adapt the organization to the "new methods," will not be enough.

In the meantime, the uneasy feeling about OR implementation continues to increase as the gap widens between the development and sophistication of OR techniques on the one hand and the managerial use of them on the other.[3] It is our aim to decrease the tension thus created by trying to gain insight into some aspects of the problem of OR implementation. In particular, we will be concerned with the researcher's side of the problem: what strategy should the operations researcher use to maximize the probability that optimal action on his research recommendations will be taken?

1.2. THE ATTITUDE OF THE OPERATIONS RESEARCHER TOWARD THE IMPLEMENTATION OF HIS RECOMMENDATIONS

Many attempts, especially in the 1950's, have been made to specify the objectives, working area, and methods of operations research. Recognizing the diversity of views on this subject, we state the following broad definition of OR's main interest: OR pursues, by using the scientific process of inquiry, the improvement of the operation of organizations. An organization can be defined[4] as a purposeful system with the following characteristics:

1. Some elements in the system are human beings.
2. The responsibility for the choice of acts is divided.
3. The elements in the system are interacting through communication or observation.
4. A control function, which compares achieved with desired outcomes, exists as part of the system.

Morse emphasizes the significance of the human element as part of the system that OR considers when he describes the evolvement of OR from the physical sciences and notes the difference:

> In OR it isn't possible to shut the worker off in his laboratory and forget about him until he is done. The thing he is studying is, in part, the organization itself and the executive, in a way, is part of the experiment [11].

---

[3] See, for example, Turban [9] on the use of maintenance models in industry.
[4] See, for example, Ackoff [10, Chapter 1, pp. 11–12].

A summary report of I.E. symposia sponsored by the American Institute of Industrial Engineers in 1961 confirms these views: the industrial engineer is distinguished from other engineers by his emphasis on the integration of the human being into the system and the greater utilization of the social sciences [12].

A logical extension of the above views leads to implementation as the final criterion to measure the success of an OR effort. This conclusion may seem straightforward, but it is certainly not as easily drawn by all in the OR profession. The following two statements are exemplary of the range of actual views:

It has been argued that the researcher is responsible for producing recommendations in applied research and that he must also assume responsibility for and leadership in carrying out these recommendations if they are accepted [13].

Professional personnel in OR strongly emphasize this distinction between the OR responsibility for analysis and the executive responsibility for decision [14][5].

There are several reasons why OR practitioners have often given no more than casual attention to the implementation of their research findings.

One can readily point out that the use of implementation as the criterion for measuring the success of an OR effort is not feasible operationally because of the problem of adequately measuring OR effectiveness. But, as these and the following pages should make clear, we simply cannot take the luxury of using this argument as an excuse to dismiss the implementation problem or even to diminish its importance. We can only call for more effort that will help to deal more effectively with the problems of measurement. Proponents of the implementation criterion have done so repeatedly,[6] making it clear that no simple solution to this problem exists.

Equally serious problems stem from the consideration of the human element as part of the system to be improved. This is the question we have chosen to address in more detail in this study. Explicit recognition of the human element still leaves the operations reasearcher with the question how and when he should include this element in his approach to a problem. Conceivably, "human constraints" could be built into an OR model in much the same way that technological constraints are handled. However,

[5] A conceptual framework for categorizing the relationships between researcher and manager and the support each of these positions has received in the literature is described by Churchman and Schainblatt [15].

[6] See, e.g., Malcolm [16].

human constraints elude the formal treatment given to technological constraints: the "black box," which should excuse the OR practitioner from considering the psychological or sociological mechanism by which a human being or group converts input into output, fails to deliver the required set of technological coefficients in this case.

"Look into the black box" is essentially the proposal of those who support the "clinical" approach as opposed to the "engineering" approach in OR.[7] If the system includes the manager, the operations researcher should include the manager in his diagnosis of the problem situation. Hence, he should not accept the manager's statement of his problems without close examination. Indeed, this is the only stand one can take in view of the chosen criterion for successful OR performance. The level of inquiry—or what can and what cannot be considered a "black box"—is no longer an arbitrary choice once one has stated one's objectives!

The actual position taken by many in the OR profession has not been to look into the black box but to forget about the "human production function" altogether. As a prominent OR scientist once stated to us: "By concentrating on the advancement of technical OR knowledge, we should get the people out of the system and thereby eliminate all problems of OR implementation." This attitude is encouraged by a parallel development: a fast-growing body of OR techniques provides an area of satisfaction (and recognition!) in itself. The growing demand for specialized knowledge puts extra strains on the OR practitioner and drives him in the direction of the natural scientist, who is hardly concerned about the implementation of his research findings. The OR engineer thus becomes more and more an OR scientist (cf. Lerner [18]). He should realize that this happens at the price of giving up, at least in part, his original objectives.

We doubt that the tremendous "pure" research effort in OR—whatever its contribution to science as wisdom—has paid off in terms of an "improved operation of the system" (cf. Turban [8]). While OR was finding its place in the American university, it became totally preoccupied with the intriguing features of its mathematical models. Ultimately, this should benefit the efficient operation of systems. This development has not been accompanied, however, by an equal interest in the advancement of a theory of system design on the one hand and a theory of implementation on the other. The OR *practitioner* is not free to choose to deal with only one of these three aspects of his problems. His "product," unlike, for example, a compound newly synthesized by an industrial chemical

---

[7] See for example, Gouldner [17]. We realize that our interpretation of the "clinical" approach (see text) goes further than some supporters of this view have in mind where they urge the researcher to find out the manager's "real" ends rather than taking his statement of these ends as given.

researcher, cannot be handed over to a production or marketing organization so that he can return to his "laboratory."

The social scientists Katz and Kahn have drawn their conclusion from the factual imbalance they observed in the development of OR. They equate OR with "satisficing," and see it as concerned solely with the improvement of technical operations [19]. "Systemic research," in their terminology, refers to the study of the total system and the interaction of subsystems; but this is exactly what OR set out to do! To give up this goal not only understates OR's potential, but threatens its viability.

The new function of "implementation agent,"[8] who would bridge the gap between the manager and the purely technical operations researcher, has been proposed as a way out of the OR practitioner's dilemma. (See, e.g., Breton [20], or Mann and Neff [21].) The implementation agent assists the managers directly responsible for a change in accomplishing their task. The agent, being separated from the direct management of the functions affected by the research recommendations, should be able to follow a project in all its aspects and their interrelationships, cutting through established barriers in the organizational structure wherever necessary. But to do this, his function must be strictly advisory, and to be effective as an advisor the need for his assistance should be discovered by the manager who carries the implementation responsibility. The implementation agent's immediate initiative is therefore restricted to signaling misinterpretations or shortcomings of the recommendations, observing developing conflicts and proposing possible remedies, and creating an awareness of his availability for advice. This description of the implementation agent already indicates what personal characteristics will most likely lead to successful performance in this function:

> The change catalyst should probably be an older and accepted member of top management who would be recognized as having organized the product of his years of operating experience in line and staff positions into a useful body of wisdom . . . . The change catalyst's ability to work with people and to help others face and solve problems confronting them would probably also require that he had some years of experience as a staff man, working without the direct sanctioning and rewarding power of a line position, but fully conversant with the use of expert and referent power . . . . [20, p. 56]

Notwithstanding his possible usefulness, the introduction of an implementation agent affects a symptom rather than its causes. The symptom in our case is the observed existence of an implementation gap. The implementation agent might be able to close the gap temporarily by

---

[8] Alternatively called "implementation consultant" [2] or "change catalyst" [21].

seeing to it that the research recommendations are used. To reach the point of *understanding* use of the research recommendations, we may have to delve deeper, as we will see later on.

Ackoff [13] provides us with two additional reasons why implementation should be of *direct* concern to the operations researcher. First of all, OR is never "value free." The manager may not know his values or he may hold incompatible ones, which makes a value-free science inoperational. In addition, "with the development of an adequate technology of problem solving, a solution carries with it the prestige of science and is interpreted as a recommendation whether or not the scientist wishes it to be so considered." (Ackoff [13], p. 407). Second, implementation is often the only real test of the validity of research conclusions and as such should be part of the research.

Hence, we decide to open the black box of the "human production function." It seems only natural to first turn to the social scientists for information about what we will find in it (cf. Creelman and Wallen [22]).

1.3. THEORY, EXPERIMENTS, AND CASE STUDIES IN THE SOCIAL SCIENCES RELEVANT TO A STUDY OF OR IMPLEMENTATION

The new directions that social scientists have taken in the study of initiating, diffusing, and controlling change are most significant to our study. Earlier writings in sociology deal with change mainly as a process of restoring a somehow disturbed equilibrium or as a necessary condition for the existence of an equilibrium (see, e.g., Etzioni [23]). More recently the processes that can decisively change the state of equilibrium itself have been included. A whole range of new questions arise when the framework of nonchange within which change is studied is abandoned.

A useful framework for further discussion is provided by Lewin [24]. Lewin's field theory as a conceptual system (rather than as a theory) allows us to relate to one another the different approaches to change and to highlight similarities and differences in their emphasis on parts of a bigger system. Lewin describes the relationship of the individual to a concrete situation as a field of psychological forces that jointly determine the individual's behavior, that is, the directional outcome of the individual's transactions with his internal and external environment. The individual is an equilibrium-maintaining system, but this notion of equilibrium is dynamic and based on the total situation rather than a fixed framework. What constitutes the field of forces or the "lifespace" for an individual at a certain moment is the totality of facts that influence his behavior. The lifespace thus forms a psychological reality of different dimensions (time, reality, feeling) of which nonpsychological elements can only indirectly, through the individual's perceptions, be a part. The psychological field of forces is more or less differentiated as a cognitive structure of regions, which forms a "tension system": the tensions are created by the counteracting forces and maintained by the negative or positive "valences" of the elements in the psychological field. When the resultant force in the field differs from zero, we have change or "locomotion": either the individual—pursuing equilibrium—will move into the direction of the driving force or a change in cognitive structure equivalent to this locomotion will take place.[9]

Festinger's theory of dissonance elaborates on the notion of an individual as an equilibrium-maintaining system [26]. He considers different sources of dissonance arousal and different means of dissonance reduction and is especially interested in predicting behavior in case the equilibrium has been disturbed. Ample evidence for the validity of his theory has been given. It is hard to see, however, how his theory can be used for the prediction of a *specific* response as a means of dissonance reduction outside controlled situations (see, e.g., Festinger and Aronson [27]).

The condition for change is therefore the disturbance of the equilibrium in the psychological field. This is generally recognized as the existence of a "perceived need" as a condition for change. The field-theoretical formulation indicates that disturbance of the equilibrium is reached by adding or eliminating forces resulting in a system of higher, lower, or equal tension, depending on the type of response. The actual response chosen— locomotion or cognitive change—depends on the interrelation of forces: the relative strength of goals, the attractiveness of activities to reach goals, the probability of reaching goals by a given path, the presence of authoritative pressures, and other forces. The relative importance ascribed to the different forces is mirrored in the existence of different approaches to the process of change, the most important distinction being between the individual-oriented and the group-oriented research (see, e.g., Cartwright and Zander [28]).

The individual-oriented research in social psychology has concentrated on the individual's perceptions of stimuli—that is, disturbances of his equilibrium—and their effect on his attitude toward certain issues. The main hypothesis in the attitude studies is that equilibrium will be maintained between a subset of forces, in particular between the cognitive, affective, and behavioral components of attitude, and that therefore a maintained disturbance of one component will lead to an adjustment of

---

[9] For further review of Lewin's theories see Deutsch (25).

other components to reduce inconsistencies. Support for this hypothesis in specific instances is presented by Hovland and Rosenberg [29]. The order of communications and the organization within each communication have been studied and used to predict specific responses, such as the acceptance of a certain opinion. The findings suggest that the probability that a certain response is chosen by an individual can be increased under certain circumstances by increasing the attractiveness of that response (e.g., need-arousal before presenting information that can satisfy the need) or by adding other stimuli (e.g., the requirement of public commitment to an opinion, a favorable conditioning of the individual toward the communication source by presenting, for him, desirable communications before undesirable ones). (See Hovland [30] and Hovland et al. [31].) The findings of these studies have to be qualified by the fact that in a laboratory setting the presence of forces other than those controlled is often deliberately minimized; for example, in most communication experiments the subjects under study had no prior knowledge of the topic involved (see [30], p. 139).

The increased awareness of the forces at interplay in creating behavior called for their measurement. Measurement techniques are a major contribution of the so-called "interactionists," whose basic hypothesis is that organizational systems are built on the interactional properties of individuals (see Chapple and Sayles [32] and Bales [33]). This point of view and the added diagnostic skill of measurement appears useful in studying organizations (Chapple [34]). The new techniques made it possible to demonstrate that often neglected variables such as "interpersonal competence" form significant constraints on the effective operation of organizations (Argyris [35]). But oversimplifications are likely to appear if the limitations of this point of view are not realized; such is the case, in our opinion, when the implementation of change is made a mechanistic function of the existence of adequate controls, that is, of an adequate interactional system (Sayles [36]).

One of the most successful recent efforts to apply social sciences to the organizational situation deals with the stage of "unfreezing" necessary for bringing about change. The group, called a training group, is used as a medium to increase the awareness of one's own and others' perceptions of expressed behavior (Bradford et al. [37]). The individual learns and tests new behaviors in off-the-job group meetings: he is stimulated to experiment, using feedback on his behavior given to him by the group trainer (Miles [38]). The individual's tendency to rely on a familiar "safe" but not always appropriate behavior pattern is mitigated in the training situation by minimizing the forces of threat, punishment, or criticism that he would normally anticipate in case some chosen nonfamiliar behavior should fail. It is implied that the acquired skill of diagnosing one's own behavior results in greater flexibility and therefore more willingness to consider behavior activities unused till now. The approach leans on the primacy of the rational-level forces to which all other level forces, once recognized as such, can be subdued.

The group as a target of change builds on a rich tradition of experiments and field studies. Experiments have on the one hand demonstrated the dependence of group performance on such variables as communication network, group size, problem characteristics, and perceived status of the group. On the other hand, the study of the processes at work during the operation of a group has unveiled many intermediate variables and processes that determine individual and group behavior: group attractiveness, cohesiveness, and sense of belonging, group norms and conformity, group leaders, and followers (see for reviews, e.g., Kelley et al. [39] and Sprott [40]). The significance of these forces as determinants of the individual's behavior, feelings, and beliefs has led to the suggestion that it might be easier, more effective, or even essential to gain control over the group forces to influence the individual's behavior than to try to influence his behavior in a more direct way (e.g., Cartwright [41] and Lewin [42]). Several field studies used the group approach successfully to bring about change. The Hawthorne studies [43] form the classical example of group processes—viz., morale, friendship—intervening in such "technical" relationships as that between wage incentives and productivity. Another well-known example, the Harwood experiments, shows that internalizing the source of change to a group, that is, by participation in decision making, may bring the group forces into support of the change: "Thus, although a process of guided experiences which are equally his own, a person may be reoriented so that he gradually takes on within himself the attitudes which he would not accept from others." (Marrow and French [44]). Lawrence [45], in his comments on some of the Harwood experiments (Coch and French [46]), emphasizes that it is not the technical change per se but the social change, by which it is accompanied, that is resisted. Social and human considerations became serious obstacles for the implementation of the technical change in Coch and French's "no-participation group." The participation method, in contrast, stressed the continuity of existing social and human relationships. Workers in the "participation group" did not perceive any social change, which explains, according to Lawrence, that no implementation problem developed. Lawrence's explicit recognition of the dual aspects of change, technical and social, is particularly significant in view of the more recent developments in change research that focus on organizations as integrated socio-technical systems (see below).

The relative importance of specific factors that determine the effectiveness of group influencing was tested in Bennett's experiments: her conclusion were that the need to reach a decision and the degree of consensus in the final decision, rather than group discussion or public commitment, are important for its implementation [47].

Special mention should be made here of the Asch experiments (see, e.g., [46]), that, to our knowledge, give the best single illustration of the importance of group pressures for the explanation of individual behavior. Asch's subjects showed a remarkable tendency to conform to a strongly favored judgment in their environment, even if the judgment (controlled by Asch) was obviously wrong. (Industry-wide acceptance of operations research and, even more likely, of computers may be due to a similar "bandwagon effect.")

The importance of the group task—of prime interest to the operations researcher—as a determinant of behavior tends to be neglected in view of the rich complex of group forces whose interactive play is only beginning to be understood. Homans [49] brought task and interactions together in the relationship between his "external" and "internal" systems: the interactions required by the task (the external system) are the source of explanation for the extended interactions (beyond what is required; the internal system) and the resulting group forces. The interdependence of forces on different levels is clarified by his framework and is explained as a system of economic exchanges of cost and reward [50].

The external relations of groups in their organizational setting have had relatively little attention. Mann [51] proposed to take account of the interdependencies of subgroups in a system by the formation of "organizational families." The organizational family would be ideally conditioned for change by presenting it with feedback of survey-results about its own performance and the performance of the greater unit in which it is embedded. The discussion of relevant information at the appropriate levels in terms of immediate experience may reveal possibilities to improve operations (by creating awareness of a need for change), while participation in the analysis and interpretation of the information would motivate the change.

A next step is to look at an organization as a socio-technical system, an idea developed by Trist and his associates at the Tavistock Institute [52]. Recognizing the primacy of technical change as a cultural constraint, they have convincingly argued that the introduction of each technical change should be paralleled by an adaptive social change such that the motivation for efficient performance will remain (Trist [53] and Rice [54]). In other words, technical improvement can only be implemented when some social constraints are respected. The social constraints reflect the findings of experimental and field research: the need for a task that can be meaningfully completed (this may require group rather than individual assignment), control over and responsibility for the activities related to the task, and satisfactory interpersonal relationships with those performing related tasks.

Finally, there exists a rich tradition of innovation studies in which the reference point is taken to be the innovation rather than the organization or individual (Rogers [55]). The usual approach in these studies is to correlate the time of introduction of an innovation (relative to comparable other units) with characteristics of the innovating individual and of his reference groups (such as his family, village, or professional colleagues). The latter have been shown to change with the different stages, from awareness to final complete adoption, of the diffusion-process.

The Change Agent

It is clear that the change agent becomes a new set of forces in the changee's field. In what direction these forces will operate and how they will affect other forces depends on the strategy followed. The foregoing discussion can properly be adapted to include the change agent. The managerial perception of the change agent will be affected by the agent's status, reputation, past performance, and personality. The change agent may be perceived as having direct personal valence, using his expert and referent power as a basis for influencing, or he may influence more indirectly through, for example, the authoritative power of top management. His task is to reach the proper balance between attractiveness and approachability in order to make the situation maximally conducive to the proposed change (Blau [56]).

Conclusion

The findings reported in the social science literature have important implications for the implementation of operations research:

1. A study of the relationships between a manager's stated goals, the environment, and the decision alternatives should be embedded in a study of the organizational and individual managerial values and their interrelationships, that is, the "clinical" rather than the "engineering" approach is required if implementation of the research outcome is to be attained. It is not enough to find the "right" solution; the researcher who aims at implementation of his findings has to come up with the *right* solution to the *relevant* problems.

2. The individual manager cannot be considered in isolation, since interactional activity leads to phenomena that have a life of their own. A class of organizational constraints has been revealed by social scientists

that is usually neglected by operations researchers. The social sciences are only beginning to formulate these constraints, however. A continuous refinement of theories and an increasing rigor in defining terms is taking place in order to deal with the many interactive forces determining action-behavior. Audacious attempts to state "general laws" have until now served only to generate the research that disqualified these laws as being too indiscriminate to be of any practical value. For example, Lund's Law of Primacy in Persuasion has been shown to hold as well as not to hold depending on the values given to other parameters (see Hovland [30, pp. 129–138]). Similarly, the productivity effect of participation in decision making has been qualified for personality characteristics (Vroom [57]). On the other hand, it cannot always be established in what way a described relationship operates. For example, the relationship between group cohesiveness and the group's ability to produce conformity to group standards among its members as studied by Festinger, Schachter, and Back [58] allows different explanations. Do group members conform because they are reluctant to leave or cannot leave the group, or does conformity merely reflect the increased information-sharing through increased communications in highly cohesive groups? (See Kelley and Thibaut [39, p. 675].)

3. Change is an integral part of an organization; the perceived forces that determine behavior are continuously changing. However, our interest is not so much in change per se as in the direction and mode of change, that is, in *specific* responses to equilibrium disturbances. In most studies encountered the proposed technological change was a "given" for the social scientist. This explains why social science research concentrates on what is misleadingly called "resistance to change": the resistance to adopting a specific response—the change proposal—has been studied not so much in terms of the elementary environmental forces that gave rise to it, but solely in terms of the individual and group variables mentioned above. Manipulation of these variables leads then to more or less mechanical relationships that demonstrate ways to make behavior conform to the change proposal. "Principles" for effecting change merely describe the relevant variables and processes to reach this conformity (e.g., Ginzberg and Reilley [59]).

To be more explicit, operations research—as we defined the profession—claims that its proposals (which often imply change) are a direct response to the elementary requirements of a decision-making situation that will improve the total operation of an organization. Our review of the change literature reveals that social scientists have taken an interest in the OR proposal as a proposal for change, but that they leave its claims of improvement unchallenged or even undiscussed. This attitude implies a silent assumption that an organization's total operation can be decomposed into two functions, a technical and a social function, that are to a large extent independent. Even the emphasis on the interrelationships between behavioral variables and the *end product* of the technical function has helped to condeal the fact that also the *creation* of the end product —e.g., by the operations researcher as part of the technical function—is, or should be, affected by these interdependencies.

To say that the usual social science approach is therefore irrelevant is as unfair as to say that the study of individual characteristics, without taking group determinants of behavior into account, has not taught us anything. It is by systematic exploration of a restricted topic that science progresses. However, the choice of a specific, restrictive point of view should be based on the problem to be considered: "Planned change" and operations research as a technical specialty have been distinguished (Bennis [60]), but implementation requires that they be brought together. What we propose to do is to compare specific aspects of the origin and processes of managerial behavior with the origin and processes by which an operations research proposal comes into existence. Thus we would like to bridge the gap between social scientist and technical operations researcher that underlies the gap between scientist and manager.

1.4. THEORY, EXPERIMENTS, AND CASE STUDIES ON THE IMPLEMENTATION OF OPERATIONS RESEARCH

Several case studies on the implementation of OR are reported in the literature. We will discuss some of the successes and failures and see what the interested practitioners themselves have to say about the causes of success or failure and what can be done about them.

1. *Successes in OR implementation.* Vazsonyi [61] reports the successful introduction of new decision rules, derived with OR methods, that increased production control. He points out that at the time of starting the work, there was a widespread desire on the part of management for improvements in production control and the feeling that it was possible to do better. Apparently the researcher's analysis formed a readily accepted extension of management's thinking. The McKinsey report mentioned earlier [7] comes to a similar conclusion in explaining the impressive success of OR approaches in the refining function of the oil industry: OR formed a logical extension of the analytical calculations that refinery engineers had made for many years and OR found, therefore,

a sympathetic and understanding management. Ackoff [62] reports that of 48 technically successful projects undertaken by the OR group at Case, only one remained completely unimplemented: in this case an organizational change in management took place. The importance of a stable top management that from the outset takes a serious interest in the OR effort is underscored by the reasons Ackoff mentions for partial nonimplementation in 8 other cases: A reorganization of management, the lack of involvement of a high enough level of management, the use of research for the manager's personal rather than organizational objectives, and economic pressures that led to abandonment of the study. The need to deal with the highest executive and with corresponding authority is also mentioned in a successfully implemented cargo containerization study for a shipping line (Weldon [63]). Weldon in particular emphasizes the importance of "selling" to convince management that the OR recommendations rest on an adequate consideration of all important factors that affect the decisions involved. It should be noted, however, that containerization was equally supported by the engineering department of the firm.

2. *Failures in OR implementation.* The failure to introduce sampling methods for the interaccount clearing system of railroads—which would have led to big savings—is reported by Churchman (64). Middle management was used to thinking in terms of percentage error and did not want to accept sampling for smaller populations for which the percentage error, but not the dollar error, increased.

A boxcar information system, designed to optimize the operation of boxcars for a railroad, showed potential savings of $5 million per year, but was abandoned two years after its introduction (Hicks [65]). The system itself was not the cause of the failure, however. Insufficient communication with middle management, which had arrived at its position through experience rather than formal training and was already suspicious of quantitative methods and research, created a climate of distrust and uncertainty. A lack of understanding of the new system also led to a continued one-sided policing of those instances in which shortages required the overworking of facilities, whereas surpluses (which did not result in immediate stress situations) were overlooked.

We note that in the two last examples lack of understanding was the major reason for OR failure. Turning once more to the literature, we find numerous determinants of OR implementation described and stressed to varying degrees. Miller and Starr [66] emphasize the characteristics of the research proposal as determining the "degree of belief" on the part of management. On the one hand, there is the degree to which the strategy and tactics of a proposal have been specified, the degree of certainty of the anticipated outcome, and the corresponding degree of control over the outcome. On the other hand, there is the degree of commitment that is required for implementation, which differs for repetitive and nonrepetitive solutions, the degree of reversibility of a procedure once introduced, and the degree of permanence of the solution proposal. Ackoff [62] emphasizes the relationship of the operations researcher to the manager. The operations researcher should communicate directly with the authority capable of controlling all functions involved in his research. The manager, on the other hand, should be committed to pay sufficient attention to the operations research proposal by making the research available only at a cost. However, the conditions under which research is performed are not always under the researcher's control to the extent required by Ackoff's proposal (see, e.g., Stimson [67]).

Top-management support for the researcher is often isolated as the critical factor by the OR profession, and it is often implied that implementation will follow automatically if the researcher is adequately backed by top management's authority. In view of the discussion in the foregoing section on the field of forces that determine managerial behavior, this view is at least naive. In the case studies we described above, implementation did not take place *despite* top management's support.

Being aware of the multidimensionality of the problem of implementation, we note that a recurring theme—as illustrated by the cases mentioned above—is the way of thinking and understanding on the part of management. Implementation appears to have been most successful in environments that are "in tune" with the analytical OR approach long before the operations researcher appeared on the scene. Miller and Starr seem to have this in mind when they say that the manager's "belief will further depend upon the extent to which the decision criterion expresses his intuition and attitudes" ([66, p. 419]). Churchman [68] points to the aspect of understanding in order to explain why information together with analysis do not yet imply implementation. Understanding is also the basis for distinguishing four basic attitudes with respect to the manager-researcher relationship by Churchman and Schainblatt [15]. As a conclusion to his study, Rogers [55] attempts to give an outline of a "theory of diffusion and adoption of innovations." His "generalizations," indicate what is to be the body of his theory and leave no doubt about the central role of perception, the key dimension of understanding.[10]

---

[10] An example of Rogers' generalizations: "The relative advantage of a new idea, as perceived by members of a social system, affects its rate of adoption."

The small group experiments by Churchman and Ratoosh [69,70] are explicitly designed to test implementation behavior. Since this study is a direct outgrowth of the Churchman-Ratoosh experiments, they deserve more attention.[11] The most remarkable result of these experiments has been that implementation—defined to be understanding, not merely acceptance of the research proposal—was so seldom reached. Although afterward the subjects often blamed the poor communications system (written messages) for their poor performance, performance was no better when face-to-face meetings were introduced between decision periods. The introduction of *more* restrictive communications did result in more expressions of concern about the underlying causal relationships of the firm's problem, but did not result in an earlier or more complete adoption of the optimal solution presented by a confederate. The mode of presentation of the optimal solution as well as the role and status of the confederate were varied in many ways. Experimental evidence gave clearest support to "sociometric status" as a variable that directly affects the implementation of the optimal solution. (In this series of experiments the choice of the confederates was based on a sociometric network derived from a questionnaire given to the subjects after a meeting that preceded the main experiment.) A strongly "chosen" confederate appeared to have fewer problems than a strongly "underchosen" confederate in getting the optimal solution adopted by his fellow team members.[12]

The Churchman-Ratoosh experiments explored a much wider range of variables than we have mentioned above. Although several variables could be identified as affecting the implementation process, no manageable set of critical "control" variables (except at their extreme values) could be located. The whole gamut of individual and group phenomena, discussed in the previous section, became an inextricable whole. The standard answer to such a problem has been to tighten experimental controls, which at some point *inescapably* leads to clear results in the form of cause–effect relationships. There is no doubt that these relationships are worth studying. However, to decide *in what direction* control ought to be increased is to decide the implementation problem at the outset. It would mean to equate a study of implementation with a study of leadership, of conformity, of influence, or whatever aspect one chooses to consider.

---

[11] The author worked as a research assistant on the Churchman-Ratoosh project during 1964–1966. The C.R. experiments have the format of a business game in which the firm's problem has a strong OR solution. The solution covers the complete activities of the firm and adoption of the solution therefore requires a coordinative effort of all managers. The behavior of a group of subjects with respect to the optimal OR solution is tested by having one team member, a confederate, present the solution to his colleagues after a number of experimental periods.

[12] This series of experiments was conducted by J. Mueller [71].

Churchman and Ratoosh chose not to focus on some specific aspects, but to continue their exploratory effort. Elsewhere [72], Churchman gives an explicit justification for this approach. Talking about solipsism, he states: "The implied strategy is one of starting with simple, well-defined problems and working up to complicated ones, but how can one know which simple problems provide the correct starting points without having some idea of the nature of complicated problems and their solutions?" ([70, p. 248]).

Conclusion

Human problem-solving behavior has been looked at from many different angles. The different approaches we have discussed in this and the

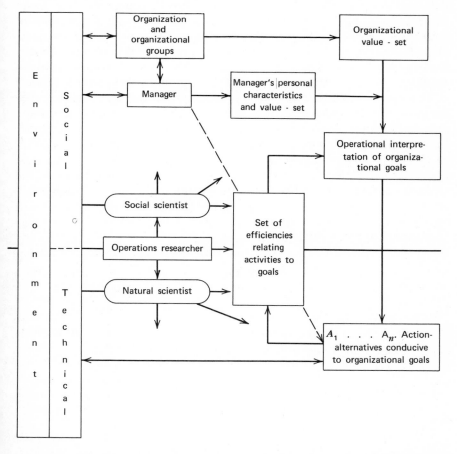

Figure 1   The OR worker's interest in organizations should cover social *and* technical aspects.

foregoing section are reflected by alternative selections of arcs and nodes in Figure 1. The solid horizontal line separates the areas of interest to the natural and social scientist, respectively. The operations researcher has often chosen to align himself with the natural scientist, who is primarily interested in the discovery and exploration of technological relationships and whose goal is to provide the manager with action-alternatives of ever-increasing technical efficiency relative to the manager's objectives.

We have argued that, in order to improve the operation of an organization, the operations researcher's proper place is on the dividing line that separates social and technical disciplines. He should be an expert in properly balancing his attention between all links in Figure 1. Emphasis on improving the strength of one of the links, for example, between manager and organization as in the T-group, between manager and environment by providing information, or between manager and a chosen set of actions by persuasion, may be the appropriate approach in a given situation. The operations researcher should have no a priori preference for any of these "solutions," however. In fact, the OR method—seen as a way of thinking—is eminently suited to guide him in any particular situation.

The operations researcher should realize that the OR method itself becomes a new variable in the system which may cause inadequate managerial understanding of the OR recommendations. By "understanding" we mean the process by which the decision-maker knows why his method of decision-making is correct (cf. Churchman [68]); as we have seen, the nature of most OR recommendations is such that managerial understanding is essential to obtain full value from their adoption.

1.5. A FORMAL STATEMENT OF THE IMPLEMENTATION PROBLEM

To formalize our statement of the implementation problem that we have chosen to consider, we introduce the following symbols:

V = the "true" set of values of the organization. This is an "ideal" set, which actually only exists through the perceptions of the members of the organization.

V_M = manager's perceived organizational value set[13]

V_R = researcher's perceived organizational value set

A = action set. A forms the set of all possible actions that may contribute to realization of the organization's values.

---

[13] The term "manager" represents the whole decision-making structure with respect to the problem at hand. In reality this is usually a part of middle or top management, consisting of one or more managers.

A^t = specific subset of actions chosen at time t.

A_R = action strategy proposed by the researcher.

$A_R{}^t$ = Specific subset of actions proposed by the researcher at time t.

A_M = action strategy currently adopted by the manager.

$A_M{}^t$ = actual subset of actions taken by the manager at time t.

$\bar{V}_R$ = expected degree of realization of the researcher's value set V_R, when A_R is followed

$\bar{V}_M$ = expected degree of realization of the manager's value set V_M, when A_M is followed

C_R = expected cost of applying A_R.

C_M = expected cost of applying A_M.

T_{MR} = transition cost of switching from A_M to A_R.

E = the organizational environment, that is, the set of constraints under which the organization is operating. Four subsets of E can be distinguished:

$E_1 = T_1(A)$ = technological constraints considered by the operations researcher in the model upon which his recommendations are based. T_1 can be interpreted as a known matrix of technological coefficients that transforms the action space into the constraint space.

$E_2 = T_2(A)$ = technological constraints not considered by the operations researcher. The transformation matrix T_2 will usually not be explicitly known.

$E_3 = H_1(A)$ = psychological, socio-environmental, and political constraints considered by the operations researcher in the model upon which his recommendations are based. Similar to T_1, H_1 can be interpreted as a known transformation function that takes the action space into the constraint space.

$E_4 = H_2(A)$ = psychological, socio-environmental, and political constraints not considered by the operations researcher. H_2 is an unknown or not exactly known transformation function that takes the action space into the constraint space.

Thus we have:

$E = \{E_1, E_2, E_3, E_4\}$ and

$E = E(t)$, that is, the values of the environmental constraints may change over time. Only the changes that are beyond the control of manager or researcher are included here.

The following relationships exist among the above variables:

$$A_R = f_1(E_1, E_3, V_R)$$
$$\bar{V}_R = f_2(A_R, E)$$
$$A_M = f_3(E, V_M)$$
$$\bar{V}_M = f_4(A_M, E)$$

These functions should be interpreted as being observed by a neutral outside observer. They will not always be realized explicitly by the individuals involved.

Finally, we have:

$$T_{MR} = f_5(A, E_2, E_4).$$

The transition cost includes the opportunity cost that may result from foregone actions as well as the cost of relaxation of the constraints E_2 and E_4, which the research recommendations require.

The implementation problem that we will consider in the remainder of this study exists if the following conditions are fulfilled:

1. The set of constraints $E_2 = T_2(A)$ is an empty set; or these constraints are not effective.
2. $A_R = f_1(E_1, E_3, V_R)$ is a well-defined function, that is, for all possible combinations of E_1, E_3, and V_R and for all t we can determine $A_R{}^t$ from f_1.
3. $V_R \sim V_M$, that is, manager and researcher are working on the same premises.
4. $\bar{V}_R - C_R - T_{MR} > \bar{V}_M - C_M$
5. The set of constraints $E_4 = H_2(A)$ is nonempty and contains some constraints that are effective.

The conditions stated above are sufficient but not necessary for the existence of an implementation problem. Abandonment of the third condition ($V_R \sim V_M$) would open up an area of implementation problems that are perhaps far more interesting than the one we will consider here. However, the problem to which we restrict ourselves seems a good starting point to attack this field of study. The problem we have defined is not only a real one—it also forms the most immediate extension of the OR function as it is currently interpreted by many (see Section 1.2). It allows us to bring to bear upon it the bodies of knowledge of two separated disciplines. And finally, the approach that we will develop here may prove useful in a further exploration of less manageable problems in this area such as the ones we mentioned above.

The first two conditions state the requirement of the *technical adequacy* of the research. Any technological constraints that were not or could not be handled by the researcher should not have any remarkable effect on the research proposal, if considered. Also the research proposal must have been made explicit for the present situation in concrete actions that are sufficiently spelled out to be usable by the manager. The third condition states that the research should be *relevant;* that is, the manager's and the researcher's perceptions of the organizational objectives should be sufficiently close. This really means that the researcher has used the "clinical" rather than the "engineering" approach in his research. This does not exclude the case in which the manager's personal and the organizational objectives conflict, which would be considered an effective constraint of E_4. The fourth condition requires that the research recommendation is *superior* to the manager's present policy, even if the transition cost is considered. Note that superiority may be based on an increased degree of control (smaller variance) if control itself is valued by the organization. This condition—based on the organizational value system—is therefore broader than requiring superiority of the mathematical "expected outcome."

$\bar{V}$ and C form a stream of discounted revenues and costs. The transition cost T_{MR} may consist of, for example, the cost of eliminating, reschooling, or reallocating personnel. In general, the transition cost includes the costs of relaxing those constraints that were not considered by the researcher and that therefore may not be effective, since this would make the research recommendation infeasible. Moreover, the transition cost should include the opportunity cost of any foregone actions, which generalizes the superiority conditions to policies other than the one currently used by the manager. It should be realized that the division between objectives, constraints, and transition cost factors is a matter of choice: objectives could be formulated as constraints, but have been singled out for optimization because of their particular importance with respect to the value set; transition cost factors are constraints not directly considered in the researcher's model and whose relaxation is therefore required in order to make the research proposal feasible. In other words, the transition cost is the cost of relaxing unconsidered constraints (= 0 if the constraints are ineffective). The last condition merely states that there should be a remaining problem, which we then call an *implementation problem.*

Full implementation is reached when $A_M = A_R$. In this case the manager adopts the research proposal and $A_R = f_1(E_1, E_3, V_R)$ is predictive of the manager's behavior. If $A_M = A_R$, we say that the manager *under-*

stands the research proposal. He properly adapts to changes in the environmental parameters.[14] On the other hand, if $A_M{}^t = A_R{}^t$ for the present t but not necessarily all t, we say that the manager *accepts* the research proposal. Since $A_M = A_R \Rightarrow A_M{}^t = A_R{}^t$ for all t, adoption with understanding implies adoption at all times and corresponds to the limiting case of acceptance. That is, the manager is sensitive toward changes in the parameter values of the environmental constraints and will adjust his actual actions to them as required by the strategy A_R. Conversely, $A_M{}^t = A_R{}^t$ for some $t \not\Rightarrow A_M = A_R$, that is, acceptance does not imply implementation.

The discussion in Sections 1.3 and 1.4 has made it clear that the social scientist has concentrated his effort on formulating and manipulating the constraint sets E_3 and E_4, that is, the psychological and socio-environmental constraints. The natural scientist, on the other hand, has worked on the formulation and manipulation of constraint sets E_1 and E_2, the technological constraints. The operations researcher has mainly used the knowledge of one set—the technical—in formulating the organizational problem. He has given occasional attention to some psychological constraints (constraint set E_3), but this has usually been restricted to those constraints that could be formulated by methods familiar to him, that is, the methods used for technological constraints. (An example is the job-assignment problem, solved by linear programming.) The *de facto* decomposition of the organizational problem in two parts neglects the interdependencies among the constraint sets. Interdependence between two constraints exists if output, that is, furthering of any one of the organization objectives, requires both constraints as input. It is clear, therefore, that many interdependencies among the four distinguished contraint sets exist. Their impact in practical operation is diminished by the sequential attention given to objectives and by so-called satisficing which leaves sufficient slack in organizational constraints to make them ineffective. (See, e.g., Cyert and March [73].)

The researcher who aims at improving the organization's operation has to consider these interdependencies. Social science research has indicated how psychological and sociological constraints can be relaxed, for example, by improved personal relationships, participation of the manager in some aspects of the research, or an improved presentation of the researcher's recommendations. Successful application of these techniques will lead to a more intensive use of the researcher's proposal. To the extent that a distance in the ways of reasoning between manager and

---

[14] Note that our definition of implementation goes beyond the common interpretation of this term. In particular we want the term implementation to include *deviations* from the OR proposal if changes in environmental parameters dictate such deviations.

researcher exists and is disregarded, a more intensive use of the researcher's proposal means merely a higher degree of *acceptance* of the proposal. Acceptance, however, does not imply *understanding* of the proposal and therefore contains no guarantee that the research recommendations will continue to be used. When we state the operations researcher's goal more explicitly as that of bringing about *long-range* improvements in the organization's operations, it is clear that mere acceptance of his recommendations may be very unsatisfactory. Gaining acceptance without gaining understanding leads to organizational instability. The importance of gaining understanding is measured by the degree of instability introduced by mere acceptance of research recommendations. This degree of instability in turn depends on the characteristics of the research proposal, such as the degree of repetitiveness and the sensitivity of the recommendations relative to changing environmental parameters.

Chapter 2

RESEARCH AND RESEARCH IMPLEMENTATION: A FRAMEWORK

2.1. RESEARCH RECOMMENDATIONS AND MANAGERIAL ACTION

In the remainder of this study we will concentrate on the extent to which differences in cognitive style, or a distance in ways of reasoning, between manager and researcher influence implementation behavior. Three questions will be considered:

1. How can we determine or measure the distance in ways of reasoning?
2. Is it possible to predict the distance in ways of reasoning, with respect to some research project, from characteristics of the situation *before* the research is done? If so, what are these characteristics?
3. How can we use this prediction, if at all, to design an implementation strategy for the researcher?

The first and second questions will be dealt with later. The third question is considered in this chapter.

In Section 1.5 we mentioned the ways of reasoning in the case in which the research recommendations are adopted. We stated that if $A_M = A_R$, that is, if the manager's behavior can be predicted by the functional relationship that maps environmental parameters into managerial action, the manager understands the research recommendations. More generally, we will say that managerial understanding of the research recommendation exists if the distance in the way of reasoning between manager and researcher is zero. The larger the distance in ways of reasoning, the less understanding there exists. Understanding can only be equated to the condition $A_M = A_R$ if the research is adequate, relevant, and superior to present managerial practice. These were the conditions we stated for the

26

existence of an implementation problem. Managerial understanding can therefore result in rejection of the research recommendations if these conditions are not satisfied. On the other hand, if no understanding exists, that is, if the distance in the ways of reasoning between manager and researcher is large, the conditions for the existence of an implementation problem can be satisfied regardless of the managerial action.

The possible behavioral reaction of the manager to the research recommendations as a function of managerial understanding can be classified in one of four categories:

1. Rational Rejection

The manager understands the research recommendations, but rejects them on rational grounds. The research may be inadequate, irrelevant, or not superior to present practice (transition cost considered). Irrelevance of the research often takes the form of an improper consideration of a subsystem of the total system. That is, the wrong constraints have been singled out for optimization in view of the total organizational value set. An example of rational rejection is given by Bavelas and Strauss [74]. The operation of a painting department of a toy factory was considerably improved as the result of a research study. The plan was nonetheless abandoned, because of its impact on the bigger system (the factory). Production pile-ups in front of the painting department and vacuums behind it impaired the operation of adjoining departments. As a consequence of the plan, the wage structure in the factory was also upset, which had adverse effects. Hence our first condition for the existence of an implementation problem (see page 22) is not satisfied.

Rational rejection is related to the problem of project selection, that is, the choice of a subsystem to be considered in the research. The problem of project selection is of a higher order than the problem of implementation and is not considered here. It should be realized, however, that the evaluation of potential implementation problems should be an important determinant of project selection.

2. Resistance

The manager rejects the research recommendations and his way of thinking about the research problem deviates considerably from that of the researcher's. Rejection in this case may very well be caused by a lack of managerial understanding. If the research is adequate, relevant, and superior to present management practice there exists an implementation problem. The manager may fail to recognize the advantages of the research recommendation for various reasons. He may not have paid sufficient attention to the research proposal; he may incorrectly evaluate the proposal's return, cost, or transition cost; his personal goals may conflict with and take precedence over organizational objectives; or he may have insufficiently resolved the inconsistencies in his perception of organizational objectives. An example of resistance is the failure to introduce sampling methods for the interaccount clearing system of railroads, mentioned in Section 1.4 [64]. Although middle management recognized net dollar profits as an organizational objective, it had mistakenly— through a long-existing system of interaccount clearing on the basis of percentage errors—operationalized this objective as "to get what other railroads owe us."

3. Acceptance

The manager adopts the research proposal, but does not understand it. Acceptance was discussed before in Section 1.5. An implementation problem exists to the extent that instability is introduced by mere acceptance of the research recommendation. An example of acceptance is the introduction of the boxcar information system by a railroad, mentioned in Section 1.4 [65]. The disproportionate attention given to boxcar shortages compared to surpluses was intuitively sound and in accordance with past practice, but it wiped out the gains expected from the research.

4. Implementation

The manager understands the research proposal and adopts it. It is useful, for reasons that will become clear later, to divide this category into two subcategories:

a) *Sustained Implementation.* Managerial understanding of the research recommendations is integral, that is, the manager has good overall understanding of the critical factors underlying the recommendations, but this understanding is acquired at the cost of continued involvement of the researcher. The manager realizes that changes in environmental parameters may require changes in his actions. He is able to identify the change points, but proper reaction to the changes is only assured if the researcher stands ready to provide his continuous support.

b) *Autonomous Implementation.* Managerial understanding of the research is explicit and complete. No continued support of the researcher is required. Autonomous implementation corresponds to what Kelman calls "internalization" [75]. Adoption occurs because the researcher's proposal is consistent with the manager's perspective and solves a problem for him. The source of the proposal is of minor importance in this case.

An example of sustained implementation is the introduction of a linear programming system for the scheduling of production in different plants of a lumber industry.[15] The proper use and necessary adjustments over time of the system are guaranteed, since the researcher continues to control the running of the programs. To arrive at internalization of the research recommendations, the company started the policy of hiring OR-trained people in the managerial departments rather than expanding the operations research department. Examples of autonomous implementation, referring to the refining function of the oil industry, are given in the report mentioned in Section 1.4 [7].

A summary representation of the manager's action with respect to a research proposal as a function of managerial understanding is given in Figure 2. The introduction of other dimensions of the implementation problem would, of course, result in a further breakdown of the above categories. In Figure 2 the impact of other constraints is reflected by the

[15] Information from private interview.

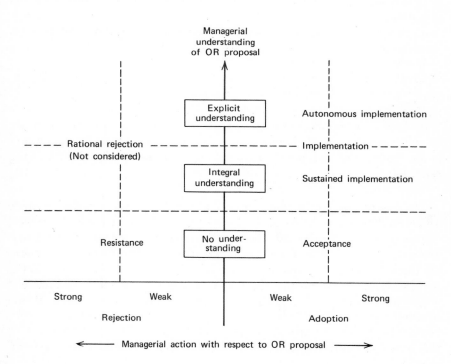

Figure 2

strength of the managerial action. For example, *strong* resistance may be caused by the lack of concordance between the manager's personal and the organizational objectives.

2.2. STRATEGIES OF IMPLEMENTATION: THEORY

In Chapter 1 we have discussed a number of determinants of managerial behavior with respect to a research recommendation. We have seen that the relative importance of different factors has been assessed in many different ways. The emphasis on some behavior determinants usually leads to an undue neglect of other factors, but is sometimes necessary to make progress in scientific understanding of a complex situation. The different aspects that have been considered are:

1. individual factor (e.g., personality, personal values, age, intelligence).
2. organizational factors (e.g., type of organization, organization values, leadership).
3. characteristics of the research proposal (e.g., divisibility, complexity, repetitiveness).
4. characteristics of the researcher (e.g., status, expertise).
5. relationships between these factors (e.g., individual–organizational objectives, research–organization–manager).

A strategy of implementation is a plan that outlines how to take care of those constraints (behavior determinants) that were not taken care of in the research proposal. This definition gives rise to the following remarks:

1. The strategy of implementation is complementary to the research and should therefore be considered at the beginning of a research project. On the one hand, the greater the number of constraints considered in the research proposal, the less of an implementation problem will remain. On the other hand, the fewer the number of constraints considered in the research proposal, the higher the degree of objective realization possible.[16]
2. The strategy of implementation should also be considered at the beginning of a project because some constraints are created by its very beginning. Examples are the location of the researcher with respect to the manager—internal or external to the organization, the degree of

---

[16] Of course, these statements hold only for *effective* constraints.

managerial participation in the research, and the communication links between manager and researcher, which determine his possible use of legitimate, expert, or referent power.

Previously proposed implementation strategies, being mainly the work of social scientists, have usually centered around the problem of relaxing the human constraints that inhibit managerial adoption of a research proposal. Argyris [35] aims to relax the constraint of decreased "interpersonal competence" that inhibits the realization of organization effectiveness. Mann and Neff [21, pp. 61–86] start with the change proposal as given to outline an implementation strategy based on the estimated impact of the change—and the divergence of these estimates among estimators—on each member of the organization. The training group, in separation from the organization or in its more recent form of "organizational family," has often become the instrument by which the relaxation of human constraints is achieved (Bennis [60, pp. 131–166]).

More generally, we conclude that an implementation strategy specifies ways of relaxing those constraints that were neglected in preparing a given research proposal, and that would prevent proper use of the proposal, if not considered at all. There is no obvious reason why only technological constraints should be considered in the research proposal, while human constraints should be left as implementation problems, other than the fact that the researcher does not know how to integrate the human constraints in his research. In fact, if the operations researcher excludes constraints only because he has no techniques to formulate them adequately, his research proposal is likely to be quite irrelevant to the problem it is supposed to solve.

Similarly, the sole concentration on the *relaxation* of human constraints by social scientists implies more than a *de facto* subordination of these constraints to the impersonal and task-oriented values of the organization. It implies subordination *at any cost*. From the OR point of view, a constraint should be relaxed only if the cost of relaxing the constraint is smaller than the shadow price or opportunity cost of the constraint. As a byproduct of finding ways to relax human constraints, the social scientist provides the operations researcher with information on what the costs of relaxation are. If relaxation of human constraints leads directly to the fulfillment of some organizational objectives—as frequently will be the case—the relaxation is partly "paying for itself" and the net cost should be considered. On the other hand, precisely *because* the operations researcher cannot formulate the human constraints in a familiar way, that is, in terms of the basic activities specified in his research, he has a clue to what the joint shadow price of these constraints is. The human constraints, being of a higher order, inhibit the research implementation as a whole and not just the accomplishment of some gainful objectives. The shadow price of these constraints, if found effective, is therefore represented by the net value of the research proposal or a fraction thereof.[17]

In the case that relaxation of some constraint is not gainful (as explained above) or is impossible (i.e., an infinite cost of relaxation makes it unprofitable), the realization of the objectives, as estimated by the research proposal, has to be adjusted in order not to violate this constraint. This means that a different research proposal or different tactics that specify a research and implementation strategy—under which different implementation constraints will be effective—is necessary.

The interdependency of research proposal profitability and implementation cost, that is, the cost of relaxing implementation constraints, is illustrated by Figure 3. The horizontal axis represents the different research proposals relating to a certain problem (or the degree of realization of one research proposal) ranked in order of profitability. At the

[17] We realize that our discussion necessarily leads to value theory. Since this is a large topic in itself, we will not discuss it here. Suffice it to say that, from an OR point of view, a proposal for action implies that operational threshold measures of values can be formulated.

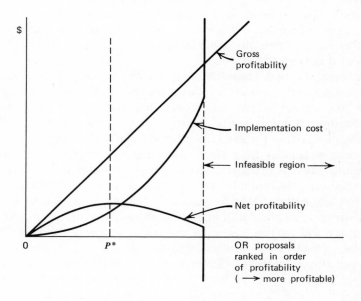

Figure 3   Implementation costs reduce the value of an OR proposal.

origin, 0, all relevant constraints are respected in the research proposal and the degree of realization of the objective is at a minimum. The implementation cost at this point is, of course, zero. Moving to the right, fewer and fewer effective constraints are respected in the research proposal, which means that the proposal's profitability increases. But the implementation cost increases as well, since more and more constraints need to be relaxed before implementation of the proposal can take place. If we consider only *efficient* research proposals—the proposal with lowest implementation cost at a given profitability—the implementation cost curve will be upward sloping. To the extent that more "difficult" implementation constraints have to be dealt with as higher degrees of realization of a research proposal are achieved, the slope of the implementation cost curve will be increasing. Finally, the implementation cost curve will become completely inelastic: some implementation constraints cannot be further relaxed and the remaining degrees of proposal realization are infeasible.[18] Correspondingly, the net profitability of the research project will initially increase, reach a maximum and then decrease until the implementation cost becomes prohibitively high and the net profitability of the project is reduced to zero.

Figure 3 also illustrates what choice should be made between the two possible ways of action: relaxation of implementation constraints or adjustment of the objective function. To the right of the "optimal" research proposal P^* the objective function is adjusted; otherwise the implementation constraints are relaxed. In actual situations the best that can be expected is an interactive process of adjustment of the objective function and relaxation of the implementation constraints, since the functional relationships of Figure 3 are usually unknown. An example of this interactive process is the implementation of the proposal to eliminate no longer needed fire crews from trains. Immediate union opposition formed an implementation constraint with a prohibitively high (infinite) cost of relaxation. Adjustment of the objective function (temporary foregoing of profits) led to another constraint (union opposition over time) with a reasonable cost of relaxation. Both actions took place simultaneously: railroads postponed the elimination of fire crews and worked on the relaxation of the constraint by keeping pressure on unions and providing schemes for reschooling and new employment for the personnel to be eliminated.

What time do we allow a research proposal before we consider it, on the basis of the implementation criterion, unsuccessful? Gross and Ryan

---

[18] An example would be the requirement that top management has to be removed in order to get a certain proposal through.

[76] estimate the duration of a complete adoption process, from awareness through trial to adoption, to be around nine years. A change program proposed by Blake et al. [77] is estimated to take around five years. Bennis ([60, pp. 127–129]) reports on a change program that takes two years. Even recognizing the differences in definition of the beginning and end point of a change process, the various estimates give hardly any indication of what can be considered a proper implementation period. We will not add our estimate, since the question asked above loses its meaning in view of our foregoing discussion. The myth that we can give meaningful content to the "implementation period" is based on the assumption that a research recommendation can be considered as an *isolated, unchangeable* given. As our fire crew example clearly illustrates, the research and implementation proposal are one organic whole; implementation at a later point in time really means to change the research proposal, since it means to consider some added constraints in the research proposal and shift the objective function correspondingly rather than to relax these additional constraints.

Does this mean that a research/implementation proposal can never be unsuccessful? Not necessarily. The postponement of introduction of a recommendation may kill its relevance and make it no longer worthy of consideration. In general, we say that the researcher's abandonment of the *intention* to introduce a research/implementation proposal indicates its failure. Accordingly, the "rediscovery" years later of an old research proposal is considered a new proposal, unless the rediscovery is part of a planned process and occurs more than by chance.

Our view of the research and implementation problem as a continuous dynamic process is in line with modern organization theory which emphasizes cognitive restrictions (applying to manager *and* researcher!) as well as satisficing (e.g., March and Simon [78]). Instead of the illusion of an always optimally behaving system, we consider the potential reality of an optimally adapting system. (Theories of "marginal innovation" that say that innovation is only possible in small steps take a similar point of view.) A schematic flow diagram of this dynamic process is given in Figure 4. The subscript i refers to iteration i: at subsequent iterations, more constraints from the set E_4 are shifted to the set E_3. The process stops when a satisfactory solution, for which the cost of implementation is smaller than the net profit from the project, is found.

If this scheme is to be operational, the researcher has to make a continuous effort during his research to sense ahead of time what constraints of the set E_4 will be effective and what the cost of their relaxation will be. Corrective action in his research, if needed, should be taken before the final recommendations are made.

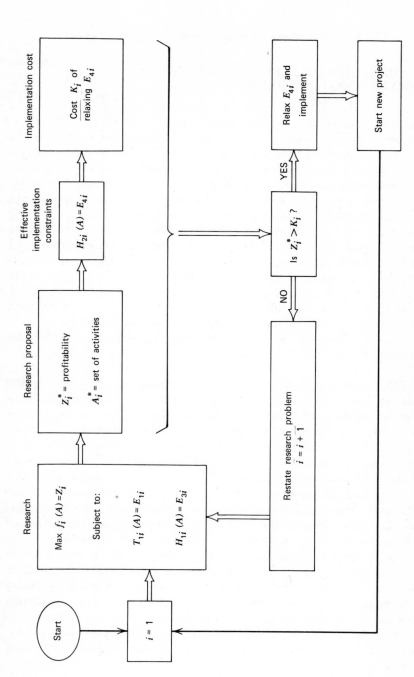

Figure 4 Rearch and implementation strategy are interdependent.

2.3. STRATEGIES OF IMPLEMENTATION:
OPERATIONAL PROBLEMS

Having presented a theoretical framework of research and implementation strategy, the task remains to give operational meaning to the processes described. The level of abstraction in the discussion, in the last section especially, was necessary to enable us to grasp the whole problem with which we are dealing. Going into details necessarily implies limitation to a special case, but with a general theory in hand the approach can be extended to factors other than those to be considered here.

The constraint singled out for further consideration has been labeled before as "the distance in the ways of reasoning between researcher and manager," which, for short, can also be called the "cognitive-style constraint." For the moment we rely on the discussion of the first section of this chapter for an understanding of the meaning of this constraint. A more elaborate discussion follows in the next section and explicit meaning is given to the constraint for a test case, which will be discussed in the next chapter. There are several reasons why we want to consider this constraint in particular:

1. The distance in ways of reasoning is typically an implementation constraint, that is, a constraint of higher order than those usually considered by the operations researcher in his research. The constraint may be recognized by operations researchers as being effective in many cases, but will just as quickly be discarded because of its unmanageability. It is hard to see how this constraint can ever be formulated in terms of input coefficients of individual activities; it is rather the proposal as a whole that is affected. We might attempt to give a formal statement of the constraint in terms of input coefficients proportional to the coefficients of the objective function. But even then a number of as yet unresolved problems remain to which we will refer at the end of this section.

2. The research in the social sciences discussed before has concentrated on finding ways to induce adoption of a research recommendation. But, to the extent that a distance in the ways of reasoning between researcher and manager exists and is disregarded, adoption of a recommendation means merely a higher degree of acceptance of the recommendation. *Implementation* is required to gain long-range improvement in organizational operations if mere *acceptance* implies organizational instability (cf., p. 25).

3. Many of the remarks we found in case studies of OR implementation can be reduced to the effectiveness of this constraint (see Section 2.1).

The questions asked in the beginning of Section 2.1 can now be seen in the proper light. In order to sense ahead of time if the understanding constraint will be effective—a condition we stated at the end of Section 2.2 (p. 34)—the researcher should be able to measure and to predict what the distance in the ways of reasoning will be and of what significance this is for the given project. In case the cognitive style constraint is expected to be effective, the researcher has to consider the cost of relaxation compared to the profitability of the research. Possible ways of relaxing the constraint are:

(a) Educating the manager. It is uncertain to what extent education can affect a person's approach to problems. Also, education may be extremely costly or time consuming.

(b) Introducing understanding by expanding the managerial function. New constraints, that stem from the added power and communication relationships, may become effective this way.

(c) Introducing understanding by replacing the manager. In most cases the cost of this alternative will be prohibitively high, because of its impact on the whole organization through creating an atmosphere of job insecurity.

(d) Attaining sustained implementation, that is, the researcher remains connected to the project in a supervisory function. This alternative introduces the same problems as the second one, and also restricts the capacity of the research function to do other research.

(e) Adapting the research proposal to the manager's way of thinking. This will be possible only to a limited extent lest the value of the research recommendation be lost.

In case the cost of these alternatives exceeds the profitability of the research proposal, the remaining alternative is:

(f) Changing the research proposal so that currently effective implementation constraints, which now prohibit the implementation of the proposal, are no longer violated in the new proposal. This means that rather than relaxing the implementation constraint, it might be more profitable to adjust the realization of the objective function.[19]

The operational problems that arise when applying the research and implementation strategy we have outlined above are problems of measurement, prediction, and control. In particular, the questions to be answered

---

[19] It should be realized that in all the above cases the discounted stream of all expected future revenues of the research proposal is to be compared with the discounted stream of implementation costs.

in any given situation before one can apply the implementation part of the strategy are these:

(a) How does one measure the net profitability of different research proposals or of different degrees of implementation of one research proposal?

(b) How does one measure the extent to which an implementation constraint is effective?

(c) How does one measure the cost of relaxing an implementation constraint?

(d) Can one determine and how does one measure variables that can adequately predict the future effectiveness of an implementation constraint?

(e) Can one devise controls to cope with effective implementation constraints?

In the remainder of this study, we will illustrate the possibility of predicting the effectiveness of the cognitive style constraint as an implementation constraint in an experimental situation. At the same time we will propose two alternative implementation strategies whose successfulness critically depends on the degree to which the cognitive style constraint is effective. Obviously, we can only deal with these questions after having given an adequate answer to the measurement problems that arise.

2.4. THE COGNITIVE-STYLE CONSTRAINT AND THE HYPOTHESES OF THIS STUDY

The hypotheses of this study all deal with the "distance in the ways of reasoning" between manager and researcher, alternatively called the "cognitive style constraint." The following quotation—apart from its conclusion—may help to understand what we mean by the understanding constraint:

> . . . The search for a semblance of certainty can be overpowered by the techniques of search. . . . Today, we have developed a whole range of decision-making methods that are basically mathematical. And because they employ a methodology that is unrelated to common experience, they are beginning to endow planning with all the characteristics of an exclusive cult. The danger, of course, is that findings become uncommunicable to the man who must make the ultimate judgment.
> What we are confronted with is virtually a new language of stochastic processes, minimax, algorithms, heuristics, parameters, models, and simulation, all of which are somehow related to systems analysis. This is simply another name for operations research. . . .

But unfortunately, operations research is becoming a fad. In the process, the admission is beginning to leak out that, regardless of the precision achieved by the new aids and tools, policy decisions still rest fundamentally on intuitions and human judgment. . . .

The decision-making process, in short, must remain with the chief executive. That is why I tend to mistrust the studies that purport to show that small companies don't plan or that the biggest block to planning in the larger companies is the front office. . . . [Spencer [79]].

We can identify two ideal types of "ways of reasoning":

1. Analytic Reasoning.

This type of reasoning reduces problem situations to a core set of underlying causal relationships. All effort is directed toward detecting these relationships and manipulating the decision variables (behavior) in such a manner that some "optimal" equilibrium is reached with respect to the objectives. A more or less explicit model, often stated in quantitative terms, forms the basis for each decision. Factors not included in the model, perhaps because they could not be quantified, are considered only insofar as they may require a significantly different course of action than the one suggested by the model solution. Available alternative courses of action are evaluated primarily in terms of the significance of their deviation from the model proposed course of action. In this study the way of reasoning of the operations researcher is assumed to be the analytic way of reasoning.

2. Heuristic Reasoning.

A person using this type of reasoning emphasizes workable solutions to total problem situations. The search is for analogies with familiar, solved problems rather than for a system of underlying causal relationships, which is often thought illusory. Common sense, intuition, and unquantified "feelings" of future developments play an important role to the extent that heuristic reasoning considers the totality of the situation as an organic whole rather than as a structure built up from clearly identifiable parts. It is extremely difficult, if not impossible, to uncover the mechanisms at work that lead to a decision under heuristic reasoning. If one had to characterize the resulting decision, however, it would be by consistency of the decision with its internal and external environment as opposed to the optimality orientation of the decision of an analytic reasoner.

As stated, these two ways of reasoning should be interpreted as ideal types. We clearly deal with a continuum of which the ideal types form the extremes. It would be a gross oversimplification to assume that people take a fixed place on this continuum, even apart from the question whether we are or are not able to locate this position. Factors such as time, intelligence, education, type of problem dealt with, relevance of the problem, and deadlines for solving the problem—all play a role in determining what approach a person might use in any particular situation. Our characterization attempts to classify people—in point, managers—according to their *tendency*, other things being equal, to use one or the other approach in a decision-making situation.

We arrived at the cognitive style constraint as an interesting variable for further study of the implementation process from our evaluation of numerous histories of actual OR studies. It is important to note, however, that the distinction we proposed between the two ways of reasoning has its parallels in the psychological literature. Tyler [80, p. 221] relates how individual differences in perceptual characteristics were already a subject of study in the 19th century. Interest in this topic slackened during the first half of this century, when psychologists turned, en masse, to general intelligence studies and to the development of intelligence tests. More pertinent to our discussion is the increased activity that recently developed in the research on cognitive styles. (See for a summary of present positions: Messick and Ross [81].) Witkin et al. [82] distinguish between field-dependent and field-independent subjects with regard to the ability to keep an item separate from a field or embedding context and make a corresponding distinction between global and analytic styles of functioning. It was shown on several occasions [81, ch. 10, pp. 171–181] that this distinction is not specific to perceptual situations, but extends to intellectual functioning as well. Studies by members of the "Perception Project" at the Menninger Foundation have further identified variables that act as cognitive controls of response behavior (in particular: scanning, field articulation, and leveling-sharpening) and have demonstrated the close relationship between these variables and the field dependence–independence distinction of the Witkin group [81, ch. 11, pp. 183–198].

The experiments by Roy and Miller [83] confirm the existence of fundamental differences in the approach to a completely deterministic but complex problem-solving task. Their ". . . analysis showed a consistent pattern of difference between Ph.D. level individuals trained in the natural sciences and those trained in the social sciences or humanities. These differences were such as to generate less redundant[20] performances by those trained in the natural sciences, although those trained in the

---

[20] The writers define redundancy as the ratio of inferable questions to the total number of questions asked (information gathered). An inferable question is defined as a question whose answer could be derived from the already available explicit or implicit information.

social sciences on the average reached solutions faster." Roy and Miller's conclusion that the time needed to solve a problem might therefore not be as good a measure of performance as the measure of redundancy that they proposed is of course inspired by the writers' own bias toward analytic reasoning.

We should be cautious in comparing our proposed distinction between "ways of reasoning" with the various dichotomous characterizations of individuals in other studies, some of which are mentioned above. As Wallach points out [81, pp. 208–211], the analytical-global (or field dependence–independence) construct is not refined enough and hence allows different interpretations (e.g., conceptual versus perceptual field independence), which in turn lead to sometimes baffling inconsistencies when different test results are compared. At this point we want to emphasize that our measure for distinguishing individuals according to their reasoning style will concentrate on the individual's attitudes and preferences. His actual reasoning behavior may be expected to coincide with his preferences, although not necessarily so, as we will see when we discuss our classification procedure in the next chapter. The importance of the above studies to us is that they have clearly demonstrated the consistency over different tasks and the stability over time of various characterizations similar to the one we propose here. The main hypothesis of our study is based on this consistency and stability assumption.

We conclude this section with a general statement of our hypotheses. A more precise statement in the context of the testing situation will be given in the next chapter.

Hypothesis I. If the researcher attempts to create explicit and complete understanding of his research on the part of the manager, autonomous implementation will follow if the manager's way of reasoning is analytical, but strong resistance will follow if the manager's way of reasoning is heuristic.

Hypothesis II. If the researcher attempts to create integral or general understanding of his research on the part of the manager, sustained implementation will follow, regardless of the manager's reasoning style.

Hypothesis III. If the manager's way of reasoning is heuristic, the researcher's explicit-understanding approach will lead to suppression by the manager of analytic arguments. The researcher's integral-understanding approach, on the other hand, will encourage the manager to include analytic arguments in the preparation of his decision.

Both hypotheses I and II assume that the researcher uses "adequate" techniques of presentation of his results. We will call a proposal presenta-

tion technique "adequate," if the attained level of managerial understanding is satisfactory or, if not satisfactory, cannot be improved by a
feasible increase in the exposure to or explanation of the research.

We hasten to add that we by no means make the rather presumptuous
assumption that the researcher is always "right." In Section 1.5 we have
explicitly excluded from consideration the cases that would lead to
"rational rejection" by the manager (see also Figure 2, p. 29). Finally,
we refer to Section 2.1 for a definition of the terms explicit versus integral
understanding, and autonomous versus sustained implementation.

The significance of the first two hypotheses stems from the fact that
autonomous implementation is less costly and thus preferable to sustained
implementation. Sustained implementation requires more or less continuous involvement of the researcher to assure continual implementation and
organizational stability. However, sustained implementation is in turn
preferable to no implementation at all, which might follow if the explicit-
understanding approach is used.

Our third hypothesis may give some insight into the underlying causes
of the behavior we hypothesized for heuristically oriented managers.
We hypothesize that the explicit-understanding approach is perceived
as a threat by the heuristically reasoning manager, which leads him to
suppress completely any communications related to this approach. In a
broader context, this hypothesis attacks the relevance of information
measures that stress informational content or, more recently, the value
of information with respect to some objective but do not concern themselves with differentiating between potential users of the information.

2.5. ALTERNATIVE APPROACHES TO THE STUDY OF AN IMPLEMENTATION CONSTRAINT: A LABORATORY EXPERIMENT VERSUS A CASE STUDY

Before describing our experimental design, we would like to consider
the reasons that led us to choose an experiment rather than another
approach, in particular a case study, as testing ground for our hypotheses.
It might be argued that, if one likes to extend one's conclusions to real-life
situations—as we obviously do—a case study or several case studies form
a more valid starting point for such generalizations. The following considerations, in our opinion, more than offset this argument:

1. To the extent that we are interested in nonimplementation, we
would often be looking for no longer existing or deliberately suppressed
cases. As a consequence, most of our information would have to come

from interviews. In view of the next points, the interview is of questionable reliability as a source of information.

2. In many instances, problems of secrecy make it difficult to gain insight into why some cases were or were not implemented.

3. The sensitivity of the individuals involved may cause serious distortion of information. Nonimplementation is readily linked with "failure," for which nobody wants to take the responsibility.

These observations stem from our contacts with industrial organizations, their managers, and their OR department officers. Based on the very limited theory and experience in the area of implementation research, we may add two more arguments:

4. The state of the art is such that a lot of groundwork is needed before a field study could be undertaken with a reasonable chance of success. We mentioned already the needed clarification of concepts, the derivation of implementation measures, and the need for a theory of implementation. In the foregoing, we started out to set the stage for such a theory. A well-defined laboratory situation seems better suited to test the operationality of concepts and theory than a field study in which many confounding factors may obscure the meanings of behavior.

5. Perhaps the most compelling reason for restricting ourselves to laboratory experimentation is that even highly controlled experimental studies (relative to real-life situations), such as those by Churchman and Ratoosh (70), have rarely uncovered definite causal relationships underlying the implementation of research recommendations.

We conclude therefore that a laboratory study may fruitfully precede a field study in which the laboratory-tested concepts can be applied. As our discussion on validation of the results (see below, Section 3.9) will show, a field study remains necessary as a next step in validating the laboratory results despite the reservations we have with respect to the possible success of such a study.

Chapter 3

EXPERIMENTAL DESIGN

3.1. INTRODUCTION AND SUMMARY

The laboratory experiment we designed has the format of a business game. Our subjects were graduate students in business administration who served as managers of a hypothetical firm (see Section 3.3). Our main considerations in formulating the firm's problems were to ensure that the conditions for the existence of an implementation problem (see Section 1.5) were potentially fulfilled and that this problem would materialize in the vast majority of our test cases. On the one hand, this required a strong analytic structure underlying the firm's problems. A rich decision-making environment, on the other hand, should effectively conceal this analytic structure, while the basic analytic problem, once discovered, should be complex enough to evade immediate formulation and solution. We will show how these requirements are fulfilled in Section 3.2. The above considerations separate our experiment immediately from thev ast majority of small-group experiments involving problem-solving tasks.

In reviewing the social science literature (Section 1.3), we objected on several occasions to the fact that many of the causal relationships found in experiments by social scientists are crucially dependent on the elimination of variables that might very well be significant in those cases to which one would like to extend the experimental results. An example in point would be the study of an isolated individual, while one is interested in making inferences about the individual's social behavior from the experiment. Given our interest in implementation behavior in its social setting, a group experiment was an imperative. However, the study of a rich and complex problem in a group setting might make a formal test of our hypotheses—our stated intention—an elusive undertaking. The problem seems to get completely out of hand, if we consider that, in view of the poor knowledge available about implementation problems, an extremely

44

rich[21] experiment is desirable in order to minimize a priori experimental bias. We resolved this problem by simulating the environment of our subjects such that in each experiment the firm's management was made up of one live and four simulated and hence controlled managers. The simulation of the environment enabled us to gain control over a rich experimental situation without being forced to eliminate a large number of potentially significant variables.[22]

Within this setting we studied the interactive effects of our two central variables, the subject's reasoning style and the researcher's (one of the simulated managers) approach to the subject in presenting an optimal solution to his problems. The classification criteria to distinguish reasoning styles are discussed in Section 3.5. The interpretation of two alternative implementation approaches is given in Section 3.6. A complete review of the experimental design and a discussion of how the experiment was actually conducted follows in Section 3.7. The two last sections of this chapter deal with measurement problems (Section 3.8) and problems of validation (Section 3.9).

3.2. THE TASK

The formal structure of the firm in our experiments was patterned after the design of the Churchman-Ratoosh experiments discussed above (see footnote 11, p. 18). A group of five persons formed the firm's management (one president and four functional managers) and was requested to make periodic (half-yearly) decisions in the areas of finance, marketing, production, and purchasing. The firm's objective was explicitly stated to be the maximization of long-run profits. (See Appendix 1 for complete experimental instructions.) Different teams did not interact directly, although this was not necessarily clear to the experimental subjects.

The new task we designed involved the purchasing of raw materials as well as the production and sale of six products. Three of the products (*A*, *B*, and *C*) were produced and marketed during the summer seasons (the odd periods), while the other three products (*D*, *E*, and *F*) were produced and marketed during the winter seasons (the even periods). The type of problem to be dealt with was the same for all six products and differed only in the setting of parameter values. The most significant dis-

---

[21] With a rich experiment we mean an experiment in which a large number of variables is considered.

[22] Elimination can be seen as an extreme kind of control, i.e., with the value of the parameters set equal to 0. When we contrast elimination to control, we have in mind control within a range of acceptable parameter values.

tinction was that the demand for two products (B and D) was deterministic, while the demand for all the other products was stochastic. The odd and even periods were completely unrelated except for the financial function; the three products produced within one period were only related through a joint capacity constraint. The subjects might, of course, not be aware of this structure and in fact often saw relationships where none existed. The existence of these near independencies allowed us to distinguish clearly between implementation and mere acceptance, as defined in Section 1.5, in our experimental situation (the method is explained in Section 3.8, below). Because of the high degree of independence between periods, the timelag of one period, needed to calculate financial feedback-results, did not create undue problems for our subjects, even though the experiment was conducted in a continuous fashion. We may give credit to the same independence characteristics for minimizing the harmful effects of grave errors committed in the early part of the experiment, which otherwise might leave the subject with a firm whose outlook for the future would only generate his apathy, and the experimenter with a ruined observation.

The firm's central problems could be analyzed formally in a mathematical model. An optimal solution to this model in terms of the explicitly stated objective function exists and is presented in Appendix 2. The experimental instructions (see Appendix 1) contain all information needed to construct the model. In the instructions as well as during the experiment the subjects' attention was drawn to the fact that the experimenter would perform any computations the subjects requested as long as the instructions for the computation were sufficiently specific. Hence, even though solutions to the model were difficult to obtain manually within the time available to the subjects, the relevance of the optimal solutions was not reduced because of undue time pressures.

In a research proposal, one of the simulated managers, the accounting manager, recommended, after some period of time, the optimal solution to the subject, who was made president of the firm. The research proposal provided the optimal solution to the firm's major problems and was therefore *technically adequate and relevant*. The problem proved sufficiently difficult to ensure *superiority* of the proposal over actual managerial behavior in nearly all cases; "stumbling" upon the right solution without analysis was extremely improbable, while at the same time the solution is highly sensitive with respect to different decision values. Transition problems were formally eliminated, since the periods could be considered as repeated trials of the same problem (subjects often did not realize this!). Finally, the experimental richness in terms of the number of relevant variables introduced and the number of action alternatives realistically available to the subject (see Instructions, Appendix 1) was certainly sufficient to ensure that revelation of the optimal solution would not *automatically* be followed by its adoption merely because of a lack of realistic alternatives. The questionnaire findings discussed in the next chapter confirm this statement. We conclude therefore that the conditions for the existence of an implementation problem as they were stated in Section 1.5 were unambiguously satisfied in our experimental situation.

3.3. THE SUBJECTS

The subjects for the experiment were selected at random from the current "roster of M.B.A. students" of the Graduate School of Business at the University of California, Berkeley. Each person selected received a letter inviting him to participate in our experiment. The subjects received financial compensation for the time spent in preparation for and participation in the experiment. We concealed our interests in problems of implementation from the subjects by inviting them to participate in a "communication efficiency study." The experiment kept this label until the debriefing, which took place after the experiment was over.

Master's students in business were chosen as subjects, because, of all people to whom we could have access, they come, in our opinion, closest to the population of our interest, the industrial managers. When compared to undergraduates used in similar experiments, the use of mature graduate students as participants also seemed to increase the degree to which a serious commitment of effort was made.

An invitation letter was sent to a total of 160 students, of whom 10 participated in test runs and 40 in the final series of experiments[23] (five of which had to be discarded due to technical failures). Since most of the experiments took place after the end of the academic year, many refusals to participate were due to holiday absence or summer jobs, which accounted for approximately $\frac{2}{3}$ of our total. Eliminating these cases, we had a favorable response rate of slightly more than 85%.

3.4. THE EXPERIMENTAL GROUPS

3.4.1. Experimental Control in a Small Group Experiment

For a closed[24] group experiment we can identify three main sources of variables, stemming from the group's activities or task, the individual

---

[23] Twenty students, all attending a class in organization behavior in May 1966, were invited for the first four trial experiments. These participants are in addition to the ones mentioned in the text.

[24] A group experiment is closed when there exist no interactions with an external environment.

members of the group, and the interactions between these members, respectively. Experimental control[25] can correspondingly be split up into three areas. To what extent and at what levels control should be exerted depends on the objectives of the experimenter. How we formulated a task in accordance with a number of stated requirements was discussed in Section 3.2. We now turn to the control over the individual group members and their interactions.

Each of the three central hypotheses of this study (see p. 41) focuses on one aspect of this question: How does an individual decision-maker react to a research recommendation that requires him to alter his current decision strategy? As stated, we intend to observe his reaction in a group environment. To reduce the between-group variance, however, we decided to gain explicit control over all aspects of the four remaining group members. This decision obviously set a limit to the degree of freedom we could allow in the interactions between the members of the group. We attempted to keep the restrictions on free interaction to a minimum, however, since such restrictions might prevent, to various degrees, the impact of the group environment from becoming felt.

We are not aware of any other experiment that uses the same mixture of control settings as we outlined above, but several studies are pertinent to different aspects of the design we used. The use of confederates or robots in experimentation by social scientists is, of course, well known. Asch's experiments [48] are an example. The large group experiments conducted by Rome and Rome [84] include a large number of live as well as computer-simulated subjects. One of the players in Hoggatt's duopoly games [83] is a computer-simulated robot. The interaction between the live and simulated subjects in Hoggatt's and Asch's experiments, however, is restricted to symbol exchange. In the Romes' experiments, a tree-like language is used, which allows the live subjects to communicate with their simulated subordinates and each other; but it remains highly restrictive because of its specific question-format [86]. Hare [87] reports on the work of the Laboratory of Social Relations at Harvard to control and to predict the interaction processes between the members of a small group. But these efforts are directed toward *pure* computer simulation. Other nonbehavioral studies have attempted to approach the natural richness of face-to-face interaction, while remaining in complete control over the communications that take place. At this end of the spectrum, the

[25] The term "experimental" control is best understood when contrasted with "statistical" control. The former type of control fixes the value of a variable at a certain predetermined level before the experiment starts; the latter observes the value of a variable as it occurs in the experiment and considers it only when the experimental data are analyzed.

partner relationship between live and simulated subject is usually replaced by a rigid question–answer relationship. The syntactical and grammatical problems that arise at this point are phenomenal, as a program like "Baseball" of Green et al. [88] clearly illustrates.

The next two subsections describe in some detail the way we exerted control over four managerial functions (Section 3.4.3) and the communication restrictions that we imposed (Section 3.4.2). The role of the computer in establishing these controls is explained in Appendix 3.

3.4.2. Communications between Team Members

We will discuss the communication system in our experiments from the point of view of the one live subject on each team. For the duration of the experiment, all interactions were restricted to teletype communications. As viewed by the live subject (the "president" of the firm), there existed an all-channel communication system between the five members of his team, but contents of the communications were severely restricted by the required use of a limited vocabulary, the "formal language." Instructions for use of the communication system and the vocabulary are given in Appendix 4 of the instructions (see Appendix 1), which also gives some examples of messages that might be sent. A program (to which we will refer as the monitor) written for the PDP-5 computer monitored the communications.

Summarizing, the steps to be taken by a subject for each message sent were the following:

(a) Indicate intent to communicate by pushing the carriage return (CR) button on the teletype. If free to handle his message, the monitor asked the subject to specify the destinations of his message. If not, the subject was notified that he could not communicate at that time, but might try again later. (The messages received were: ** TO WHOM? ** or: ** PLEASE WAIT **, respectively).

(b) Specify the destinations of the message. Each team member was identified by a code (a number between 1 and 10). The experimenter could also be addressed (code 0). If at least some of the destinations specified were "legal," that is, if they were the codes of other team members or of the experimenter, the monitor advised the subject to start his message. (The message received by the subject was: ** GO AHEAD **.) If none of the destinations specified were legal, the monitor again asked for destinations until some legal destination was specified.

(c) Send the message. The subject would normally construct his message from words (or "message elements") available to him in the vocabulary. Upon its recognition, the monitor completed each message element and also caused the teletype to shift to the beginning of a new line. A "nonformal" message element, that is, a word or string of words or symbols that was not part of the vocabulary, could be included in a message, but only if the subject gave the monitor advance notice by pushing a special button on the teletype (the ALTMODE button). The subject could include as many nonformal message elements (each element never being more than one teletype line) as he wished merely by having ALT-MODE precede the typing of each nonformal element. However, the monitor would interrupt a message as soon as it became clear to him that the subject had attempted to include a nonformal message element without having announced his intention by pushing the ALTMODE button. (The message that would interrupt the subject was: ** NON-FORMAL **, which meant that the last message element would not be included in the message.) A message could have a maximum length of 30 message elements, while no messages could contain more than 20 nonformal message elements. The monitor would interrupt if either of these limits were exceeded.

The subject was able to correct a message while sending it by pushing the RUB OUT button on the teletype, which would cause the last message element entered to be erased. Several message elements or even the whole communication would be erased by repeatedly pushing the RUB OUT button.

(d) Indicate the end of a message by pushing the delimiter (↑). As soon as the delimiter was pushed, the message was taken out of the hands of the subject, to be delivered by the monitor. It is at this point that we, the experimenters, inserted the major and final control over the communications. That is, the monitor would not blindly deliver the message to its indicated (legal) destinations, but would first test the message for its acceptability. Each formal message element was acceptable. A nonformal message element was acceptable only if it consisted of numbers (with or without their unit specification) and/or a mathematical expression. Only if the message, that is, *all* its message elements, was found acceptable, was it delivered to the legal destinations specified by the sender. If the message was found unacceptable, it was sent to the experimenter (code 0). The sender always received a copy of his message, which in its heading indicated to whom the message had *actually* been delivered. The sender would therefore find out immediately if his message did not reach the destinations he requested. (Of course, he could know beforehand, since the acceptability rules are stated in Appendix 4 of the instructions.)

It was at the experimenter's discretion to forward or reject a message that was directed to him because it was found unacceptable by the monitor. The experimenter could thus prevent, by forwarding a message, undue harassment to the subject resulting from apparent shortcomings in the vocabulary or small errors in its use.[26] The subject was immediately informed about the action taken on an "unacceptable" message.

Two requirements had to be observed in creating the vocabulary:

(a) the vocabulary could not be so rich that simulation of the four functional managers would become infeasible;

(b) the vocabulary could not exceed the available space for it in computer memory. In order to perform its function as described above, the monitor program required the complete vocabulary to be stored in the computer. The last requirement limited the vocabulary to a maximum of about 250 words.[27]

The first requirement led us to create a vocabulary that would allow only task-oriented communications. The actual communications of a series of four trial experiments, with all live subjects (i.e., 20 in total) and no restriction on the communications other than the required use of teletypes, provided the basis for a core vocabulary. Through a second series of trial experiments, with all live subjects but the communication restrictions described above, the core vocabulary was modified and extended to its final form. (See also footnote 26 on this page.)

3.4.3. The Simulation of Managers

The experiments consisted of 12 periods of one-half hour each. The first two periods served to familiarize the subjects with the firm and its monitor-controlled communication system. (See also Section 3.7.) The remaining 10 periods were each divided into two segments of 20 and 10 minutes, respectively. During the first 20 minutes of a period, the five team members were allowed to communicate under monitor control.

[26] The same feature was an important aid in the on-line development of the vocabulary in the early test runs. Starting with a small core vocabulary, subjects in the test runs would often use unacceptable nonformal message elements in their messages. These elements gave the experimenter a clue as to what additional formal message elements were needed. The experimenter could add a new formal message element to the existing vocabulary at any time *during* an experiment.

[27] The computer used was a PDP-5 with a magnetic-core memory of 4096 12-bit words. The monitor program uses about 2800 words of memory space. The last page of memory (consisting of 128 words) is reserved for a program to call tapes.

The remaining 1170 computer words allowed 2340 characters (two per word) to be stored. This corresponds to 260 English language words, assuming seven characters per English word on the average and allowing for two characters per English word to indicate the end of that word (or "message element").

This segment was concluded with the four functional managers sending their decision proposals for the current period to the president of the firm. Each proposal was restricted to decisions in the functional area of the manager who sent it. The last 10 minutes of a period were used by the president to prepare final decisions, which he in turn sent to the experimenter (see form, Appendix 4).

All activities of the four functional managers were under explicit control of the experimenter. The people actually serving in the roles of these managers were therefore no more than a human interface, an "editor" if one likes, between the set of explicit rules prescribing their behavior and the one uncontrolled subject, the president of the firm.[28] Had we relied solely on a strict computer simulation of the managerial roles, we could never have attained the so desirable relative freedom of communications in view of the tremendous grammatical and syntactical problems that would have forced further restrictions on the interactions. Moreover, pure computer simulation would have forced us to create an even more restrictive treelike language and a strict question format in the communications (cf. our remarks at the end of Section 3.4.2.).

How the functions of the marketing, production, and purchasing managers were controlled is discussed in this section. A separate section (Section 3.6) is devoted to the function of the accounting manager, since the treatment variable of this study—the researcher's approach to the manager—finds its experimental realization through this function.

In the simulation of the firm's managers, we distinguished three aspects of control:

(a) Rules governing the autonomous or initiative part of a manager's communications during each period.

(b) Rules governing the induced or response part of a manager's communications during each period.

(c) Rules governing the decision proposals sent to the live subject (the president) at the end of the communication segment of each period.

We turn first to the rules that governed the decision proposals, since the autonomous and induced communications were often made contingent on the actual values of these decision proposals for the current period.

A period's decision proposals were calculated from four functional relationships—one per manager—which are stated in Appendix 5. The func-

---

[28] This statement does in no way diminish our appreciation for the help received from the "editors"!

tional relationships were formulated such that the proposals would have the following characteristics:

(a) A proposal should demonstrate a common sense and cautious approach to management. Examples of common sense would be "aim at full use of production capacity," and "set the price as high as the market can bear." Cautiousness was interpreted as an unwillingness to change proposals if the firm's present results seemed satisfactory. Such cautiousness was guaranteed by weighing heavily the last available proposals, if they had been successful, in calculating new ones. More generally, heuristic reasoning, as defined in Section 2.4, guided the managers' decision proposals.

(b) The above approach did not imply extreme rigidity with respect to the president's ideas. Rather than creating an extreme situation of social pressure—as, for example, explored by Asch [48]—we were interested in creating a well-balanced environment to the extent that this was possible. The deviation between the previously proposed decision and the president's actual decision of the same period received therefore some positive weight in calculating the decision proposal for the current period.

(c) The decision proposals were designed to reflect increased familiarity with the firm's operations after the first few periods. A very simple stepwise learning effect was built into the decision-proposal functions, which assured that consistency between the proposals from the different areas increased over time.

(d) The decision proposals were made more sensitive to the financial feedback results the more the actual results deviated from the expectations.

(e) The decision proposals were reasonable but not optimal, or at least not all optimal at the same time. We term a proposal "reasonable" if a live subject would have no reason to believe that the proposal was not generated by another live subject. By observing conditions (a) through (d), we did, in effect, satisfy condition (e).

The autonomous and induced messages—the two other aspects of control mentioned above—centered around the arguments that contributed to the formulation of the decision-proposal rules discussed above. A scenario, containing all autonomous messages to be sent to the president during the course of an experiment as well as the time of sending them, was prepared for each manager (see Appendix 6). The scenarios were mutually coordinated such that interactions between simulated managers, often implied by scenario messages, did not actually have to take place. Most messages in the scenarios were contingent on observed values of

Table 3.1. Number of Messages Autonomously Initiated by Each Simulated Manager During the Course of an Experiment

Manager	Period 3	4	5	6	7	8	9	10	11	12	Total
Accounting	3	2	3	3	3	3	2	1	4	3	27
Marketing	3	3	2	2	2	1	1	1	2	2	19
Production	3	2	2	2	3	2	1	2	2	2	21
Purchasing	2	2	1	2	2	1	2	1	2	2	17
Total	11	9	8	9	10	7	6	5	10	9	84

certain parameters that reflected recent developments and current status of the firm. The scenarios thus formed the framework of the discussion as initiated by the simulated managers and the basis of its continuity. Table 3.1 shows for each manager the number of messages that were autonomously initiated and sent to the president during the course of an experiment (from period 3 on).

The frequencies of initiated messages shown in Table 3.1 are based on the averages of frequencies observed in four unrestricted test experiments conducted in May 1966.[29] The formal-language test experiments of February 1967 did not indicate a need to reduce these frequencies, as one might have expected. However, the length of the formal messages was generally shorter in this last series of experiments, and this we considered in constructing the messages of our simulated managers.

Except when necessary to comply with an explicit instruction of the president, usually involving the transmission of some data or of a request, monitor-controlled communications between the simulated managers did not actually take place. This brings us to the rules that governed the simulated managers' response behavior with respect to the incoming communications from the president. Incoming messages were immediately classified into one of three categories:

A. Priority messages. An incoming message was classified priority if it contained an *explicit* instruction, request, or question to which the sender expected a reaction. Appropriate action, with due observance of a time-lag, always had to be taken.

---

[29] The number of messages to be sent by the accounting manager had to be raised somewhat to ensure an adequate presentation of the optimal solution through his scenario.

B. Nonpriority messages. This class is most easily defined as containing all messages that were not classified *A* or *C*. Such messages were suggestions, recommendations, and opinions. The messages in this class might or might not get a response (see below).

C. Nonresponse messages. An incoming message was classified nonresponse if the message contained an answer to a prior question or a statement to which the sender could not possibly expect a reaction. No response was given to such messages.

After a message had been classified, a response lagtime determined when a response was to be released. A table of such lagtimes basically generated from a normal distribution[30] accompanied each scenario. The response was then constructed in accordance with response rules specific to each manager and each period (see Appendix 7). A response expressed agreement or disagreement with the president's message and/or supplied the information requested. If the response rules did not lead to a unique response, the message was answered with a request for clarification. For example, if a president asked: "What are our costs?" he would get in reply: "What costs? Explain." Our effort to create a well-balanced environment for our subject stood central in determining the response rules for the managers. A message from the president usually met with some favorable and some negative reactions. In general, heuristic arguments were supported by the production and purchasing managers, while analytic arguments were favorably greeted by the accounting and marketing managers.

Different individuals participated in the experiments to represent the simulated managers. Without previous knowledge of the instructions or the communication system, an individual could be an efficient operator as simulated manager within two to four experimental periods. After the first series of test experiments, uncertainty about the action to be taken by a simulated manager seldom arose. This seems to confirm our earlier statement that the introduction of a human interface did not result in any significant loss of experimental control.

---

[30]A series of values was randomly drawn from N ($\mu = 3$, $\sigma = 1.5$) and divided into blocks of 10 values. The first block of 10 values that contained at least two values among the first four within 2σ-limits from the mean was used for the first manager, etc. Values outside 2σ-limits were set equal to ∞ (corresponding to no response). A minimum response lag-time of 3 min, 10 min for messages requiring the processing of not readily available information, was observed. Response lag-times were used sequentially (if a priority message met with an ∞ lag-time, the next value was used). By using this procedure to generate response lag-times we intended to eliminate immediate subjective controls as well as to generate a pattern of lag-times that represented fairly what we observed in the test experiments.

3.5. THE CLASSIFICATION OF SUBJECTS ACCORDING TO THEIR COGNITIVE STYLE

We now turn to the question how to measure differences in cognitive style between manager and researcher, the president and accounting manager, respectively, in our experimental situation. The researcher's style, by definition analytic (cf. section 2.4), is made explicit experimentally in the scenario of the accounting manager (see Appendix 6). For the purpose of this study we will restrict ourselves to the two types of reasoning styles—analytic and heuristic—we distinguished in Section 2.4.[31] The question at the beginning of this paragraph can therefore be restated: How do we classify a subject as belonging more to one than to the other of these two categories?

G. W. Allport [89] has already pointed out that attitudes should not be defined as types of overt conduct, nor merely as verbally expressed opinions or beliefs, but rather as directing or motivating tendencies that lie behind both behavior and opinion. The tests we used to measure cognitive styles have two desirable characteristics in view of the fact that Allport's statement equally applies to the definition of stylistic differences:

(a) Our measurement of reasoning style was based on both behavior and verbal statements.

(b) Rather than taking behavior or verbal statements at face value, we attempted to discover the intentions of the subject that caused them. In particular we used the interpretation of judges rather than immediate test scores as the basis for classification.

Our subjects were given three tests during the first session of the experiment. The tests are reproduced in Appendixes 8 and 9 and shortly discussed below:

A. The HAT test (Heuristic–Analytic Tendency test) consists of two behavior tests:

*A*1. The water jar problem.[32] This problem requires the subject to measure exactly a certain number of quarts given the capacity of two jars, which are the only measures he has available.

---

[31] This point will be elaborated upon in Section 4.2.

[32] This problem is a version of Sam Loyd's moonshiner's problem [90]. The same type of problem is known by social scientists as the water jar problem, used by Luchins [91] and later by others, e.g., Stedry [92], but, as far as we are aware, was never used for the purpose described here.

*A*2. The weighing problem. This problem requires the subject to detect the one heavier coin from a given number of otherwise indistinguishable coins. The only measure he has available is a scale, which may be used only a limited number of times.

Two sets of problems of each type, of about equal difficulty within each set, had to be solved by the subject. The first set in each case consisted of problems that were easily solvable or proved nonsolvable, no matter what approach was used. The subjects were required to give a step-by-step solution to the problems in this set. The second set of problems of each type was considerably harder. As an answer the subject only had to state whether a given problem was solvable or nonsolvable, but he could use the paper (the only paper available to him during the test) to keep track of the steps in his solution. Both tests were followed by a brief questionnaire that asked the subject about his previous experience with this type of problem, his attitude toward it (like–dislike) and the procedure he had used to solve the problems.

Both tests have a strong analytic structure[33] and seem more appealing to analytic subjects. Heuristic subjects, we conjectured, would feel frustrated by a problem that is obvious, that is, without any element requiring a subjective evaluation, and hard to solve at the same time. To analytic subjects, on the other hand, the problem seemed a challenge to find an underlying analytic relationship. We did, therefore, expect that the cognitive style would reveal itself through the procedures used or tried to solve the problems—formula-oriented for analytic, trial-and-error for heuristic subjects—and through a person's expressed like or dislike for this type of problem. These elements, together with other clues from the subject's comments on the tests, jointly formed the basis for the judges to classify a subject as basically heuristic or analytic. Being more an indicator of ability than of tendency, performance measured by the number of problems solved correctly received little immediate attention. (See the end of this section for a more complete discussion of the instructions given to the judges.)

B. The ATLAS test[34] confronted our subjects with a decision-making problem for which no solution in a strict analytic sense existed. The first

---

[33] Analytic solutions to the two tests are given in Appendix 10.

[34] This test was adapted from an experiment conducted by Dr. Richard O. Mason, then a Ph.D. student in Business Administration at the University of California at Berkeley. His comments and help in developing the ATLAS test are gratefully recognized.

part of this test describes ATLAS Joist Manufacturing Company considering five different plant capacities to construct upon their entry into the West Coast market. The subject was asked to assume the role of ATLAS's management, to study the situation and data concerning the problem, and to state what decision he would make in the given situation. The subjects then received two types of management reports. Half of the subjects received one type of management report first while the other half received the other type first. The two reports corresponded to the distinction between a heuristic and analytic approach to management's problem. After each report the subject was asked to restate and possibly revise his decision and to evaluate the report. A final questionnaire then asked the subject to compare the two reports, and to state his preference for one or the other type. It was made clear to the subjects that the data as well as the reports supplied were necessarily simplified representations of the actual situation.

The judges were again asked to classify a subject according to his reasoning style as they were able to determine from the questionnaires. The subject's own initial arguments as well as his later expressed preference for one type of report (analytic: American Marketing Consultants; heuristic: Allston Management Consultants) were both considered in this judgment.

Prior to the judging, the criteria for judgment were discussed in a joint meeting of the three judges and the experimenter. The following rules were agreed upon:

(a) Each test would be considered independently.

(b) The overall impression obtained from a test would prevail over the explicit answers given if there appeared to be a conflict between the two. For example, a subject might state in the ATLAS test that he applied analysis to determine the plant size. The subject would not be classified as "analytic," however, if his responses to other questions did not confirm this statement.

(c) The judgment would emphasize a subject's tendency in approaching problems as opposed to his ability in solving them. This requirement implied that the score reached in the pitcher test and in the coin test (i.e., the number of correct answers) was subordinated to the answers to the final questionnaire of these tests and to the inferences on methodology that could be made from the worksheets (they might of course be correlated).

(d) The judges must make a decision, that is, a "don't know" judgment would not be allowed.

(e) For the ATLAS test, the following classes within the 2 categories "analytic" and "heuristic" were distinguished:

1. Strictly analytic. The subject proceeded in his solution to the test problems in a rigid, analytic manner. The solution was sought by laying bare all implicit information before new explicit information was gathered.

2. Basically analytic. The subject approached the solution to his problems by analysis, but did not go to an extreme. A certain alternation between analysis and the use of heuristic procedures took place, but analysis remained his focusing point.

3. Weakly analytic. The subject seemed to jump from one approach to the other in a fairly haphazard manner. No strong tendency in either direction was apparent, but the analytical tendency was judged to dominate slightly.

4. Strictly heuristic. The subject gave little or no attention to analysis, but proceeded in the solution to his problems by gathering a maximum of explicit information (trial and error). He concentrated on the immediate concrete aspects of a situation. Information and decision were linked by "insights."

5. Basically heuristic. The subject relied mainly on heuristic procedures to arrive at a solution to his problems, but was inclined to include analysis if faced with it or if the problem at hand seemed particularly suited for analysis.

6. Weakly heuristic. Like the "weakly analytic" class, but now the heuristic tendency was judged to be dominant.

The above classification was found to give a satisfactory description for the ATLAS test. The information obtained from the pitcher and coin tests was insufficient to justify the distinction between "strictly" and "basically" heuristic and analytic, respectively. Hence we decided to distinguish only two classes for each category for these two tests.[35]

3.6. THE TREATMENT VARIABLE: THE OPERATIONS RESEARCHER'S APPROACH

Since the operations researcher's[36] approach to management's problems is basically analytic, he cannot simply observe the manager's rea-

---

[35] A subject's ability to solve problems and the difficulty of the problem have been mentioned as two confounding variables influencing a subject's style in approaching a given problem. No attempt was made to isolate the impact of these variables formally through statistical analysis, but the judges were explicitly instructed to consider their impact.

[36] In the following discussion, the term "researcher" is used in short for "operations researcher."

soning style and adapt his problem approach to it. However, we suggested that the researcher may take advantage of his knowledge about the manager's cognitive style by varying the degree of managerial understanding of his research, as defined in Section 1.5, that he attempts to reach. The higher the degree of understanding reached, the less post-research involvement will be required from the researcher to attain implementation of recommendations. But, on the other hand, the more a manager is heuristically oriented, the more difficult or costly it will be to reach a high degree of managerial understanding. The hypotheses of this study make an even stronger claim: If the researcher does *not* include the manager's cognitive style as a codeterminant of his implementation strategy, he risks complete rejection of his recommendations. That is, a heuristically oriented management may resent an overemphasis of analytic arguments—intended to establish the independence of the research results from the researcher—to a point that it turns against the researcher's recommendations. (The reverse situation—an analytic management annoyed by a too patronizing attitude of the researcher who conceals too many technical aspects of his research and thus keeps management dependent on his function—seems less likely to occur.)

In our experimental situation the researcher was represented by the accounting manager. We did not introduce the role of researcher as such, because this label might have had prior connotations—appearing in our study as confounding variables—for the subject. The two versions of the scenario of the accounting manager (see Appendix 6) correspond to two different implementation strategies, one aimed at gaining explicit, the other at gaining integral managerial understanding of the research. In our experiment either one approach or the other was applied. The experiments did not differ otherwise.

We have repeatedly made the distinction between two forms of adoption of the research recommendations, called implementation and acceptance, respectively. The former is adoption with, the latter without, understanding of the research proposal. In the experiments, the parameter changes that were announced after period 10 could cause a merely accepting subject—unable to see the relevance of such a change—to drop the hitherto adopted optimal solution. Thus, these changes were designed to separate to some extent the accepters from the implementers. To have the distinction between the two types of adopters appear even more explicitly, the presentation of the optimal solution for products C and D was initially withheld from the subject. We reasoned that an implementing subject would be able to compute the optimal solution himself or, in view of the time-constraint, to give explicit instructions for its computation to the accounting manager or the umpire. Only after such explicit instructions were received was the optimal solution for products C and D provided. The optimal solutions for products A, B, E, and F, on the contrary, were provided to the subject under any circumstance.[37]

In order to put our hypotheses to as strong a test as possible, we retained a maximum of similarity in the two versions of the accounting manager's scenario. Both versions contained sufficient (and similarly presented) arguments to enable our subject (the president) to gain a general appreciation for and an at least limited understanding of the research done. The only essential difference consisted of the inclusion of the formulas to support the research findings in case the "explicit understanding approach" was being used (see Scenario Accounting Manager, Appendix 6 and Appendix 11). Hence, one might say, subjects receiving "explicit-understanding" treatment were given an advantage over those receiving "integral-understanding" treatment, since the former received information withheld—at least initially—from the latter. It is exactly this statement that is challenged by our hypothesis stating that, in certain cases, such a seeming advantage may turn out to be a real disadvantage.

3.7. A SUMMARY OF EXPERIMENTAL DESIGN AND PROCEDURE

A schematic overview of the experimental design, that shows the interrelationships between the design elements discussed in the previous sections, is presented in Figure 5. Some details that we did not yet discuss completed the design and are discussed below. A chronological review of a typical experiment is given in Table 3.2.

The three sessions of the experiment were held on different days (with the exception of the A-series, see below). During the first session of the experiment the two tests were administered to a group of 5–10 subjects simultaneously. The subjects were also made familiar with the teletype communication system, the firm's problems, and its formal language by actually operating the firm for the first two experimental periods. The functions during this first session were arbitrarily assigned, while the assignments were changed after the first period. Subjects were told at the end of this session that their colleague team members and their

---

[37] The distinction between acceptance and implementation was already made by Churchman and Ratoosh [70]. In their experiments, they defined implementation as a subject's ability to compute an optimal solution for a new product (which meant a change in parameters), introduced toward the end of the experiment.

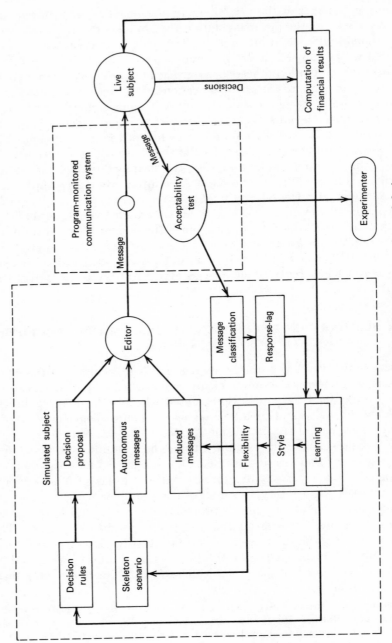

Figure 5 Schematic overview of the experimental design.

Table 3.2. Chronological Review of the Experiment

Session	Description	Duration
—	Subjects receive instructions before the experiment and are asked to read them at home	1 hr
1 (4 hrs)	Introductory briefing on experiment	20 min
	HAT test	50 min
	First two periods of the experiment to familiarize subjects with problem and communication system	2 hrs
	ATLAS test	50 min
2 (3 hrs 40 min)	Periods 3 and 4	1 hr
	Break	15 min
	Periods 5 and 6	1 hr
	Break	15 min
	Periods 7 and 8	1 hr
	Questionnaire 1	10 min
3 (3 hrs 20 min)	Periods 9 and 10	1 hr
	Break	30 min
	Periods 11 and 12	1 hr
	Questionnaire 2	10 min
	Meeting	20 min
	Questionnaire 3	10 min
	Final decisions (periods 13 + 14) ⎱	10 min
	Debriefing ⎰	
Total		12 hrs

function in the team would not necessarily be the same for the next two sessions of the experiment.

The subjects were kept strictly separated during the remaining two experimental sessions, which were conducted with up to four subjects simultaneously. Each subject was told, individually, that he was given the function of the firm's president. He was left unaware, of course, that he would be assisted by programmed managers. The situation as seen by subject and experimenter is illustrated in Figure 6.[38]

During the second and third session the firm ran through ten more

---

[38] To handle more than four subjects simultaneously would have resulted in an overloading of the confederates (the "editors") as well as of the communication system. Precautions were taken in the monitor program to prevent subjects from becoming aware of the simultaneous existence of several presidents.

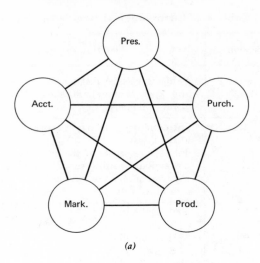

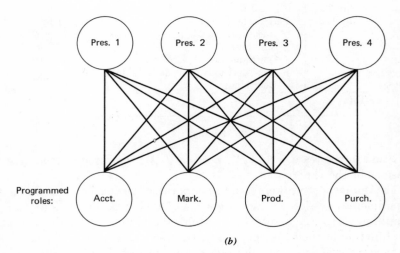

Figure 6 The firm's organizational structure and lines of communication as seen by (*a*) the subject, (*b*) the experimenter.

periods. At the beginning of each period the subjects ("all team members") received information about current expectations with respect to demand, prices, and cost. The demand information was supplied in the form of a market survey, which stated the quantities sold of each product at a range of different prices. At the beginning of each period the subjects also received a detailed income statement referring to their decisions of the period before the last one and an updated position statement. That is, when starting session two with period three, the subject received the financial report of period 1; at the beginning of period 4 the report of period 2 came in; etc.[39] The financial reports of periods 3 and 4 were the same for all subjects, that is, they were based on the same decisions for the first two periods.

For each period, the actual demand for the products with a stochastic demand was generated with the aid of a table of random normal numbers from the relevant normal distribution of demand. The same series of random normal numbers was used in all experiments (see Appendix 12). A study of the effect of the actual sequence of deviations from the expected demand on the subject's behavior was thus placed beyond our experimental design. Evaluating the possible increase in between-experiment variance due to such an effect, however, might have required conducting a prohibitively large number of experiments.

Parameters remained unchanged for the first ten experimental periods. After period 10, it was announced that some parameter changes had occurred (see Appendix 13). The changes required only a recalculation of the optimal solution. The same model applied.

Most of the experimental controls were abandoned in a face-to-face meeting that took place after period 12 between the four subjects and two confederate managers. At this point it was revealed that two "subjects" had been selected to act as accounting and production managers, respectively, for four teams simultaneously. These two subjects were now allowed to present their views on the firm's operations to the four presidents without being restricted by teletype communications or formal language. The presidents were free to interrupt these 10-min presentations of each manager with questions. Three confederates alternated in the roles of accounting and production manager during the meetings. The

---

[39] An IBM 1460 computer, located near the laboratory where the experiments were conducted, could be used to prepare the decision feedback in the form of financial reports. The same computer was used to calculate specific decision proposals for two periods ahead which were to be used by the confederate managers. With priority use of the computer, it took about 20 min between the moment the four presidents handed in their decisions and the moment that feedback reports and decision proposals returned.

scenarios for the presentations were immediate extensions of the accounting and production managers' scenarios used during the experiment.[40] The subjects were thus once more confronted with the conflicting issues resulting from the different ways of reasoning used by their managers.

It was felt that this less structured part of the experiment might shed more light on the subject's behavior during the previous experimental periods, and in particular on the way his behavior had been modified in reaction to the experimental controls that were instituted. The three questionnaires given during the experiment[41] were also intended to gather some direct reactions from the subject about the impact of the experimental design on his behavior.

A series of 35 experiments was conducted during April, May, and June, 1967,[42] in the Laboratory of the Center for Research in Management Science at the University of California, Berkeley. The experiments were subdivided into two groups according to the approach used by the accounting manager:

Series A and C: The "explicit understanding" approach was used in these two series. The second and third sessions were held on the same day (morning and afternoon) for some experiments (series A). The three sessions of the experiments in series C were held on three different days. In the analysis of experimental results no distinction is made between the experiments of these two series.

[40] See Appendix 14 for the meeting instructions.
[41] See Appendix 15 for a specimen of the questionnaires.
[42] The final series of experiments was preceded by two trial series that served as a basis for and test of the experimental design. The first series of four trial experiments was held in May, 1966; the second series of two trial experiments was held in February, 1967.

Table 3.3. Number of Observations per Cell in a Two-Way Layout of the Experimental Design

Subject Classification	Treatment		
	Explicit Understanding Approach	Integral Understanding Approach	
Analytic	6	9	15
Heuristic	11	9	20
	17	18	35

Series B: The "integral understanding" approach was used in this series of experiments. The three experimental sessions took place on three different days.

Subjects were randomly assigned to the two treatments conditional upon the requirement of proportional representation of each combination of type of subject (as determined from the test) and type of treatment (approach by accounting manager). (The requirement could not be fully met due to a lag in determining a subject's reasoning style classification and the procedure of conducting four experiments simultaneously). The subdivision of experiments is given in Table 3.3.

3.8. MEASURES

The measurement of a subject's adoption/rejection behavior with respect to the OR recommendation was constantly kept in mind when we designed the experiment. We were in particular interested in being able to distinguish between mere acceptance and understanding of the OR recommendation. The measures we propose below are based on four sources of information: (a) the subject's decisions in the areas of finance, marketing, production, and purchasing, made each period for each product; (b) the subject's messages sent during the experiment; (c) the questionnaires; and (d) the meeting recordings.

(a) *The subject's decisions in the areas of finance, marketing, production, and purchasing, made each period for each product.* Our measure of the *degree of adoption* of the optimal proposal is based on the last three decisions. The financial decision (investment/borrowing) is not directly related to the OR proposal and is therefore excluded. The measure, specified below, summarizes a subject's reactions, in behavior and attitude, toward the optimal proposal presented to him during the experiment. The decisions of the different experimental periods do obviously not all have the same relevance with respect to this overall adoption measure. Four groups of periods can be distinguished:

I	II	III	IV
	Confrontation with Arguments	Confrontation with	Final
Training	for Optimality	Optimal Proposals	Attitude
Period: 1 2	3 4 5 6	7 8 9 10 11 12	13 14

The decisions of the last two periods were made after the meeting between the presidents and the accounting and production managers took place. They are therefore a good indicator of a subject's final attitude with respect to the optimal proposal and they provide a clue to the interpretation of the decisions made by the subject when he was actually confronted with the optimal recommendations during the six periods before (periods 7–12). The decisions of periods 3–6 served to determine the degree of optimality already reached by the subject prior to the actual presentation of the optimal proposals.[43] This level should, of course, be considered if one is interested in the effect of the accounting manager's presentation of the optimal solution. The decisions of the first two periods were not considered in the analysis.

A subject could choose either of three courses of action when making his decisions:

(1) Follow the proposals of each of his managers
(2) Follow the optimal proposal of the accounting manager
(3) Make an independent decision (this may be a mixture of the two foregoing alternatives).

The degree of adoption may be said to be higher, the closer the actual decision made (A) is to the optimal decision (O). However, the reliability of the measure $|A{-}O|$ as an indicator of the degree to which a subject's decisions are influenced by the optimal proposals becomes doubtful if its value is large or if the divergence of the actual decision from the *managers'* proposals (P) is small. These last two situations might equally well reflect a high degree of independent action or a high degree of following the managerial proposals, respectively. If $P = O$, which may occasionally occur, a subject will in fact make the optimal decisions, even if he intends to follow his managers' proposals, that is, if he would also have followed P if $P \neq O$.

Our basic measure of the degree of adoption of the optimal recommendations is based on the considerations we have discussed:

$$D_{jk} = \frac{1}{2} \sum_{\substack{i = \text{prod.} \\ \text{purch.}}} \left[\text{Max} \cdot \left\{ 1 - 10 \cdot \frac{|A_{ijk} - O_{ijk}|}{O_{ijk}}, 0 \right\} \right] \quad \text{if } |A - P|_i \geqq |O - P|_i \text{ for at least one } i$$

$$= 0 \qquad\qquad\qquad \text{if } |A - P|_i < |O - P|_i \text{ for all } i.$$

---

[43] In all trial experiments improvements in the decisions that might be ascribed to a learning effect occurred before period 6.

where:

D = degree of adoption of the optimal proposal
A = actual decision
O = optimal decision (proposed by accounting manager)
P = proposed decision (of marketing, production, or purchasing manager)
and subscripts i = type decision; i = marketing, production, purchasing
j = product; j = A, B, C, D, E, or F
k = period; k = 3, . . . , 14

This measure has the following characteristics:

1. Its value ranges from 0 to 1, from no to full adoption.
2. There is only one measure per product and per period. The two measures for marketing and production are pooled to increase the reliability of the adoption measure. For each of these two decisions it occurred in less than 5% of the cases that the managers' proposals were optimal or near-optimal and this never happened for the production and marketing decisions simultaneously.
3. The purchasing decision is disregarded in determining D, but serves to decide on the ranking according to D in the case of ties. Since the purchasing decision can only take a small number of integer values, marginal changes in this decision would result in strong fluctuations of D. Such fluctuations would not be justified in view of the low sensitivity of the optimal solution with respect to the purchasing decision. Moreover, the relative simplicity of the purchasing manager's problem made the optimal decision often the only acceptable proposal and thus the reliability of D would be reduced if the purchasing decision were included in its calculation.
4. The proposed measure D implies a cutoff point at 90% of optimality. If the actual decision deviates more than 10% from the optimal decision, we consider the actual decision not to be influenced by the optimal proposal. Moreover, as the condition in the definition of D states, the value of D may be set equal to zero even though the deviation of an individual decision from optimality is less than 10%. (This happens when the deviation from the managers' proposals is less than the deviation from optimality for both the pricing and production decision.) These safeguards give us maximum assurance that no spurious ranking of the subjects according to D will result.

An overall measure of the degree of adoption of the optimal proposal,

M, can now be formulated for each product:

$$M_j = \text{Max} \left[D_{j,11/12}, \sum_{k=7,12} \frac{D_{jk}}{3} \right] \text{ if } D_{j,13/14} \geq .50$$

$$= \sum_{k=7,12} \frac{D_{jk}}{3} \qquad\qquad \text{ if } 0 < D_{j,13/14} < .50$$

$$= \text{Min} \left[D_{j,11/12}, \sum_{k=7,12} \frac{D_{jk}}{3} \right] \text{ if } D_{j,13/14} = 0$$

where:

M = Product measure of adoption of the optimal proposal; other symbols were defined above (see page 69).

The subject's final attitude toward the optimal decisions, as expressed through the decisions of periods 13 and 14, determines our interpretation of the actual decision behavior observed in periods 7 through 12 when the subject was immediately confronted with the optimal solution. In particular we realized that many different modes of behavior may accompany the phase of gaining understanding (if this is the subject's objective) of the optimal solution. A subject could wait to adopt the solution until he fully understands it, or he could start with "giving it a try." He could, still only half convinced, drop the initially adopted solution, only to return to it at a later moment. Assuming that the experiment consisted of sufficient periods to allow understanding of the optimal solution to be reached by any of these paths, the last decision period before the meeting between presidents and managers should give the best impression of a subject's overall adoption of the optimal solution. If understanding was not the subject's aim, however, there is no reason to expect that the stable equilibrium of optimality would ever be reached. Hence, we preferred to use the average of the measures D over three periods (7–9–11 or 8–10–12) as a point-estimate of the degree of adoption, unless a subject's final attitude—as expressed through his decisions of periods 13 or 14— outspokenly[44] confirmed his actual behavior of the last period before the meeting.

A stronger indication of a subject's intention that underlies his reaction to the optimal solution is obtained when we consider the distinction between implementation and acceptance as two possible forms of adop-

[44] The term "outspokenly" is operationally defined as at least some degree of acceptance of both the optimal price and production proposal and strong acceptance of one of them ($D_{j,13/14} \geq .50$) *or:* complete rejection of the optimal proposal ($D_{j,13/14} = 0$).

tion. We recall that the optimal solution for the products C and D is initially withheld from the subject and is only made available to him if he gives explicit instructions for their computation. An *acceptance* measure is therefore given by the values of M_j for products A, B, E, and F. An implementation measure is given by the values of M_j for products C and D. If adoption merely means acceptance, the value of the acceptance measure will be high, but the value of the implementation measure will be low.

It might be argued that the sole consideration of decisions does not take into account the sensitivity of the financial results with respect to these decisions. Superior performance, not adoption of the optimal proposals, was stated as the subject's goal. A high level of performance might be reached, even though the decisions are far from optimal if the decision sensitivity of the results is low. Our measures ought therefore, this argument goes, to be based on the results reached with decisions rather than on the decisions themselves. Since the *actual* results reflect the randomness of the actual demands, the *expected* results could be proposed as the basis for a superior measure of performance. However, why should a subject who is able to calculate correctly the expected results of his decisions not use the *readily available* optimal decisions? (We may note that the optima are unique, not local.) The usually proposed argument of satisficing to explain nonoptimal behavior is turned against itself in our situation: it takes the subject less effort to obtain an optimal than a near-optimal result! The former only requires a checking of the accounting manager's proposals, the latter a new involved computation. (Strict following of the managerial proposals never resulted in a less than, but near, optimal result.)[45] Our measure remains with the advantage that a subject's corrections of the optimal proposal based on heuristic arguments are easily identifiable (see e.g., Section 4.3.2).

(b) *The subject's messages sent during the experiment.* Content analysis of the messages sent by the presidents was expected to give some further insight in the process by which a president arrived at his final decisions. All messages were coded according to:

1. The message-mode (opinion/suggestion–request/question–reply)
2. the attitude of the message (agreement–disagreement)
3. the products mentioned $(A/D–B/E–C/F)$
4. the main concern expressed in the message (analytical–functional–organizational)

[45] If satisficing implies a threshold of performance below which improvement is sought by the subject, *much* lower than the optimal results, neither of the two measures discussed in the text is meaningful to compare the subject's performance!

The restrictions imposed by the required use of the formal language facilitated greatly the coding of messages. One message could consist of several "message units" that could each stand in isolation. All four coding categories did not always apply and neither were the classes within the four categories necessarily mutually exclusive with respect to a message unit.

The last category (concern expressed) may need some clarification. A message unit was considered "analytical" if it contained a clear indication that the subject was interested in the underlying relationships of the firm's problems. A message unit was classified "organizational" if the main intent of the message was to establish responsibility and authority relationships or to transfer information received from others. All other messages were classified "functional" (exclusively).

The measures derived from these codings are relative frequencies of classes within each category.

No formal measures were derived for the questionnaires or the meeting recordings, but informal use of this information was made to clarify the significance of the values of the formal measures.

3.9. VALIDATION

Before turning to a judgment of the experimental results given the assumptions made in the experiment, we turn to a judgment of the experimental assumptions themselves. This is the validation problem. The experimental assumptions are to be validated with respect to the instances to which the experimenter wants to extend the experimental results. No general agreement exists on the criteria on which such a validation should be based. The superiority of one set of assumptions over another is often derived from the degree of isomorphism or closeness of the experiment to the "real world," that is, to the instances to which one wants to extend the experimental results. We prefer to adopt a more flexible criterion, however, that bases validation on the usability of the information produced by the experiment for gaining understanding of the processes underlying some "real world" situation.[46]

The implementation behavior of industrial managers with respect to OR recommendations may be called the "real world" we had in mind when designing our experiment. More specifically, we should refer to the information aspect of an OR recommendation, where we defined informa-

---

[46] Guetzkow and Jensen [93] discuss different ways of establishing the validity of simulation models. Two of them are mentioned in the text.

tion in terms of its relevance as perceived by the receiver of the information with respect to his choice between decision alternatives. The complexity we introduced in the experimetal design should be evaluated in terms of this ultimate objective. In fact it hides our claim that the experimental design allowed sufficient codeterminants of implementation behavior to operate simultaneously to meet successfully the test of validation—in the broad sense we defined this term above—of the experimental results. Whatever the results of the experiment, their significance is bounded by the degree to which the experimental design can be validated. We will have more to say about validation in Chapter 5. At this point our remarks should suffice to place the discussion of the experimental results, to which we turn next, in its proper perspective.

Chapter 4

ANALYSIS OF THE
EXPERIMENTAL RESULTS

4.1. INTRODUCTION AND SUMMARY

The introduction of elaborate controls in the experimental design serves not only to satisfy the requirements of validation, but also to assure a rigorous test of our hypotheses. The tight controls and the quantitative adoption measures we introduced in the previous chapter have patterned the way for the use of strict statistical techniques to analyze the experimental results and a subsequent reliance on probability statements to either support or deny our hypotheses. We are keenly aware, however, that this type of rigor conceals a number of prior judgments with respect to the level of measurement we are willing to accept, the test assumptions we assume satisfied, such as continuity, normality, independence (and they often go unchecked!), and, of course, the probability level below which we call a result significant. A claim of rigor can therefore only be maintained if sufficient caution is applied in making these judgments. And even then rigor cannot be interpreted to mean that we increase the likelihood of coming up with the *correct* answers to the questions asked in our hypotheses, but only that we increase the evidence required before we are willing to accept the data as being in support of our hypotheses. [47]

In line with this discussion, we will make only nominal or ordinal use of our measurements. Cardinal use of, for example, the adoption measures, defined in Section 3.8, would imply a denial of the fact that these measures represent a concept—the degree of a subject's adoption of an OR recommendation—which at most allows ranking of the individuals concerned. This decision rules out the use of parametric statistical tests such as the

[47] If our hypotheses are true (in statistical terms: if the alternative hypothesis is true), we decrease the likelihood of showing so if we introduce the type of rigor we discussed in the text!

otherwise appropriate analysis of (co)variance. The nonparametric tests that were used are introduced as they appear in the analysis. Their choice depends on the way we resolved the problems of simultaneous statistical inference and of dependence between observations as well as on the considerations already mentioned. Significance levels of 5 and 10% are used merely for convenience. We will not hesitate to bring in evidence if this seems appropriate, even though the above significance levels are exceeded.

In Section 4.2 we present the results of classification of our subjects according to their reasoning style. The experimental evidence is presented in the order of emphasis we gave to it in the previous chapter, that is, first the decision measures (Section 4.3), next the communication measures (Section 4.4) and finally the remaining information obtained from questionnaires and the meeting discussions (Section 4.5). A discussion of the results (Section 4.6) concludes this chapter.

4.2. THE CLASSIFICATION OF SUBJECTS

Three judges were asked to independently classify each subject according to his style of reasoning as inferred from the three tests given to the subject. The criteria for judgment were discussed in Section 3.5. The individual judgments are summarized in Table 4.1. The entries in this table refer to the number of subjects assigned by each judge to each of the classes. (No distinction between strictly and basically analytic or strictly and basically heuristic was made for the pitcher and coin tests.)

The relatively high number of persons classified as "weakly analytic" or "weakly heuristic" for the pitcher and coin tests compared to the num-

Table 4.1. Classification of Subjects with Respect to Reasoning Style

Class \ Judge	Pitcher-test			Coin test			ATLAS test		
	1	2	3	1	2	3	1	2	3
Strictly analytic	10	14	9	11	15	9	5	4	5
Basically analytic							10	10	9
Weakly analytic	5	3	4	8	2	4	0	2	1
Strictly heuristic	13	12	13	10	13	12	7	8	11
Basically heuristic							12	9	7
Weakly heuristic	7	6	9	6	5	10	1	0	3

ber classified as such for the ATLAS test indicates some inconclusiveness of the first two tests. The judges indicated that their confidence in the classification according to the ATLAS test was higher than for the other two tests. The classes "weakly analytic" and "weakly heuristic" for the two behavioral tests were felt to represent more often a judge's inability to classify a subject on the basis of the available information than his strong feelings that the subject so classified was not inclined to prefer either heuristic or analytic reasoning.

The internal consistency of judgments among tests for each judge can be interpreted as a measure of the reliability of the tests as complementary measures of the concept "cognitive style." The results of pairwise comparisons are given in Table 4.2 in the form of contingency coefficients.[48] The first figure in the table refers to a breakdown of categories into six (ATLAS test) or four (pitcher and coin tests) classes as in Table 4.1. The figures in parentheses refer to the simple classification in two categories (analytic versus heuristic) without further distinction of classes within each category.

The high correlation between the judgments for the pitcher and coin tests reflects in part an actual dependence of judgments. Joint answers were often given by a subject to the final questionnaire of the two tests which made independent judgments practically impossible. The low correlations between the judgments for the pitcher and ATLAS tests and the coin and ATLAS tests mainly reflect the above-mentioned uncertainty of judges [in as many as 35% of the cases (see Table 4.1)]. This can be shown by eliminating those cases for which an uncertain classification (i.e., "weakly analytic" or "weakly heuristic") was given which causes *all* contingency coefficients of Table 4.2 to become significant at the 1% level. As shown in Table 4.3, a similar increase in agreement between the judgments for the ATLAS test on the one hand and the pitcher and coin tests (considered jointly) on the other hand is observed when we consider

---

[48] The contingency coefficient, C, is defined as: $C = \sqrt{\chi^2/(N + \chi^2)}$, where

$$\chi^2 = \sum_{i=1}^{r} \sum_{j=1}^{k} \frac{(O_{ij} - E_{ij})^2}{E_{ij}}$$

is the sum of the squared differences of observed minus expected frequencies divided by the expected frequency in a $(k \times r)$ contingency table. (See e.g., Siegel [94, p. 197].) If $k = r$, the upper limit for C is equal to $\sqrt{(k - 1)/k}$. If $k \neq r$ the upper limit for C is not exactly known. Different contingency coefficients are comparable only if they are based on the same size contingency table!

Table 4.2. Internal Consistency of Judges as Measured by Contingency Coefficients

	Judge					
Test	1		2		3	
Pitcher − Coin (P-C)	.78*	(.62)	.81*	(.66*)	.87*	(.71*)
Pitcher − ATLAS (P-A)	.55	(.38)	.56	(.25)	.43	(.17)
Coin − ATLAS (C-A)	.51	(.31)	.48	(.14)	.43	(.17)

* Significant at .01 level.

Note: The contingency coefficients in this table are not all comparable.[47] The first entries in each column are based on 4 × 4 (P-C) or 4 × 6 (P-A and C-A) contingency tables. The entries in parentheses are all based on 2 × 2 contingency tables. The maximum value of C is .91 for a 6 × 6 table, .85 for a 4 × 4 table, and .71 for a 2 × 2 table.

the majority vote rather than the individual judgments in each case[49] (in this table the pitcher and coin tests are taken together in view of the dependence we observed above).

Thus we conclude from Table 4.3 that preference statements (as solicited in the ATLAS test) and actual behavior (as observed in the pitcher and coin tests) are to some extent complementary measures of the reasoning style of an individual.

The external consistency of judgments among judges for each test forms

[49] The majority vote will tend to correct for individual errors of judgment and is also likely to improve the classification in uncertain cases. Ties were resolved by considering the strength of judgments as indicated by the classification.

Table 4.3. Classification of Subjects According to Majority Vote

Pitcher + Coin Test	ATLAS Test		
	Analytic	Heuristic	
Analytic	10	5	15
Heuristic	5	15	20
	15	20	35

$\chi^2 = 6.07$ (significant at .02 level).

a measure of the sufficiency of the judgment guidelines that we discussed in Section 3.5. Table 4.4 contains the contingency coefficients that resulted from pairwise comparisons between judges. The first figures in the table again refer to a breakdown of categories as in Table 4.1. The figures in parentheses refer to the 2 categories "analytic" and "heuristic" without a further breakdown within each category.

The guidelines given to the judges proved certainly sufficient as the strong agreement between judges (Table 4.4) indicates. To the extent that these guidelines are a proper representation of the underlying concept of cognitive style (as we intended them to be), we also may conclude to conceptual[50] validity of the tests.

To what extent previous experience, attitude, and test score in the pitcher and coin tests played a role in the classification by the judges is demonstrated by the correlations between the majority judgments and these factors (Table 4.5). The subjects who were classified "analytic" on the basis of the majority judgments appeared more likely to have had previous experience with the type of problems presented in the pitcher and coin tests. It might be questioned to what extent the analytic procedure used by the experienced subjects was their own and to what extent it was derived from the environment in which they had obtained their previous experience. On the other hand, having had experience might itself be taken as an indication of a basic interest of analytic subjects in the type of problems presented in the pitcher and coin tests. The subjects who said that they liked the coin problems and those that were successful

---

[50] Different types of validation can be distinguished. The main distinction that is made is between conceptual and predictive validation. (See e.g., Cronbach [95].) In our case we are, of course, restricted to the first type of validation.

Table 4.4. External Consistency of Judges as Measured by Contingency Coefficients

Judge	Pitcher Test		Coin Test		ATLAS Test	
			Test			
1–2	.64*	(.61*)	.69*	(.55*)	.77*	(.58*)
1–3	.60†	(.54*)	.65*	(.58*)	.78*	(.66*)
2–3	.59†	(.56*)	.60†	(.56*)	.74†	(.64*)
Max. C Attainable	.87	(.71)	.87	(.71)	.91	(.71)

* Significant at .01 level.
† Significant at .05 level.

Table 4.5. Correlation between Classification of Subjects According to Majority Vote and Their Experience, Attitude, Test Score (Pitcher and Coin Tests) and Order of Presentation of Reports (ATLAS Test) as Measured by Contingency Coefficients

Effect	Test			Max. C Attainable
	Pitcher Test	Coin Test	ATLAS Test	
Previous experience	.42*	.29†	—	.71
Like/dislike	.25	.31†	—	.71
Score	.31	.39†	—	.87
Order of presentation of reports	—	—	.26	.71

* Significant at .05 level.
† Significant at .10 level.

in solving them were more often classified as "analytic" than as "heuristic," as we did expect (see p. 57). Similar relationships could not be shown for the pitcher test, however.

As Table 4.5 further illustrates, no significant effect could be ascribed to the order in which the two consultant's reports of the ATLAS test were presented to the subject.

In conclusion, the results of our classification procedure according to majority judgment strongly support the reliability and validity of a simple two-way classification of subjects as either primarily "analytic" or primarily "heuristic." (See also our discussion in Section 5.1.) In the subsequent analysis we will therefore mainly use this two-way classification. Only in case the use of the more detailed classification categories can shed some more light on the observed behavior, will we come back to them in our discussion of the experimental results. Finally, we will use the ATLAS test to decide on the classification in cases of conflicting judgements, because this test appeared more reliable than the pitcher and coin tests.

4.3. ANALYSIS OF THE DECISIONS IN THE EXPERIMENT

4.3.1. Introduction

Based on the results of the previous section, Table 4.6 summarizes the experimental design. Approximately one-half of the subjects of each

Table 4.6. Summary of the Experimental Design

Subject Classification	Treatment		Total
	Explicit Understanding Oriented	Integral Understanding Oriented	
Analytic	4 + 2	6 + 3	10 + 5
Heuristic	9 + 2	6 + 3	15 + 5
Total	17	18	35

category received the "explicit understanding" approach; the other half received the "integral understanding" approach. The first number of each entry in Table 4.6 refers to the subjects whose classification according to the ATLAS test on the one hand and the pitcher and coin tests on the other was the same; the second number refers to the subjects for whom the tests resulted in opposing classifications.

Before we proceed with presentating the measures we proposed in Section 3.8, we should make some comments on the statistical techniques used in this section. The basic information on the decisions made during the experiment can be transformed into measures of adoption of the optimal proposal per type of decision per product and per period. We have argued before (Section 3.8) that joint consideration of the three decisions per product and per period leads to improved reliability of the adoption measure D.[51] For the analysis of differences between groups of measures D, we rejected multivariate analysis,[52] which would have considered the (psychological) interdependence of adoption measures over time and between products because this would have required us to make the unrealistic assumption of consistency in adoption patterns (see the discussion of Section 3.8). Instead we will focus on the measure M, which we proposed in Section 3.8 as an overall measure of proposal adoption. Moreover, a period-by-period analysis of measure D is made to gain some insight into the actual adoption patterns that were followed. (The values of D for each product are presented in Appendix 16). In all analyses, the products are treated independently.[53]

---

[51] The loss of information due to this aggregation of information is discussed in Section 4.3.2.

[52] Nonparametric multivariate analysis has only recently received attention from statisticians. Multivariate extensions of nonparametric location tests have been proposed by, e.g., Bhapkar [96].

[53] Under the null hypothesis (no difference between subjects), the six adoption

In fact, one would expect dependence of adoption measures among products if implementation is reached by a subject, since implementation implies insight in the underlying structure of the problem, which is similar for all products. In the case of mere acceptance, however, the question of dependence can only be answered if we are able to discover what exactly causes a subject to accept the proposal.

The many pairwise comparisons we intend to make between groups of adoption measures with repeated use of the same group in different comparisons raises the problem of simultaneous statistical inference. The proposed procedure may lead to statistically fallacious conclusions, since the actual significance level of a test is raised above the stated one if the test is used repeatedly.[54] Any individual comparisons of groups of measures are only made, therefore, if a preceding overall test indicates the existence of differences between the groups. We will use the Kruskal-Wallis H-test for the overall comparison and the Mann-Whitney U-test for the individual comparisons between groups of adoption measures[55] (see Siegel [94, pp. 184–193 and pp. 116–127]).

4.3.2. Loss of Information Due to Pooling of Decisions

In order to increase the reliability of the proposal-adoption measure, we proposed in Section 3.8 to pool the measures for pricing and production decisions and to use the purchasing decision solely to resolve ties in ranking. If incomplete adoption exists, however, the resulting measure will not tell us whether the adoption refers to the pricing proposal, the production proposal, or to both.

We used the Wilcoxon matched-pairs signed-ranks test (see Siegel [94, pp. 75–83]) to test for differences between adoption measures[56] for the pricing and production decisions for each period (Periods 7–12). The results of the test, performed per product, are given in Table 4.7.

measures (one per product) for each subject can be considered as six statistically independent drawings from the total population of adoption measures. The questions raised in the text refer to psychological dependence between these measures. If psychologically interdependent, the measures really are different dimensions of one observation and multivariate analysis would apply.

[54] What constitutes new and what repeated use of a test is a matter of judgment. See, e.g., Miller [97, pp. 31–35] for a discussion of the concept of families of statistical statements.

[55] Alternatively we could have derived simultaneous confidence regions from the Krushal-Wallis statistic (Miller [97, pp. 165–172]). The serious disadvantage of this procedure is, however, that the outcome of the comparison between two out of k populations depends on the observations in the other $(k-2)$ populations.

[56] See Section 3.8, p. 69 for a definition of the measure D. For comparing the adoption of the optimal pricing and production proposals, the constituent elements of the measure D are treated separately.

Table 4.7. Scores of Wilcoxon Matched-Pairs Signed-Ranks Test
Applied to the Differences between Proposal-Adoption Measures
for the Pricing and Production Decisions in Periods 7–12

Statistic	Product					
	A	B	C	D	E	F
T	41.5	142	76.5	13.5	65*	198
T_c	25	59	35	6	89	89

* Significant at .05 level.
T = Wilcoxon test-statistic.
T_c = Critical value of T at .05 significance level.
H_0: There are no differences between the proposal-adoption measures for the pricing and production decision.

Table 4.7 shows a significant difference in behavior with respect to the subproposals for product E. The degree of adoption of the optimal pricing proposal for product E—if some degree of adoption of the optima occurred at all—was consistently higher than the degree of adoption of the optimal production proposal for the same product, regardless of a subject's cognitive style. Product E turns out to be the only product of the six whose optimal solution requires production *below* the demand expected at the optimal price. In view of the simultaneously existing overcapacity when optimal decisions are made, many subjects were tempted to increase the production to at least the expected demand, which causes the adoption measure for the production decision to be lower than the measures for the pricing decision. No difference could be demonstrated between the analytic and heuristic subjects in this respect. Wide fluctuations in the difference of adoption measures for the two types of decision were observed for product F. The optimal proposal for product F requires a relatively high production *above* the demand expected at the optimal price. In this case subjects attempted "to correct" for this discrepancy by either directly decreasing the production or, indirectly, lowering the price, which causes an increase in the expected demand.[57] Again we did not find differences between "analytic" and "heuristic" subjects in this case. "analytic" and "heuristic" subjects in this case.

[57] The Wilcoxon test is a central tendency test and not designed to reveal differences due to extreme, but compensating, values of the observations, which explains that we did not find a significant difference for product F in Table 10.

In conclusion, partial adoption of the optimal proposals appeared due to some "corrective" action by the subject in case a most compelling (although false) heuristic argument for such correction (such as the elimination of discrepancies between production and expected demand) existed. This statement equally applies to analytic and heuristic subjects and should be considered when we make inferences about differences between these groups on the basis of the aggregative adoption measures in the next sections.

4.3.3. Analysis of Adoption Behavior Based on the Overall Measures M

The first two hypotheses of this study (Section 2.4) predict a manager's attitude and need for support with respect to a research recommendation as a function of the interactive effect of the manager's reasoning style and the researcher's mode of presentation and degree of continued support of the recommendation. The hypotheses can be stated formally in terms of the adoption measures of Section 3.8. To do so, we introduce the following notation:

A = subject classified as analytical according to tests
H = subject classified as heuristic according to tests

C = the complete "explicit-understanding" approach is used by the researcher
G = the general "integral-understanding" approach is used by the researcher

In our further discussion the four groups of subjects that are distinguished in the experimental design will be labeled AC, HC, AG, and HG, respectively. The above symbols are also used as subscripts to the measures defined in Section 3.8:

M = overall measure of proposal adoption per product
D = period measure of proposal adoption per product

Finally, we symbolize an equal, higher, or lower degree of adoption by the signs =, >, or <, respectively.

The first two hypotheses of Section 2.4 and their corollaries can now be stated formally. In each case the strongest formulation of our prediction is chosen. A brief explanation, following each statement, will make it clear whether our prediction is positively or negatively formulated. In the former case we expect a statistical test to be significant, which leads to the acceptance of the alternative hypothesis H_1. In the latter case we do not expect significance, which means that we have no reason to reject the null-hypothesis H_0.

Hypothesis I.

(a) $H_0: M_{AC} \leqq M_{HC}$ $H_1: M_{AC} > M_{HC}$ for products C and D

and $H_0: M_{AC} < M_{HC}$ $H_1: M_{AC} \geqq M_{HC}$ for all other products

Analytic subjects will reach a higher degree of implementation than heuristic subjects, and at least as high a degree of acceptance, if the accounting manager uses the explicit-understanding approach in presenting the operations research proposal. Moreover, hypothesis I claims that the degree of proposal adoption reached by the analytic subjects is high relative to all other classification-approach combinations,[58] that is,

(b) $H_0: M_{AC} = M_{AG}$ $H_1: M_{AC} \neq M_{AG}$ for all products

(c) $H_0: M_{AC} = M_{HG}$ $H_1: M_{AC} \neq M_{HG}$ for all products

In other words, there should be no reason to suspect that the integral-understanding approach reaches a significantly higher or lower degree of adoption than the explicit-understanding approach when the latter is applied under the most favorable circumstances.

Hypothesis II.

(a) $H_0: M_{HG} = M_{AG}$ $H_1: M_{HG} \neq M_{AG}$ for all products

If the integral-understanding approach is used, there should be no reason to suspect that the degree of implementation or acceptance is higher or lower for the analytic subjects than for the heuristic subjects. Moreover, hypothesis II claims that the integral-understanding approach will lead to a relatively high degree of proposal adoption. Especially the heuristic subjects, who are predicted to adopt poorly under the explicit-understanding approach, should benefit from the integral-understanding

---

[58] The absolute level of adoption of a research proposal that one may expect to reach, depends on a number of factors, such as the quality of the proposal, the quality of alternative (in particular: current) decisions and other factors related to effecting change in general. We may expect these factors to be operating to an equal extent in all cases. We therefore analyze initially the adoption behavior of the experimental groups relative to each other. The factors that affect the absolute level of adoption are discussed in the next section.

approach, that is,

(b) $H_0: M_{HG} \leqq M_{HC}$ $H_1: M_{HG} > M_{HC}$ for products C and D

and $H_0: M_{HG} < M_{HC}$ $H_1: M_{HG} \geqq M_{HC}$ for all other products

or: the heuristic subjects should be positively inclined to accept and implement the optimal solution if the integral-understanding approach is used, while they are definitely not inclined to do so when the explicit-understanding approach is used. The final and less interesting implication is that the analytic subjects receiving the integral-understanding treatment will be more inclined to adopt the researcher's recommendation than a heuristic subject who received the explicit-understanding approach and is expected not to respond at all to the research recommendation, that is

(c) $H_0: M_{AG} \leqq M_{HC}$ $H_1: M_{AG} > M_{HC}$ for products C and D

and $H_0: M_{AG} < M_{HC}$ $H_1: M_{AG} \geqq M_{HC}$ for all other products

It should not be concluded from the above hypotheses, especially IIb, that the integral-understanding approach dominates (in the game-theoretic sense of this word) the explicit-understanding approach. The hypotheses refer only to the subject's behavior (the return of a certain implementation strategy) and not to the amount of effort or commitment required from the researcher in each case (the cost of the strategy). The integral-understanding approach, requiring continued involvement on the part of the researcher, is more costly than the explicit-understanding approach and hence it is not a priori clear which approach is preferable.

The Mann-Whitney U-statistic was calculated for each pair of comparisons, while the Kruskal-Wallis H-statistic was used for the overall test. The test results are given in Table 4.8. The first column of Table 4.8 refers to the hypotheses stated above. The second column states the alternative hypothesis in each case.[59] The product measures are divided into two groups according to their classification as measures of acceptance (products A, B, E, and F) or measures of implementation (products C and D). The column labeled "Prediction" indicates whether we predicted the test to be significant or nonsignificant. The starred entries in the body of the table indicate when significance at .05 level actually occurred.

As Table 4.8 indicates, our hypotheses are strongly supported by the experimental data. The analytic subjects turned out to be strong adopters no matter what approach was used. The heuristic subjects, on the other hand, were only attracted by the researcher's recommendations if the

---

[59] Note that hypotheses Ib, Ic, and IIa are two-tailed tests, while the other tests are one-tailed.

Table 4.8. Results of Kruskal-Wallis H-Test and Mann-Whitney U-Test Applied to Measures of Overall Adoption Behavior

| Hypothesis | H_1 | Critical Value of Statistic at .05 Level | Acceptance Measures Product | | | | | Implementation Measures Product | | |
			A	B	E	F	Prediction	C	D	Prediction
Overall Differences		7.82	7.08†	8.19*	1.96	2.47	(S)	10.97*	6.13†	S
Pairwise Differences:										
Ia	$AC > HC$	16	13.50*	21.00	30.50	29.50	(S)	19.00†	15.00*	S
Ib	$AC \neq AG$	10	21.50	22.00	22.50	24.00	$\sim S$	21.50	25.00	$\sim S$
Ic	$AC \neq HG$	10	25.00	17.50	21.50	15.50	$\sim S$	15.00	24.00	$\sim S$
IIa	$HG \neq AG$	17	36.00	34.00	25.50	29.00	$\sim S$	24.00	39.50	$\sim S$
IIb	$HG > HC$	27	22.00*	15.50*	37.50	32.00	(S)	13.00*	27.00*	S
IIc	$AG > HC$	27	25.50*	24.50*	44.50	45.00	(S)	20.00*	28.00†	S

Note: The symbols and relationships of the second column are explained in the text. The entries in the body of the table are the computed H- and U-statistics. S = significance; (S) = sometimes significance; $\sim S$ = no significance; * significant at .05 level of significance; † significant at .10 level of significance. The significant differences are all in the predicted direction.

integral-understanding approach was used in the presentation. These conclusions apply particularly to the implementation behavior of the subjects as measured by the adoption measures for products C and D.[60]

The number of subjects in each group who reached implementation at least to some extent as well as the consistency between implementation and acceptance behavior observed within each group are shown in Table 4.9. This table confirms that the higher degree of implementation we found in Table 4.8 for the groups AC, HG, and AG in comparison to HC is not merely relative. 89% of the subjects of groups AG and HG and 66% of the subjects of group AC reached at least the level of "partial implementers" (as defined in Table 4.9).[61] On the other hand, only 27% of the subjects of the group HC reached at least the level of "partial implementers."

We did not find significant differences in adoption behavior for products E and F between the groups AC, HG, and AG on the one hand and HC on the other hand (see Table 4.8). Table 4.9 shows that this is due to the high degree of acceptance of the optimal proposals for products E and F by the HC group rather than to a low degree of acceptance by the three other groups. Moreover, Table 4.9 shows that subjects who did, at least in part, implement the optimal solution adopted the optimal proposals for all products in the vast majority of cases. The subjects who did not implement in general also rejected the optimal proposals for the acceptance products A, B, E, and F. A marked difference in consistency between the total or partial implementers and the nonimplementers was found, however. While only in 7.6% of all possible cases an implementer showed himself a nonaccepter at the same time, in 33% of all possible cases a nonimplementer turned out to be a simultaneous accepter. *What* caused some subjects to accept the optimal proposals in some, but not all, cases will be considered in the next section. At this point we take the experi-

---

[60] We recall that the subjects did not automatically receive the optimal solutions for the products C and D. They had either to compute the optimal decisions for these products themselves or they had to give explicit and complete instructions to the accounting manager for their computation. The optimal decisions for products A, B, E, and F were sent to the subject under any circumstances and did not require any initiative on his part. The products C and D will occasionally be referred to as implementation products, while the others are called acceptance products.

[61] One of the subjects in the group AC, a foreign student, was a 100% rejecter of the optimal proposals in the periods before the meeting, but became a 100% adopter in the final decisions made after the meeting. At least part of this extreme behavior (the only case of such extremity) can be ascribed to extraordinary language problems which caused the subject great difficulty in using the formal language teletype communications. When we eliminate this subject, 80% of the subjects of group AC reached at least the level of "partial implementer."

Table 4.9. Consistency of Acceptance and Implementation Behavior of Experimental Subjects

Implementation Measure > .10	Group	No. of Subjects	Acceptance Measure							
			> .10 (Accepters)				≤ .10 (Nonacceptors)			
			A	B	E	F	A	B	E	F
For Both Products C and D	AC	3	3	3	3	3	—	—	—	—
(Implementers)	HC	—	—	—	—	—	—	—	—	—
	AG	4	4	4	3	4	—	—	—	—
	HG	5	5	5	5	5	—	—	—	—
For Either C or D*	AC	1(0)	1(0)	1(0)	1(0)	1(0)	—	—	—	—
(Partial Implementers)	HC	3(2)	3(2)	3(2)	3(2)	2(2)	—	—	—	1(0)
	AG	4(3)	3(3)	3(3)	3(2)	2(1)	1(0)	1(0)	1(0)	2(2)
	HG	3(3)	2(2)	3(3)	3(3)	3(3)	1(1)	—	—	—
For Neither C nor D	AC	2	1	—	1	1	1	2	1	1
(Nonimplementers)	HC	8	2	—	5	5	6	8	3	3
	AG	1	—	—	—	—	1	1	1	1
	HG	1	—	—	—	1	1	1	1	—
Total		35	24	22	27	27	11	13	8	8

* The numbers in parentheses refer to the case that the adoption measure for product C is > .10 and for product D ≦ .10.

mental evidence to support our earlier statement that implementation implies stability, but that mere acceptance may lead to instability (Section 1.5).

We finally draw attention to the fact that no significant differences of adoption behavior were observed for products which had a deterministic demand (B and D) versus those which had a stochastic demand (A, C, E, and F). In view of the difference in the degree of difficulty between these two types of problems, we expected more rejections of the optimal proposals in the stochastic cases. In fact, the number of rejections was somewhat higher in the deterministic cases.[62]

4.3.4. Analysis of Adoption Behavior Based on the Period Measures *D*

A similar analysis as presented in the previous section was applied to the adoption measures D, computed for each period. The results of this analysis are summarized in Tables 4.10 and 4.11. The periods 13 and 14 in Table 4.11 refer to the final decisions made by the subject after the discussion meeting with the production and accounting managers. The results of the Mann-Whitney U-test are only presented if the Kruskal-Wallis H-test indicated overall differences at least at a .10 level of significance.

Together with the absolute levels of adoption (Appendix 16), the pairwise comparisons between groups made in Tables 4.10 and 4.11 give some insight into the general adoption patterns followed by the different groups of subjects. We first turn to the implementation products, C and D.[63]

The degree of adoption of the optimal proposals was generally low in periods 7 and 8, the first two periods in which the optimal decisions were presented. No distinctive features of subject-class or approach used are apparent in these periods. The development of implementation behavior in the predicted direction becomes first noticeable in periods 9 and 10. The reaction of heuristic subjects, in particular, differed significantly for the two modes of proposal presentation. The evidence remains inconclusive, however, since in these periods the degree of implementation of the optimal proposal was generally lower for the explicit-understanding than for the integral-understanding approach. The last statement no longer holds in the later periods: the analytic subjects who received the complete understanding approach ultimately reached a level of implementation

---

[62] The number of subjects who rejected the optimal proposals were: 11(A), 8(E), 8(F) and 15(C) for the stochastic products and: 13(B) and 20(D) for the deterministic products.

[63] See footnote 60, page 87.

Table 4.10. Results of H-Test and U-Test Applied to Adoption Measures of Periods 7–10

Hypothesis	H_1	Critical Value of Statistic at .05 Level	Periods 7 and 8 Product A	B	E	F	Pred.	Product C	D	Pred.	Periods 9 and 10 Product A	B	E	F	Pred.	Product C	D	Pred.
Overall Differences		7.82	2.67	2.25	3.12	2.14	(S)	2.99	3.14	S	7.83*	5.52	3.42	2.16	(S)	6.10†	4.05	S
Pairwise Differences:																		
Ia	$AC > HC$	16					(S)			S	18.00†				(S)	19.50		~S
Ib	$AC \neq AG$	10		No Significant Differences			~S			~S	20.00				~S	20.00		~S
Ic	$AC \neq HG$	10					~S			~S	20.50				~S	18.00		~S
IIa	$HG \neq AG$	17					~S			~S	40.50				~S	45.00		~S
IIb	$HG > HC$	27					(S)			S	18.00*				(S)	24.00*		S
IIc	$AG > HC$	27					(S)			S	18.00*				(S)	24.00*		S

* significant at .05 level.
† significant at .10 level.
See also note, Table 4.8.

Table 4.11. Results of H-Test and U-Test Applied to Adoption Measures of Periods 11–14

Hypothesis	H_1	Critical Value of Statistic at .05 Level	Periods 11 and 12 Product				Pred.	Product		Pred.	Periods 13 and 14 Product				Pred.	Product		Pred.
			A	B	E	F		C	D		A	B	E	F		C	D	
Overall Differences		7.82	3.64	9.32*	3.11	5.44		6.78†	6.43†	S	3.92	2.32	2.76	4.27		6.76†	10.14*	S
Pairwise Differences:																		
Ia	AC > HC	16	20.00					19.00*	15.00*	S	No					13.50*	6.00*	S
Ib	AC ≠ AG	10	23.00					26.50	26.50	~S	Significant					22.00	9.00*	~S
Ic	AC ≠ HG	10	16.00					19.00	26.50	~S	Differences					23.00	6.00*	~S
IIa	HG ≠ AG	17	29.50					30.00	39.50	~S						40.00	32.00	~S
IIb	HG > HC	27	13.50*					19.00*	26.00*	S						26.50*	45.00	S
IIc	AG > HC	27	27.00*					30.00†	27.00*	S						25.00*	37.50	S

* Significant at .05 level.
† Significant at .10 level.
See also note, Table 4.8.

that was about as high as the level reached by analytic or heuristic subjects who received the integral-understanding approach.[64] The lag in implementing the optimal proposals in the former case appears due to a more serious attempt by the subjects to understand the derivation of the optimal solution before its adoption was considered. The explicit-understanding approach enabled the subject to become relatively independent from the accounting manager, since the optimal solution was immediately supported by the complete set of formulas in this case. The receipt of formulas was apparently interpreted as a request for checking them or at least studying the relationships before turning to the optimal decisions that were based on the analysis (although such a request was never actually made).

The shock given to the system after period 10 by the announcement of a number of parameter changes did not significantly affect the development of implementation behavior we described above, but rather reinforced this development. In fact, the predicted differences in implementation behavior were strongest in periods 11 and 12. The fact that our hypotheses withstood this test indicates that the actions of implementing subjects rested on a firm confidence in the analysis and at least sufficient understanding of it to realize that the same underlying relationships still applied despite the parameter changes.

The tests for periods 13 and 14 refer to the after-meeting decisions. The adoption measures for product D increased to their maximum value for all analytic subjects and increased considerably for the heuristic subjects who received the explicit-understanding approach. Similar increases did not occur for the subjects who received the integral-understanding approach, which explains the changed pattern of significant differences for product D in period 14 (similar reactions for product C did not affect the tests, since the absolute level of adoption for product C reached during the foregoing periods by subjects receiving the integral-understanding approach was already high). The relationship between the subjects' reception of the accounting manager's arguments in the meeting and the approach used by this manager in the previous periods will be considered in Section 4.5.

The acceptance measures for products A, B, E, and F do not quite show the same consistent pattern of differences that we observed for the implementation measures. The optimal decisions for these products were made available to the subject without any initiative on his part. Hence the subject could decide to use these optimal decisions at any time even if he did not have any real understanding of the analysis upon which the

---

[64] See footnote 61, page 87.

decisions were based. We did expect, however, a fairly high level of accept-ance of the optimal solution by those subjects who were expected to adopt the optima for products C and D—the analytic subjects and the heuristic subjects receiving the integral-understanding approach—since such con-sistency should directly follow from an understanding of the optimal solu-tion. A low level of acceptance was expected for the heuristic subjects who received the explicit-understanding approach, since we hypothesized that emphasis on analytic style would alienate these subjects to a serious extent (cf. hypothesis II, Section 2.4).

Our expectations were confirmed only for product A in period 9 and for product B in period 11. The absence of significance for the other prod-ucts and periods is undoubtedly due, in part, to the different behaviors of those subjects who ultimately adopted an optimal proposal, but who varied greatly with respect to their use of the optimal decisions in the periods prior to definite adoption (see also Section 3.8, pp. 67–68). Such variations were less likely to occur for the implementation products C and D, since their optimal decisions were not as readily available to the subject. The other factor that accounts for the few cases of significance in comparing the acceptance measures between groups was mentioned in the previous section: the nonimplementing subjects were sometimes will-ing to accept the accounting manager's proposals, especially for products E and F, which caused the difference we had expected between these subjects and the implementing subjects to disappear. (See also Section 4.3.2 on products E and F, pp. 82–83.)

4.3.5. The Impact of Confounding Variables

One might expect the immediate success or failure of a decision, as reflected by the financial report sent to the subject, to be a major determi-nant of the subject's future reliance on the sources that generated this decision. Table 4.12 illustrates what the results would be if the subject always followed his managers' proposals for all periods and what they would be if the subject always followed the optimal proposals from period 7 on (period 7 is the first period in which the optimal decisions are pre-sented). The actual results depend of course on our use of one specific series of random normal numbers to generate the deviations of actual from expected demand (see Appendix 12). The expected results under the optimal proposal are also given in Table 4.12.

Table 4.13 relates adoption behavior of period t to the financial results of period $t - 2$ ($t = 7, \ldots, 12$) for products A, B, E, and F. The hypothesis that adoption or increased adoption of the optimal proposal in period t by those subjects who did not use this proposal fully in period $t - 2$ was more likely to occur if the net profit in period $t - 2$ was nega-

Table 4.12. Actual and Expected Financial Results for Two Alternative Courses of Action (Always Optimal versus Always Managerial)

Proposal followed	Period				
	3/4	5/6	7/8	9/10	11/12
1. Mgrs' Proposals: Actual Results					
A	11,200	13,200	12,400	10,700	3,600
B	2,800	2,800	2,800	2,800	2,800
C	1,600	3,000	400	2,400	600
Net Profit	−400	3,000	−400	−100	−9,000
D	14,500	15,400	15,900	15,900	15,900
E	−2,800	4,300	−4,000	−7,900	−1,400
F	300	3,400	3,000	3,400	3,100
Net Profit	−400	3,000	−400	−100	1,600
2. Opt. Proposals: a. Actual Results					
A			16,500(+)	12,100(−)	5,900(+)
B			3,100(0)	3,100(0)	3,100(0)
C			−1,400(−)	9,900(+)	5,400(−)
Net Profit			2,200(−)	9,100(+)	−1,600(+)
D			16,500(0)	16,500(0)	16,500(0)
E			3,100(+)	−600(−)	2,900(−)
F			5,200(+)	3,500(−)	3,000(−)
Net Profit			8,800(+)	3,400(−)	6,400(−)
b. Expected Results					
A				13,600	4,800
B				3,100	3,100
C				5,000	5,600
Net Profit				5,700	−2,500
D				16,500	16,500
E				1,850	4,150
F				3,900	3,400
Net Profit				6,200	8,000

Note: Net profit = sum of marginal profits-fixed cost ($16,000). The signs in parentheses refer to the directional deviation of the actual from expected results.

Table 4.13. Adoption Behavior Related to Financial Results

Group	Decision period t	Net Profit per $(t-2)$[a] +	−	χ^2	Change in Marg. Profit from per $(t-4)$ to $(t-2)$[b] +	−	χ^2	Min. (Net Profit, Marg. Profit) per $(t-2)$[c] +	−	χ^2
AC	I	8	19	.15	17	10	.05	2	5	.11
	II	19	21		21	20		3	8	
HC	I	21	22	.00	26	17	.01	8	11	.07
	II	45	40		47	38		8	6	
AG	I	26	13	.00	14	23	.03	6	5	.01
	II	38	19		25	28		7	9	
HG	I	23	20	.34	19	24	.90	3	11	.97
	II	43	15		41	13		8	5	

10% significance-level: $\chi^2(1) = 2.71$

I = Adoption or increased adoption of optimal solution in period t.

II = Rejection or decreased adoption of optimal solution in period t.

(Only the subjects who did not (fully) use the optimal solution in period $(t-2)$ are considered.)

H_1: a) The degree of adoption in period t is adversely affected by the net profit in period $(t-2)$.

b) The degree of adoption in period t is adversely affected by the change of marginal profit from period $(t-4)$ to $(t-2)$.

c) The degree of adoption in period t is adversely affected by the minimum of net profit and marginal profit in period $(t-2)$.

Hypotheses a) and b) refer to products A, B, E, and F. Hypothesis c) refers to product E only. All data refer to periods $t = 7$, . . . , 12. Example: In 19 of the 40 cases, in which AC-subjects made a net loss in period $t-2$ and did not use the optimal proposals in that period, were the optimal proposals adopted or was their adoption increased in period t.

tive than when it was positive was not confirmed by the experimental data. Neither did the data confirm the more specific hypothesis we get when we replace in the previous sentence "the net profit of period $t - 2$" by "the change in marginal profit for each product from period $t - 4$ to period $t - 2$." The conclusions remain the same if we test these hypotheses per product.

As Table 4.12 illustrates, product E is the only product whose marginal profit ever became negative, even if the optimal solution was used. The hypothesis that a negative marginal profit *or* a negative net overall profit in period $t - 2$ induced a subject to adopt the optimal solution in period t was therefore specifically tested for product E (see last 3 columns of Table 4.13).

We note that the test results of Table 4.13 only support the point that net profits or changes in marginal profit did not directly influence the adoption behavior of our subjects. Our data were inadequate to test the more general hypothesis that "source-switching"[65] is more likely to occur when immediate past experience shows the results from the current source unsatisfactory.

All heuristic subjects adopted more strongly the optimal solution for product E in period t if they had a marginal loss for that product in period $t - 2$ (see Table 4.13). The strong acceptance of the optimal proposal for product E by the HC subjects when their nonoptimal decisions used before had resulted in a marginal *profit* still stands out, however, and appears to be explainable only as the joint effect of many factors.

We were careful to supply the subjects with sufficient market-survey information before each period to ensure that their market expectations would essentially coincide with the demand distributions actually used. This assertion might be questioned in view of experimental evidence presented by Rapoport [98] who found that the presentation of extensive demand information did not significantly affect the immediate demand expectations of the subjects in his experiments. Instead he found significant dependence between his subjects' decisions and the demand in the preceding experimental trial. Our finding that subjects showed a tendency to set production close to the expected demand, irrespective of other factors (see Section 4.3.2) combined with Rapoport's results, suggest that the adoption of an optimal proposal is more likely to occur if the optimal production and the last available actual demand deviate in the same way from the expected demand (according to the demand distribution presented in the market survey). These data are presented in Table 4.14.

---

[65] In Section 3.8 (p. 68) we identified three sources of decision proposals: the functional managers (with proposals generated according to the rules of Appendix 5), the accounting manager (with the optimal proposal), and the subject himself.

Table 4.14. Adoption Behavior Related to the Degree of Apparent Agreement between Optimal Proposals and Actual Results

Decision period t		Directional relationship between the deviations (opt. production − exp. demand) and (act. demand − exp. demand) in period $(t-2)$		
		Number of agreements	Number of disagreements	χ^2
AC	I	12	10	.01
	II	15	12	
HC	I	26	18	.01
	II	37	21	
AG	I	23	15	.00
	II	22	12	
HG	I	27	17	.09
	II	18	19	

10% significance-level: $\chi^2(1) = 2.71$.

I = adoption or increased adoption of optimal solution in period t.

II = rejection or decreased adoption of optimal solution in period t.

H_1: The degree of adoption in period t is enhanced by the apparent agreement between the optimal proposal and the actual results of period $(t-2)$.

The data refer to periods $t = 7, \ldots, 12$ and products A, E and F. Example: For the AC-group, there were 27 instances in which there appeared to be agreement between the optimal proposal and the actual results of period $(t-2)$. In 12 cases such agreement was followed by the (increased) adoption of the optimal proposal in period t.

The experimental data again did not generally confirm the hypothesis that adoption in period t is more likely to occur if directional agreement existed in period $t-2$ between the deviations from the expected demand of optimal production and actual demand, respectively.[66] Analysis per product does not change this conclusion. However, some indication exists that the heuristic subjects supported their adoption of the optimal proposals by heuristic arguments (see Table 4.14). But the approach used by

[66] The immediate implications of the parameter changes after period 10 were consistent with the measure of agreement between optimal proposals of period 11 or 12 and actual results of period 9 or 10 so that no correction for this factor was necessary.

the accounting manager appears to overrule this point, as the comparison of groups *HG* and *HC* indicates.

We have already noted (footnote 43, p. 68) that, in the trial experiments, substantial improvements in performance did occur, if at all, in the early decision periods. Performance after period 6 either stabilized at or oscillated around a certain level, which in no case was high enough to result in a positive value of our performance measure D. The performance of the teams before period 7 in the final series of experiments generally agreed with our observations in the trial experiments. A more than accidentally high degree of optimality was reached before period 6 by only four subjects (BM, BJ, CE, BK), three of whom had been classified as analytic. Only one subject (BM) reached a substantial degree of optimality (as expressed by a value of $D \gg 0$) for more than one product. With these possible exceptions, we feel justified, in view of the preceding remarks, to ascribe the differential effect of performance before and after period 7, as measured by the values of D and M, completely to the presentation of the optimal proposals by the accounting manager. The exceptions, moreover, rather support than discredit our conclusions drawn from the observed behavior.

Many more factors must have influenced the subject's actual decision behavior. It was the intention of this section to highlight only those factors beyond the experimenter's control, whose impact might seem to provide us with immediate alternative explanations for the observed differences between groups. However, we could identify no single factor that had as strong predictive power of the adoption behavior as cognitive style.

4.4. ANALYSIS OF COMMUNICATIONS

All messages were coded independently by two individuals according to the coding scheme presented in Section 3.8 (page 71). The required use of the formal language left the subject little room for ambiguity in his messages, which was reflected in the extremely high degree of agreement between the coders. Disagreements, accounting for less than 2% of the total of messages coded, were resolved by consensus judgment of the two coders.

The number of interactions that the subjects initiated with their managers varied greatly, from a low of 10 to a high of 178 interactions during the periods 3–12. The interaction pattern, however, appeared strongly task- and scenario-determined, which led to a high degree of consistency between subjects with respect to the *relative* number of mes-

Table 4.15. Average Number of Messages Sent by Subjects to Each Manager with its Range (in Parentheses)

Group	Manager				
	Acct.	Mark.	Prod.	Purch.	Total
AC	24.5 (17–32)	18.3 (9–33)	20.2 (9–32)	19.3 (11–29)	82.3 (46–126)
HC	19.8 (7–51)	15.5 (0–49)	15.4 (3–41)	12.7 (3–37)	63.4 (13–178)
AG	19.3 (10–34)	15.7 (9–33)	14.6 (7–22)	11.0 (7–22)	60.6 (33–109)
HG	16.2 (5–29)	13.6 (2–29)	12.3 (2–29)	10.1 (1–24)	52.2 (10–106)

sages sent to each manager. Table 4.15 shows the average number of messages sent by subjects per group. The interaction pattern remains unchanged when we subtract the directly induced messages (classified as "answers") from the counts.

The data of Table 4.15 seem to indicate that the required use of a formal language might have been more inhibiting to heuristic than to analytic subjects. Moreover, the explicit-understanding approach led to a generally higher level of messages sent by the subjects who received this approach. The mathematical explanations sent by the accounting manager under the explicit-understanding approach might explain such an increase in activity of the subjects in the latter case. However, tests on the basic data indicate that these differences should not be overemphasized.[67,68]

The message units (the whole or part of a message) were classified according to main content in one of three categories: analytical, functional,

[67] Comparisons were made between the total number of messages sent by heuristic and analytic subjects who received the same approach from the accounting manager. The results of the Mann-Whitney U-test were both nonsignificant:

Comparison $AC - HC$: $U = 20$; U_c (6, 11) = 16 at .05 level of significance.
Comparison $AG - HG$: $U = 33$; U_c (9, 9) = 21 at .05 level of significance.

[68] The effect of the approach used was measured by comparing the two approaches for the same type of subject.
Results of the Mann-Whitney U-test were:

Comparison $AC - AG$: $U = 13$; U_c (6, 9) = 12 at .05 level of significance.
$\quad\quad\quad\quad\quad HC - HG$: $U = 42$; U_c (9, 11) = 27 at .05 level of significance.

Table 4.16. Average Number of Message Units Sent by Subjects Classified According to Content with Its Range (in Parentheses)

| Group | Message Content | | | Total |
	Analytical	Functional	Organizational	
AC	15.0 (20.1%) (6–30)	38.0 (52.6%) (12–62)	19.3 (27.3%) (2–31)	62.3 (48–100)
HC	14.7 (22.7%) (4–43)	24.0 (37.0%) (3–68)	26.2 (40.3%) (6–66)	64.9 (16–148)
AG	14.8 (21.4%) (5–28)	23.6 (34.0%) (11–43)	30.1 (44.6%) (6–67)	69.5 (35–124)
HG	10.3 (18.2%) (4–19)	22.1 (39.0%) (2–44)	24.2 (42.8%) (3–55)	56.6 (11–105)

or organizational (cf. Section 3.8, p. 71). A summary of the results of this analysis, referring to periods 3–12, is given in Table 4.16.

We note that the totals in the last column of Tables 4.15 and 4.16 are not necessarily equal, since one message may consist of more message units and each message unit is counted in the coding. Moreover, the same message could be sent to several managers simultaneously. In this case the message was counted as many times as there were receivers, but it was coded only once.

No significant differences were found between the four groups of subjects with respect to the relative frequency of message units per content category.

In our third hypothesis (Section 2.4, p. 41) we predicted that the heuristic subjects would suppress the analytic arguments in their decision preparation if the accounting manager applied the explicit-understanding approach, but that these arguments would be included if the integral-understanding approach was used. We measured a subject's consideration of analysis for his decisions by the relative frequency of analytic message units with respect to the total of message units sent by him. Our hypothesis was tested on the basis of this measure by comparing the relative frequency of analytic messages sent in periods 5–8 with the same figure for periods 9–12. The periods 3 and 4 were eliminated to discard a possible beginning effect[69] (few analytic messages could be expected in

---

[69] We did not correct for an ending effect, since the subjects were left in uncertainty about which period would be last. In view of the announced duration of the experiment, they most probably expected to manage their firm for several periods more.

these periods). The results of a two-tailed Wilcoxon matched-pairs signed-ranks test of the hypothesis are reported in Table 4.17. The null hypothesis states that the relative frequency of "analytic" message units in periods 9–12 was unchanged from periods 5–8. This hypothesis was tested for all categories of subjects. The results of a similar test with respect to "organizational" message units are also reported in Table 4.17.[70]

The hypothesis that the heuristic subjects suppress the analytic arguments in their communications when the explicit-understanding approach is used by the accounting manager is not supported by the data. However, it is remarkable that the *HC* group is the *only* group of subjects whose fraction of "analytic" message units did not significantly increase during the latter periods.[71] It is as remarkable that the *HC* group is also the *only* group of subjects whose "organizational" messages significantly increased during the later periods. Inspection of the messages sent by the presidents revealed that the *HC* subjects often referred the analytic messages received from the accounting manager to their other managers for comment, which accounted for the substantial proposition of analytic message

---

[70] Some dependence between relative frequencies of "analytic" and "organizational" message units exists, since both are part of the same constant sum. However, the existence of a third category ("functional") and the nonmutual exclusiveness of classes (see p. 71) diminish the dependency. Conclusions about either of the first two categories should therefore be based on separate tests.

[71] We note that the only one case of nonincrease of analytic message units in the *AC* group refers to the same foreign student mentioned in footnote 61 on page 87.

Table 4.17. T-Values of the Wilcoxon Matched-Pairs Signed-Ranks Test of Hypotheses Regarding Content of Message-Units

Group	Message Unit Content		Critical Value at .05 Level
	"Analytic"[a]	"Organizational"[b]	
AC	1†	4	0
HC	34.5	10.5*	11
AG	5.5*	20.5	6
HG	0*	25	6

* Significant at .05 level.
† Significant at .10 level.
(All significant differences are increases)
H_0: a) The relative frequency of "analytic" messages from periods (5-8) to periods (9-12) remained unchanged.
    b) Same as a), but replace "analytic" by "organizational."

Table 4.18. Subjects' Attitude Toward their Managers as Expressed by the Excess of Agreements over Disagreements

| Group | Excess of Agreements over Disagreements with | | | |
| | Production and Purchasing Managers | | Accounting and Marketing Managers | |
	Number	%	Number	%
AC	5	20	20	80
HC	25	31	56	69
AG	11	22	39	78
HG	13	36	23	64

units in the later periods. The data suggest to us to replace our third hypothesis by the following alternative hypothesis: Using the explicit-understanding approach, the accounting manager (researcher) will be unable to communicate directly—that is, such that both sides understand each other without the aid of an interpreter—with a heuristic president (manager). The approach may lead the president (manager) to seek interpretation of the communications received from the accounting manager. However, the accounting manager (researcher) can himself *ensure* proper consideration of his arguments by the president (manager) by using the integral-understanding approach.

The expressions of agreement and disagreement give us some indication about a president's feelings toward his managers. According to the measure of excess of agreements over disagreements the heuristic subjects tended to line up more with the production and purchasing managers, while analytic subjects agreed more often with the accounting and marketing managers. (Table 4.18.)

The absolute level of the percentages in Table 4.18 have little meaning, since the agreements and disagreements are for the most part directly induced by the scenarios. A comparison of the percentages between the groups gives some idea about the disposition of the subjects, however. Thus we see that subjects tended to favor the arguments of the accounting and marketing managers—regardless of their natural tendencies —if the explicit-understanding approach was used. But, as comparison with the findings of the earlier sections of this chapter illustrates, agreement in words obviously does not always mean agreement in deeds!

4.5. ANALYSIS OF QUESTIONNAIRES AND MEETINGS

The first two questionnaires, given to the subjects after periods 8 and 12, respectively, dealt with the problems of communication (arising from the controls we instituted), the performance of the firm, and the evaluation of the managers. The third questionnaire asked questions about the meeting between the presidents and the accounting and production managers.

There is no doubt that the subjects felt seriously restricted by the required use of a formal language and teletype communications. However, neither the approach used by the accounting manager nor the classification of the subject were found to have a systematic influence on the amount of difficulty experienced in communicating. Moreover, only four subjects of those who had reported that communications were insufficient for effective operation in the first questionnaire stated that no significant improvement in communications had occurred in later periods. Table 4.19 summarizes these answers.

Nearly all subjects stated in the first questionnaire that strong improvement in the performance of the firm would be reached if face-to-face meetings would be allowed. But only two subjects stated in the second questionnaire that face-to-face meetings would lead to significant improvement of the firm's performance. Abolition of the formal language but continued

Table 4.19. Difficulties Reported in the Use of the Firm's Communication System

Group	All Messages			Essential Messages			Improvement in Later Periods		
	No Diffi-culty	Some or Much Diffi-culty	NA	No Diffi-culty	Some or Much Diffi-culty	NA	No Im-prove-ment	Some or Much Improve-ment	NA
AC	0	6		2	3	1	1	5	
HC	0	11		4	7		2	9	
AG	1	7	1	3	5	1	1	6	2
HG	1	8		8	1		0	7	2

NA = No answer given.

restriction to teletype communications was generally not thought to lead to performance improvement in either case.[72]

Few subjects were able to maintain a profitable operation without turning to the optimal decisions. The experiment lasted long enough to ensure that the superiority of the optimal decisions—if used continuously—was reflected by the actual results. (The subjects never, of course, got a chance to make this comparison.) As a direct consequence of this structure, only four subjects of the sixteen who did not reach (near)optimality expressed satisfaction with their firm's performance at the end of period 12. Ten subjects were dissatisfied, even though they operated at optimality (they were still trying to overcome losses from previous periods). These results are summarized in table 4.20 which, for each group of subjects, relates expressed satisfaction with actual performance.

We combined the answers to the questions: "To what aspect of the operations did you pay most attention?" and "What are the firm's major problems at this point?" and divided them into three groups: functional (FNC), organizational (ORG), and optimal (OPT). The first two categories have the same meaning as in the message analysis (see p. 72); the last category refers to answers that explicitly state that the subject is seeking to adopt optimal decisions. (Table 4.21).

[72] The most serious problem in the use of the formal language (especially in the beginning periods) appeared due to a hardware feature. Under the half-duplex system —in use at the time our experiments were run—the same channel is used for receiving and for sending characters. When the monitor took over from a subject to complete his current message element, the subject often still typed one or two more characters. This led to a garbled printout of the remainder of the message element (although it was properly stored) and to confusion on the part of the subject.

Table 4.20. Expressed Satisfaction with the Firm's Performance

Group	After Period 7		After Period 12			
			At Opt.		Not at Opt.	
	Yes	No	Yes	No	Yes	No
AC	2	4	2	2	1	1
HC	6	5	3	—	2	6
AG*	3	3	—	5	1	3
HG	6	3	5	3	—	1

* Three *AG*-subjects did not answer the question after period 7.

Table 4.21. Attention Focus Reported by Subjects

Group	After Period 7 FNC	ORG	OPT	After Period 12 FNC	ORG	OPT
AC	1	5		2	1	3
HC*	2	8		2	8	1
AG		7	2		3	6
HG*	3	5	1	4	4	

* One subject of the *HC*-group did not answer the question after period 7. One *HG*-subject gave no answer after period 12.

Up to period 8 all subjects focused their attention strongly on the organizational aspects of the firm. After period 12 only the *HC* group of subjects reported organizational problems as their main focus of attention. Hence, the subjects' statements confirmed the findings we derived from a content analysis of the messages (see p. 101).

The relative ranking of the accounting and production managers after periods 7 and 12, respectively (Table 4.22), shows increased attention to the accounting manager's messages by all but the *AG* subjects.[73] The production manager received about the same attention after period 12 as

[73] With much reservation we could take this as an indication that the integral-understanding approach is less acceptable to the analytic subjectst han the explicit-understanding approach.

Table 4.22. Relative Ranking by Subjects of the Accounting and Production Managers According to the Contents of their Messages

Group	Accounting Manager After Period 7 H	M	L	After Period 12 H	M	L	Production Manager After Period 7 H	M	L	After Period 12 H	M	L
AC	2	1	3	5	1	—	—	6	—	—	2	4
HC	2	3	6	4	4	3	1	9	1	1	7	3
AG	4	4	1	3	6	—	—	7	2	—	8	1
HG	3	6	—	6	3	—	1	6	2	—	8	1

H = High; M = Medium; L = Low.

Table 4.23. Responses to Third Questionnaire Compared with Actual Behavior of Subjects

	Preferred Presentation				Suggestions actually followed							
					Before meeting				After meeting			
					Acct.		Other		Acct.		Other	
Group	Acct.	Prod.	Both	None	I	II	I	II	I	II	I	II
AC	6				3		3		5	1		
HC	7	4			2	1	5	3	4		5	1
AG	5	3		1	5	1	2	1	2	4	1	2
HG	6	1	1	1	6	1	1	1	5	1	2	

Entries in table refer to the number of subjects.
I = Suggestions actually followed agree with statements made in third questionnaire.
II = Suggestions actually followed disagree with statements made in third questionnaire.

after period 7 except from the *AC* group, whose majority discredited the production manager after period 12. In order to eliminate the absolute level of ranks used by a subject, we ranked a manager high (H) if the rank given exceeded the majority of ranks given the other managers. A manager was ranked low (L) if the rank given fell below that given to the other managers. Otherwise we ranked the manager medium (M).

After the meeting between the presidents (four at a time) and the accounting and production managers, 24 out of the 35 subjects declared themselves in favor of the accounting manager's presentation (Table 4.23). However, the presence of only one analytically oriented subject in a meeting often determined the course of the discussion, which often ended in a strong agreement between the analytic subject and the accounting manager. This obviously may have influenced the responses of heuristic subjects.[74] That statements are by no means valid substitutes

[74] We wonder if as many of the meetings would have shown a bias toward the analytic arguments, had we used businessmen rather than students as subjects. Preference for the accounting manager's presentation was "socially desirable" in a strongly analytically oriented academic community! We note also that only 12 out of 29 subjects (the B- and C-series) expressed *agreement* with the accounting manager (as opposed to preference for his presentation). (The A-series did not receive this question.) (See also Table 4.23.)

for actual behavior is illustrated by the responses to our question concerning which team member's suggestions and/or decisions a subject had used during the previous decision periods. No less than 17 out of 36 subjects gave answers that did *not* correspond to their actual behavior. In Table 4.23 we distinguish between the accounting manager versus all other sources that a subject named helpful in arriving at his decisions. The entries in the columns refer to the source actually followed to make decisions before and after the meeting, respectively. The cases in which the subject's statements agreed with his actual behavior are separated from those where they did not agree.

Six subjects (*CB, CD, CM, BB, BO,* and *BQ*) expressed in the meeting a strong awareness of being in a game-playing situation, and four of them suspected the existence of confederates as their managers. It is questionable to what extent and in what direction this influenced their behavior. Elimination of these subjects would certainly not alter our conclusions from the experiment, however.

Chapter 5

DISCUSSION AND CONCLUSION

5.1. DISCUSSION OF THE EXPERIMENTAL RESULTS

The main hypotheses of this study can be summarized as follows:

(a) cognitive style may operate as an effective constraint on the implementation of research recommendations

(b) the researcher may be able to reach implementation by properly taking this implementation constraint into account in his research strategy.

The importance of cognitive style in the approach to problem situations and its consistent operation in a variety of situations has had considerable attention in the literature [80–82]. We realize that the very choice of cognitive style as an implementation constraint has placed us in the middle of an as yet unsettled dispute among psychologists. The question that they raise is whether and how personality, in view of its apparent complexity and instability, can fruitfully be described in terms of more or less simple and stable traits (see, e.g., Allport [99]). Although our tests and subsequent experiment lend some support to the hypothesis of generality and stability over time of a once-observed cognitive style, for the purposes of this study we need not take an extreme position in this dispute. The tendency to rely mainly on a heuristic style of reasoning in a *specific* and more or less time-constrained problem situation may suffice—in our experimental as well as any real life situation—to render cognitive style effective as an implementation constraint. The dispute we referred to above finds its cause rather in the sometimes sweeping generalizations with respect to the generality and stability of an observed personality trait that psychologists would sometimes like to make on the basis of their test results. But such generalizations are of less direct concern to us.

From our point of view, the important contribution that psychologists have to make in this area is to provide us with insights into the "cost" of relaxation of psychological constraints. For example, an effective cognitive style constraint in a particular situation would meet with an infinite cost of relaxation if generality of this constraint over time and over problems could be strictly assumed.

The operations research solution to the firm's problems in our experiment was the fruit of thorough analysis. Cognitive style was therefore hypothesized to be effective as an implementation constraint if the subject's style did not match the analytic methods used to arrive at the research recommendations. The experimental evidence strongly supported this hypothesis. With two exceptions, the eleven heuristic subjects of group HC rejected—completely or in part—the OR recommendations if the accounting manager, that is, the operations researcher, supported the soundness of his recommendations by presenting to the subject his analysis of the technical problems, even though he gave all persuasive intuitively sound arguments as well. Of the two exceptions, one subject (subject CC) appeared analytically oriented from the answers he gave to the questionnaires. However, all judges agreed to classify the subject as heuristic according to his test results. The other "heuristic" subject (subject CF), who strongly accepted and implemented the optimal solutions under the explicit-understanding approach, did not give much indication of his analytic orientation in the questionnaires. He distinguished himself only by having sent very few messages during the experiment. His group ties apparently affected him little, which may have eased his decision to neglect his managers' proposals, although the reasons why he did so are not altogether clear.

The analytic subjects, on the other hand, responded more positively to the accounting manager's proposals if the explicit-understanding approach was used. We noted before that the complete rejection of the optimal proposals before the meeting by one analytic subject (subject CH) was at least in part due to his problems in understanding the experiment instructions and in communicating with other team-members.[60] The only other subject in this group (subject CB of group AC) who hesitated to adopt, and in part rejected, the optimal proposals was the one who stated most strongly his awareness of the game situation and his suspicions about the real identity of his managers during the meeting at the end of the experiment. The divergence of the HC and AC groups was accentuated by the final set of decisions made after the meeting, in which the artificial communication barriers were completely broken down. The AC group chose nearly unanimously the optimal proposals for all products (only one AC subject did not adopt the optimal proposal for product C). Of the HC group as few as three (for product C) and never more than seven (for product A) out of 11 subjects adopted the optimal proposals.

The second part of the hypotheses stated above was equally strongly confirmed by the experiment. Only one of the nine heuristic subjects who received the integral-understanding approach (subject BT of the HG-group) did *not* reach a high degree of adoption and at least some implementation of the optimal proposals. Two of the analytic subjects (subjects BA and BP) rejected strongly (although not completely) the optimal proposals. Both had been classified as analytic according to the ATLAS test, but as heuristic according to the two behavior tests. The decisions made after the meeting continued to show a high degree of adoption of optimal proposals, which ranged from four to seven (out of nine) analytic and from five to seven (out of nine) heuristic subjects adopting the optimal proposals for the different products.

Where our first two hypotheses have immediate parallels in real life situations, our third hypothesis seems to be more restricted to the specifics of the experimental situation. In Section 4.4 we modified the third hypothesis to bring it in line with the experimental results. However, it may well have been the limitation of realistically available alternatives, imposed by the experimental controls, that caused many heuristic subjects of the HC group to forward the accounting manager's proposals to their managers rather than neglect them completely as we originally hypothesized. The amount of pressure that could be (and was) continuously exerted by the accounting manager in the experiment no doubt far exceeded the amount of pressure that an operations researcher will usually be able to exert on management in reality. But even though the mode of the heuristic subjects' reaction to the analytic presentation of the research proposal differed from what we had hypothesized, the central notion of our third hypothesis still stands: the lack of implementation, observed when the accounting manager (operations researcher) attempted to gain a heuristic subject's conceptual and behavioral commitment to his research recommendations by emphasizing the analytic procedures that led to their creation, follows from the problems in establishing a direct communication link (or better; a direct understanding link) between people who differ strongly in cognitive style.

We do not consider the integral-understanding approach to be an easy and equivalent alternative way of creating a direct understanding link between an analytic researcher and a heuristic manager. Indeed, we could prevent in our experimental situation the alienation of a heuristic subject from an analytic researcher by deemphasizing the difference in cognitive styles that existed. The price of such a research strategy is, however, that the subject does not receive the full fruit of the research unless the researcher commits himself to a long-range postresearch involvement with the manager's problem. This is also the real-life parallel we would like to draw to our experimental observations. It seems to us that admonishments to the researcher such as "Be sure to speak the language of the manager," or "Put the mathematics in the appendix of your report to management" (see, e.g., Wynne [100]) do not get to the heart of the implementation problem. In our view, the entire nature of the commitment the operations researcher has to make to ensure the implementation of his recommendations depends on the implementation constraints that are found to be effective. It should therefore be of great importance to the researcher to be able to identify the potentially binding implementation constraints as well as to predict their actual effectiveness before embarking on a research project.

5.2. VALIDATION RECONSIDERED

In this section we direct ourselves to two questions:

(a) the validation of the tests we used to classify the subjects in the experiment according to their style of reasoning.
(b) the validation of the experimental results.

In Section 4.2 we justified our use of the ATLAS, pitcher, and coin tests to classify the subjects according to their cognitive style by showing the internal consistency of the judgments between tests for each judge, and the external consistency of judgments between judges for each test. Having shown consistency, we could point out that the instructions given to the judges formed a reasonable interpretation of the underlying concept of cognitive style which we had discussed in Section 2.4. For the purpose of this study we could be satisfied at this point. An attempt to tie our work to the efforts of other students of cognitive style requires further validation, however. In particular, it requires the establishment of the relationship of the tests we used with tests used by others in their studies. Although this work will not be undertaken here, we will mention some of the tests with which we would expect our test results to be highly correlated. Witkin et al. [81] used the so-called Tilting Room Tilting Chair, the Rotating Room, and Rod and Frame tests, which all center around bodily orientation as the basic variable, to measure their concept of field-dependence–independence, which we already mentioned as akin to our concept of cognitive style. Tyler ([80, pp. 228–233]) refers to studies of perceptual processes in which closure ("the act of grasping and retaining a clear, coherent pattern in the stimulus materials") plays a central role. Of the several closure factors that have been distinguished we would expect the flexibility of closure (the retention of a figure in a distracting field) to be correlated with our analytic category. It would therefore be interesting to establish the relationships between our tests and, for example, the Thurstone-Gottschaldt's Embedded Figures Test which was shown to have high factor-analytic loadings on this closure factor (cf., [79, p. 230]).

Our analytic category may also be expected to be strongly correlated with the sensing and thinking types, our heuristic category with the intuitive and feeling types of the Myers-Briggs Inventory (see, e.g., [79, p. 469]). Spranger's ideal types [99] and the subsequent studies by Allport, Vernon, and Lindzey [102] provide a basis for further comparisons. Moreover, our heuristic subject seems likely to score high on the religious and esthetic scales of the Allport-Vernon-Lindzey test [102], while our analytic subject may rather be expected to line up with their theoretical, economical, social, and political man.

We could continue our speculation on how the characteristic of cognitive style, as measured by the tests we used, relates to other tests and research in psychology. (See e.g., Cronbach [95, pp. 539–577] for other relevant references.) Actual cross validations would have to be preceded by a refinement of our tests to allow the replacement of our dichotomous distinction by a continuous scale of heuristic–analytic tendency. A greater variety of problem situations than our tests currently provide would be required in order to be able to deal effectively with the confounding variables that one encounters in the process of measuring cognitive style. Confounding variables were found to be related to the subject [ability to solve problems, motivation, rigidity in problem-approach (Luchins' Einstellungs effect)], the problem situation (difficulty and complexity of the problems, structured versus unstructured problems) and interactions between the two (degree of success with a given procedure). However, for the point we want to make in the present study this topic does not need further elaboration.

The answer to the question of validity of the experimental results can be affirmative if we accept the requirements for validation we stated in Section 3.9. We concluded from a review of real-life situations that a study of cognitive style as an implementation constraint seemed promising (see p. 36). Further investigation of the cognitive style constraint seems even more promising in view of the experimental results. A first step in this direction might be to investigate to what extent the results we have observed are specific to the point we chose in our sample space. The subjects (graduate students in Business Administration), the problem (tailored as it was for an OR application), and the specific formulation of the scenarios are only three of the parameters whose impact needs to be studied before any generalizations or even inferences to a particular real-life situation can be made from the experiment. Some of these variations could be studied within the framework of the experiment we designed at a relatively low marginal cost. "Real life," which might be studied in terms of the approach we have proposed before (see Chapter 2 and the next section for a summary) should complement and guide further steps in this research.

5.3. CONCLUSION

The time has come to focus once again on the total picture. This will soon make it clear that the effort presented here is only a small step in identifying and handling the problem of OR implementation. It may also prevent a criticism that might arise from misinterpreting the scope of this study. One might argue that the lack of implementation often stems from disagreement or uncertainty about what is the proper problem to consider or what forms a proper basis for evaluating a researcher's proposal (and any other alternative course of action). However, we explicitly restricted ourselves to an admittedly narrowly defined implementation problem for reasons stated in Section 2.5 (pp. 42, 43). Thus, the results of this study should be even more alerting to the operations researcher, who might be willing to admit the inadequacy of his techniques to approach the above-mentioned higher order problems, but who would feel quite self-assured in an environment comparable to the one we created for the experimental subjects.

The main hypotheses of this study (p. 41) were confirmed by the experimental evidence. Our conclusions therefore go a step beyond the claim that technically optimal decision rules are often poor predictors of actual behavior. (See, e.g., Rapoport [98].) First of all, we were able to identify a nontechnical constraint that appeared binding in an environment that was extremely favorable for implementation of the operations research solution. Moreover, we showed that consideration of the constraint of cognitive style—in our experiment, by properly modifying the presentation of the optimal results and making the manager more researcher dependent—indeed enhanced the chances for implementation of the optimal proposals. We realize that there may exist ways by which we could have relaxed the constraint beyond the point at which it ceases to be effective. For example, we might have tried to educate the heuristic manager to an analytic way of thinking. However, the time-constrained experimental situation hardly lent itself to a test of this alternative. Moreover, one may doubt what lasting success might be expected from such an education program in view of the deep-rootedness and consistency of cognitive style over time as well as types of problems.[75] (See also our remarks in Section 5.1, p. 109.) The comment of one of the subjects, who stated in the final questionnaire—after the meeting—"Even though I agree with the mathematical approach, I find the intuitive approach more satisfying," is most illustrative at this point.

We have stated before (see p. 44) that the desire to exert extreme control over an experiment may lead to the exclusion of so many variables from the experimental situation that the originally rich set of alternatives is no longer realistically available to the subject. The more a set of alternatives has thus been restricted, effectively though not explicitly, the less relevant will be the observance of a hypothesized behavior. On the other hand, if an extremely rich and open-ended experiment does not allow the exertion of sufficient controls in the experimental situation, no hypothesis could ever be confirmed experimentally in a satisfactory manner. The creation of a mixture of experimental richness and strong experimental controls, realized by the use of human editors in a computer-controlled environment, was our response to this dilemma. To what extent we succeeded in this task determines the relevance of the confirmation of our hypotheses in the experiment for other, especially "real life," situations. In this light, we readily recognize the relative overemphasis on the information aspect of operations research recommendations due to the near-suppression of the potential impact of many psychological variables as well as to the creation of an environment that overly favored the application of OR methods. With this reservation, we conclude that our study has given useful insights into the value of OR information under different information-processing systems or cognitive styles.

The approach we have proposed in this study as a strategy for the operations researcher may be summarized as follows. *All* foreseeable constraints that may prevent the improved operation of an organization in a given problem area, be they of a technical, economical, political, psychological, or socio-environmental nature, should form part of the initial problem formulation. Some of the constraints will be left as implementation constraints, that is, they are initially placed beyond the direct con-

---

[75] References that support this statement were mentioned in Section 2.4. Of special interest here is the remark by Roy and Miller that ". . . the qualitative differences in problem-solving performance observed between persons in the natural sciences and in other areas is not due to factors relating to the specific training received during the Ph.D. education, but rather represents the operation of factors already present before college courses have been encountered." ([97, p. 299]).

cern of the researcher. They may influence the progress of the research *indirectly*, however, in view of the ultimate necessity to relax the implementation constraints to arrive at actual improvements. The criteria for dividing the constraints into two groups, those directly included in the research and the implementation constraints, should be based on the cost of relaxation as well as the identifiability and ability to formulate the constraint. The division of constraints into two groups should be viewed as a dynamic process and may change as the research progresses. The implementation problem is thus divorced from the notion that it originates at the moment a research project is formally completed. The above approach will also guide the final problem definition itself. For example, an operations researcher might better turn to a problem for which he expects his advice will be welcome to management than to one that meets with complete disinterest on the part of management (an implementation constraint with an extremely high cost of relaxation). (Of course there may be other reasons why such an action should *not* be taken.)

The professional bias of social scientists toward psychological and sociological constraints and of operations researchers, as technicians, toward technical constraints has resulted in a serious obstacle to a well-balanced consideration of the total set of constraints in theoretical as well as practical work. In a way our proposal is a revival of the "multidisciplinary approach" of operations research, which was in vogue in the fifties but never seems to have caught on in practice. It is our hope that we have contributed to an operational interpretation of the multidisciplinary approach by a restatement of this concept in terms familiar to the operations researcher. The consideration of the cognitive style constraint in this study should serve as an example of the general approach we outlined in the preceding paragraph.

The relationship of the tests used in our experiment to other studies of cognitive style has been discussed above (Section 5.2). We now turn to establish the relationship of our findings to other research, especially of behavioral scientists. In terms of, for example, Festinger's theory of dissonance [26], the operations research may be viewed as a source of dissonance arousal. However, unlike Festinger, who (passively) attempts to predict what form the dissonance reduction will take, the operations researcher, in our view, should guide the manager in a move to a more stable equilibrium. This guidance is dynamic in the sense that the desirability of a new equilibrium may change in view of the cost of reaching it. Our handling of the cognitive style constraint in the experiment illustrates our point. A researcher-dependent equilibrium became preferable to a guidance toward independent implementation of the original OR proposal by the manager when the cost of this last alternative appeared extremely high (as was the case for heuristic subjects). In general our findings give us reason to question the absolute primacy of strictly technical proposals, which form the starting point for most of the studies we have mentioned in Section 1.3. We should immediately add, however, that many of the studies mentioned in Section 1.3 deal solely with substantial technical innovations (such as the introduction of a computer or of a new farming tool) rather than with the type of innovations—often of an organizational nature—that operations research has to offer. But even in the former situation is it more acceptable to assume the primacy of technical proposals as a cultural constraint (cf. Trist et al. [52]).

Suggestions for future research follow immediately from the above paragraphs. One can draw from a vast range of suggestions by behavioral scientists (see, e.g., Marschak [103]) to identify and formulate other possible implementation constraints. Sources of conflict (in our terms: constraints) in horizontal relationships stemming from the division of labor—our study could be put under this heading—are also suggested by Landsberger [104]. The identification as well as the observation of ways to relax constraints[76] by psychologists and sociologists forms a useful source of information in the operations researcher's total approach to a problem situation. Research is needed to find *alternative* ways of relaxing these constraints, *completely or in part,* as well as to determine *the cost* of such relaxation. As said before, laboratory experiments may be useful as a relatively inexpensive and flexible tool to gain insight in the different aspects of such constraints, but field studies should provide the ultimate test of the validity and operationality of the suggestions that stem from this research.

---

[76] Alternative ways of relaxing a constraint should not be confused with the proper identification of a constraint. For example, if Heany [105] explains the use of the intuitive approach by many managers from personal feelings of insecurity, the constraint is "fear" or "insecurity," but not "cognitive style."

Appendix 1

INSTRUCTIONS FOR
THE EXPERIMENT

COMMUNICATION—EXPERIMENT

Read these instructions in full. Ask the experimenter for any clarification. Please do not discuss these instructions with anyone else *before or after* the experiment. It is essential that no member of the firm communicate about the firm and its operations with anyone else during the running of the firm's operations, except as specified in these instructions.

Instructions

I. *Introduction:*

You are a member of a firm that processes and markets fruits (such as pineapples, pears, peaches) and vegetables (e.g., artichokes, beans, etc.) and byproducts thereof. The climatological situation is such that some of the products can be harvested at any time of the year, depending only on the planting time. In some cases, however, the quality of the product will be adversely affected when the product is planted and harvested out of its "season." The products have therefore been divided into six product groups. Products within a group have very similar characteristics (e.g., with respect to best harvesting time) and in fact the firm treats them as completely homogeneous; the terms "product" and "product group," or "product line" are used interchangeably.

The division in product groups allows the firm to operate on a year around rather than a seasonal basis. Three products (called *A*, *B*, and *C*) are processed and marketed during the summer season, the three others called *D*, *E*, and *F* during the winter season.

The fruits and vegetables to be processed are bought from small, private growers. A minimum product price is guaranteed to the growers through the institution of a "guarantee" fund which is supervised by the government. To the firm this means that the products are bought at a price that remains constant over long periods of time. (A part of the price paid may consist of a contribution to the guarantee fund.)

The perishability or loss of quality of the products when held in inventory for more than some months (sometimes weeks) has led the firm to deliver all processed products immediately to the sales points and not to hold any stock of finished products (beyond the regular working inventory) during or past the season. The harvested but not yet processed products can be held in stock during the season, but not beyond the season. Stocking of unprocessed products may take place in order to diminish the sometimes considerable fixed order costs, which are in part administrative in nature and in part result from fixed charges by the grower.

The products before processing are referred to as "raw materials," after processing as "finished goods."

The raw materials and finished goods are bought and sold by weight. In the reports of the firm the quantities bought and sold are stated in tons (called "units"). Prices are quoted per unit. The smallest quantity sold is the 20-lb case ($\frac{1}{100}$ ton). (The units are therefore reported with two decimals.)

The past management of the firm has been making the major decisions twice a year: purchasing, production, and pricing decisions were made each season (also called "period") for each product group. Any available liquid capital was considered for investment. *The firm tries to maximize its long-range net profit.* You are asked to take over the management of the firm and to prepare the biyearly decisions *for an indefinite number of years that follow.* (This is a lifetime appointment!)

The decisions that *must* be made by the firm each season ("period") are:

(a) The price per ton (unit) for each product: A, B, C in the summer season (the odd periods), and D, E, F in the winter season (the even periods).

(b) The amount of each product that is to be processed (or "produced"). The production is evenly spread out over the season and is sold with minimal delay (no stockholding of finished goods).

(c) The number of orders for raw materials to be placed with growers and the amount to be purchased per order. (All orders within one season have to be of the same size.)

(d) Investments of available liquid capital outside the firm.

Other decisions such as adding or dropping a product or adding additional capacity are optional.

Relevant information is supplied in these instructions. The chief executive may ask the experimenter for any additional information the firm might want to have about its operations. If the information is available it will be supplied, but at an appropriate cost. The cost figure of information will be supplied free at request.

The following describes how decisions are made, how members may communicate, and how information is obtained.

II. *Decisions*

The firm has five members: A chief executive who is assisted by four vice presidents, each heading one of the following departments:

1. the accounting department
2. the marketing department
3. the production department
4. the purchasing department

Each member of the firm as well as the experimenter is designated by a code number. The code number is used for all communications between members of the firm.

Code No.   *Function*

0   Experimenter

1   The *chief executive* is ultimately responsible for the firm's operations. Only he may make requests for information or for the cost of certain types of information. The vice presidents (or "managers") submit their decision proposals for the next period to the chief executive *at least 10 min* before the end of each period. The chief executive is free to alter these proposals or he may leave them unchanged. At the end of each period the final decision, written on the *Decision Sheet* by the chief executive, will be picked up by the experimenter.

Each of the following managers must send his decision proposal for the next period to the chief executive at least 10 min before the end of the decision period. In addition, the decision proposals may be sent to any of the other team members. The first decisions to be prepared are for products *A*, *B*, and *C*, which are processed and marketed during the summer (period 1). Next you will prepare the decisions for products *D*, *E*, and *F* (period 2 = winter); then again decisions for products *A*, *B*, and *C* (period 3 = summer); etc.

2   *The accounting manager* (comptroller) proposes the amount of outside investments to be made and/or the amount to be borrowed for the coming period. The accounting department also provides the chief executive and the other departments with clerical assistance: it performs all calculating activities it is asked to do by the chief executive or by the other departments *after authorization by the chief executive for this work has been obtained.* The calculating activities of the department are of a clerical type and should be completely specified by the one who requests the calculations.

   The department has a desk calculator available and may ask the experimenter for any other support needed to perform its function.

3   *The marketing manager* proposes a price per ton (unit) for each product to be marketed in the next period. Currently six products are sold, three in the summer season (*A*, *B*, and *C*) and three in the winter season (*D*, *E*, and *F*).

4   *The production manager* proposes the amount to be produced (processed) of each product in the next period. Processing of product groups *A*, *B*, and *C* takes place only during the summer season, of *D*, *E*, and *F* only during the winter season. There is no inventory holding of finished goods during the season nor beyond the season. Production—which is spread evenly over the season—is always immediately set at the disposal of the marketing department.

5   *The purchasing manager* proposes for each product the number of orders and the amount per order to be placed with the growers in the next period. All orders are equally spaced over time (within the season) and they are all of the same size. Purchasing of the products in groups *A*, *B*, and *C* takes place only during the summer season, and of groups *D*, *E*, and *F* only during the winter season. The time between placing an order and its availability for production is very short and can be neglected. Inventories of un-

processed products can be held during the season, but not past the end of the season. Any remaining end inventory is sold at a liquidation price.

Note: All managers are allowed to make any suggestions they want to the chief executive and may initiate studies about the firm's operations. The chief executive may also suggest that any of the departments undertake such a study.

III. *Communications*

For reasons of efficiency, the firm has standardized its communication system. The system *limits* the amount of possible communications between individual members of the firm severely. In the setup of the Management Science Laboratory this means the following:

All communications take place through teletype. No face-to-face meetings between team members will be allowed during the experiment. In exceptional cases, for example, when you want to transmit a graph or a mathematical formula, you may send a written message. Written messages are to be sent on the message sheets and should carry the name of the sender (code), the name of the addressee (code) *and the time of sending the message.* Message sheets and carbon paper are on your desk. Call for the experimenter to transmit the message.

The teletype communications are further restricted by the required use of the firm's standardized communication language. The standardized language can be extended, however, to better fit the needs of the members of the firm. See Appendix 4 of these instructions for a detailed explanation of the use of teletypes and the firm's standard language.

IV. *Information*

Each team member will receive a financial report at the beginning of each period *from period 3 on.* The financial report contains the results of the decisions made in the period before the last one, that is, the results of the decisions made at the end of period 1 are given at the beginning of period 3, etc. An example of the financial report is attached to these instructions (*the figures are arbitrary*).

The next pages contain information on which decisions to be made can be based. The pertaining figures are given in Appendixes 1 and 2. The financial status of the firm at the beginning of period 1 is given in Appendix 3.

1. The Chief Executive. All information made available to the department managers will also be available to the chief executive. Additional information can only be requested by the chief executive.

2. The Controller. The firm does not pay dividends. The firm may, if it wishes, invest any available cash in a long-term outside investment which pays 3% per half year. Moreover, it may borrow an amount equal to last period's owners' equity at 4% per half year. However, if the firm runs out of cash and insufficient provisions for borrowing have been made, it *automatically* borrows the additional amount needed at an interest rate of 5% per half year. If the amount required exceeds owners' equity of the preceding period, the firm is declared bankrupt and liquidated. The borrowing decision has to state the *total* amount borrowed and *should include any extensions of loans made earlier*. (All extra funds needed above what the borrowing decision indicates pay 5% interest per half year.)

It is not possible for the firm to raise money in any other way, for example, by issuing stock.

The firm does not own its plant nor equipment. It pays fixed operating expenses that include salaries, rents, and office expenses. This amount is subtracted from cash at the beginning of each period. In addition, purchase costs, labor costs, and other variable costs as well as the investments made are subtracted. Total revenue is added to cash (there are no accounts receivable).

3. The Marketing Manager. Sales are for cash, and cash generated within a period can be used to pay the same period's expenses. Sales requirements can be met by the current period's production.

The finished goods are immediately delivered to the sales points, so no inventory holding costs are incurred during the season. Because the goods produced are perishable or subject to quality deterioration, there are no finished-goods inventories held beyond the season. All goods that the firm was unable to sell on the market are sold at the end of the season at a (low) liquidation price (PLQ).

In case production does not meet demand on the market, the firm may provide for substitute buying for its disappointed customers. Contracts to this extent have been made with other producers. The arrangement of substitute buying involves a "stock-out" cost to the firm.

A part of a market survey and some pilot testing recently done by the firm are given in Appendix 1. More extensive information obtained in the survey will be made available to all members of the firm when they take over management (at the beginning of period 1). These surveys will be continued. The marketing manager and the chief executive will be informed of any changes in the market at the beginning of each period.

4. The Production Manager. The incoming fruits and vegetables are sorted, processed, and then canned or boxed. Quality control and "grading" are very important. The "units" mentioned before are chosen such that one unit of raw material corresponds to one unit of finished goods within very narrow limits.

The manual labor required for production is acquired at a given hourly wage rate. An earlier study done in the plant has shown that the labor requirement per unit processed increases with increasing production in approximately the following manner:

Labor requirement per unit produced = $[V + W \cdot \text{(amount produced)}]$
manhours, where V and W are constants (see Appendix 2 for specification)

A fixed plant capacity limits the output of the firm per season. The plant capacity is given as a maximum number of labor hours, which can be allocated to the production of any or all of the three products the firm markets each season. When the production decisions jointly require more labor hours than there can be employed with the given plant capacity, the quantities produced are automatically reduced as much as is needed. (This reduction is *proportional*.) Similarly, when a production decision requires more raw materials than there are available, the quantity produced is automatically reduced as much as is needed.

All production is evenly spread out over the season and is immediately set at the disposal of the marketing manager. The firm leases its plant capacity. A 100-year lease has recently been arranged.

5. The Purchasing Manager. Raw material purchasing involves, aside from the cost of processing and shipping a unit raw material (U), a fixed order cost that is incurred each time an order is placed (CN). The fixed order cost includes the administrative expenses for an order and any fixed charges the supplier may make.

The purchasing manager may place as many orders as he wants during one season, but all orders have to be of the same size and must be equally spaced in time. Any raw material that is left at the end of the season is disposed of at a liquidation price $PLR(U > PLR)$.

Raw-material inventories held during the season are managed by the purchasing manager. Taxes, insurance, and other charges amount to 17% of the average inventory value per season. The inventory value of raw materials is based on the purchase price per unit. The *average* inventory level during a season is calculated as $(R + RIE)/2$, where:

R = size of order
RIE = end inventory (before liquidation) = $N \cdot R - Q$
N = number of orders
Q = total production

(all symbols should refer to the same period).

Note: The calculation of inventory holding costs as described is based on the following assumptions:

1. Production is divided evenly over the season; so the production department draws upon the raw material stock at a fixed rate (as determined by the quantity produced).

2. The procurement lead time can be neglected, that is, when an order is placed it is immediately available for production.

3. Raw material cannot be held for more than one season. The remaining end inventory (*RIE*) is disposed of at a price, *PLR*.

Appendix 1 of the Instructions

Results of Market Survey.

This appendix was a computer printout which is not reproduced here. The printout showed a list of 50 prices for each product together with the corresponding quantities sold. The prices covered a wide range and were presented in arbitrary order. Quantities sold were derived from the demand distribution (Appendix 2). Deviations from expected demand were generated with the aid of a random normal number table.

Appendix 2 of the Instructions

Financial and Material Information

Symbol	Description	Product					
		A	*B*	*C*	*D*	*E*	*F*
U	Raw material cost per unit ($)	110.00	14.00	38.00	97.50	51.00	80.00
CN	Fixed order cost raw material per order ($)	121.00	24.50	368.60	3.00	72.25	5.00
PLR	Liquidation price raw material per unit ($)	40.00	12.00	15.00	90.00	15.00	20.00
CS	Stock-out cost finished goods per unit ($)	—	8.00	31.00	15.00	3.20	102.00
PLQ	Liquidation price finished goods per unit ($)	440.00	15.00	70.00	100.00	—	118.00
V ⎱	Coefficients; labor requirement for units produced (Q):	2.548	.54	7.69	3.48	1.112	7.62
W ⎰	$LA = V*Q + W*Q**2$	.15	.0002	.002	.02	.001	.002

CW	Wage rate	$5.00 per manhour
CH	Inventory holding cost	$.17 per season per $ of raw mat. held (evaluated at cost)
CF	Fixed operating expenses per season ($)	$16,000.00
K	(Initial) Plant capacity per season (manhours)	1500 manhours
CB	Interest rate on money borrowed:	
	If asked for:	$.04 per $ per season
	If not asked for:	$.05 per $ per season
PI	Interest rate on investments	$.03 per $ per season
		(Investments are to be held for at least 20 periods)

Appendix 3 of the Instructions

Financial Status of the Firm at the Beginning of Period 1

Assets		Equities	
Cash	$10,000.00	Loans payable	$ 0.00
Investments	$ 0.00	Owner's equity:	
		Capital stock	$ 7,000.00
		Retained earnings	$ 3,000.00
Total assets	$10,000.00	Total equities	$10,000.00

Appendix 4 of the Instructions

The Firm's Communication System

A. The Use of Teletypes. All messages between firm members are transmitted through the PDP-5 *Message Switching System* (the "computer"). In order to get access to this system, you have to follow the next rules *precisely:*

1. To start a communication: Hit CARRIAGE RETURN (CR).

2a. If you sent a message previously that has not yet reached *all* destinations you specified, the computer will respond with ***PLEASE WAIT***. You have to start over with 1 (see also point 6).

2b. If there is no remaining undelivered message from you, the computer will respond with ***TO WHOM?***.

3. Then type in the code numbers of the team members ("stations") with whom you want to communicate. Characters other than numbers are ignored. End the message with typing ↑ (the "delimiter"). (If no or no legal destinations are typed in before ↑ is typed, you again get: ***TO WHOM?***.)

4. The computer will respond with ***GO AHEAD***. Now you can type in your message, using the standardized language as described under part B, below. You release your message by typing the delimiter ↑.

5. You will receive a copy of any message you sent, even if you do not specify yourself as one of the destinations. This enables you to check the contents of your message and its actual destination(s). The destination(s) may differ from what you specified. (See part C-2 below.)

Note: Before you receive a copy of your own message, you may have received messages from others.

6. After the computer has delivered your message to *all* stations you specified, the computer will type 20 asterisks (***. . .). Only after you

have received these asterisks you are able *to send* a next message. (In the meantime you may very well have *received* messages from others.)

Remarks:

(a) To begin any communication, you *always* press first CARRIAGE RETURN (CR). If you forget this, you will never get any reaction from the computer.

(b) The ↑ is the delimiter of all your messages. If you forget to use the delimiter (↑), your station is incapable of receiving or of transmitting any other messages. Other stations may become blocked as well, if they sent a message to you that cannot be delivered and therefore prevents *them* from sending other messages. *If one team member forgets to use the delimiter (↑), the complete communication system may be disabled!!*

(c) All destinations specified other than the code numbers of your team members or of the experimenter will be neglected by the computer.

(d) A message may *never be longer than 30 message elements*. If you would send a longer message, the excess is chopped off and will not be received by the destination(s).

B. The Use of the Firm's Standard Language (FSL). All regular messages sent by team members should use the firm's standardized language (FSL). A library of message elements, that together constitute the FSL, is given under part E, below. The procedure to be followed is:

1. Get access to the Message Switching System following the rules described under part A, above.

2. Once you have received **GO AHEAD**, select your first message element from the list under part E, below, and start typing it. Press CARRIAGE RETURN (CR) at the end of *each message element* to shift to a new line. In case the computer recognizes the message element, it will take over from you and type out the remaining part of the message element. The teletype shifts *automatically* to a new line in this case.

3. Select the next message element from the list under part E (below), which upon recognition will again be completed by the computer (or you press CR yourself). Repeat this procedure until you have finished your message.

Do not forget to type the delimiter (↑) after the last message element!

C. Exceptions from Use of the Firm's Standard Language (FSL).

1. In case you want to send a message element that cannot adequately be handled by FSL, you have to start this "nonformal" message element with typing ALTMODE. After having typed ALTMODE at the beginning of a line, you can type any message you want.

When typing a "nonformal" message element, the computer will not take over from you. At the end of a "nonformal" message element, you have again to begin with typing ALTMODE. Hence two rules are to be followed, when you do *not* use FSL:

(a) *Every "nonformal" message element (one printed line) has to be preceded by* ALTMODE.

(b) Every "nonformal" message element (*one printed line*) *has to be concluded with* CARRIAGE RETURN. This in particular also holds if the last message element is nonformal!

Note:

(a) A "nonformal" message element may never be longer than 30 characters (about half a line). Shift to a new line and continue a second nonformal message element, if desired.

(b) A message may partly consist of "formal" (FSL) and partly of "nonformal" message elements.

(c) A "nonformal," like a "formal" message, is only released after you have typed the delimiter ($\uparrow$).

2. Nonformal messages: change of destination. If a message contains one or more nonformal message elements it is labelled as a "nonformal message" [a "nonformal message" may therefore contain some formal (FSL) message elements].

Nonformal messages (with one exception: see point 3) are sent to the experimenter for approval and any other specified destinations are disregarded. The experimenter will then decide if the message can be forwarded to the initially specified destinations and you will be notified about this decision by one of the following messages from the experimenter:

(a) MSG.-.... (Your code number and the time you sent the nonformal message are filled in). ***APPROVED AND FORWARDED***

(b) MSG.-.... (Your code number—time of sending nonformal message) ***NOT APPROVED***

If you receive message (b) your nonformal message will *not* reach the destinations you requested. The criteria for not approving a message are:

1. The message could have been stated in the formal language (FSL). If you are still interested in sending your original message, you will have to rephrase it in terms of FSL.

2. The message is considered irrelevant with respect to the firm's operations.

3. The message, though relevant with respect to the firm's operations, is not of enough importance to warrant forwarding or: a sufficiently close statement can be made using FSL.

If you receive message (a) your nonformal message has been *approved* and has been *forwarded.* An *approved* nonformal message may often point out an essential shortcoming in the firm's standardized language (FSL). In this case the experimenter may decide to expand FSL with an additional message element in order to prevent similar problems from recurring in the future. If a new message element is added, *all team members* will receive the following message from the Experimenter:

**ADDITION TO LIBRARY: (The new message-element is filled in).

3. Nonformal messages: no change of destination. In the following instances nonformal message elements do *not* need prior approval by the experimenter:

(a) Units, unit identification, and product-identification.

Example: Type ALTMODE, then: 5000 tons A. The message element should *start* with the units (numbers) and be *followed* by the unit and product identification. The unit and/or product identification may be omitted. If specified, the unit and product identification *together* may not consist of more than two words.

Note: A unit specification in dollars may precede the units

Example: $5000.00

(b) Formulas.

Formulas may consist of numbers, arithmetic operators, and symbols. The arithmetic operators are written as follows:

+	(addition)
−	(subtraction)
*	(multiplication)
/	(division)
=	(equal sign)
E..	(exponentiation)
RT(.....)	(square root)

Symbols may not consist of more than two letters (or a letter and a number). A list of symbols is supplied under part F, below. If you want to introduce additional symbols, please inform the experimenter first. The experimenter will then announce the new symbol and its meaning to all team members.

Example: Type ALTMODE, then: $(500X**2 + 300.75S)/RT(149Q) = $ L2, which means:

$$\frac{500x^2 + 300.75S}{\sqrt{149Q}} = L_2$$

where x, S, Q, and L_2 are symbols.

Note: If a message contains no nonformal message elements or *only* nonformal message elements of the type 3a and/or 3b, the message will be sent *directly* from the sender to the destination(s) specified.

Be sure to follow the rules for nonformal message elements for the cases 3a and 3b: Start message element with ALTMODE, end message element with CARRIAGE RETURN (*also if it is the last message element*).

4. Hand-written messages. A handwritten message may be sent, if the message cannot be handled adequately by the teletype system. Such messages are graphical illustrations and formulas involving complications such as higher order roots, sines, etc. Messages of this type will be limited to a minimum and should occur only *exceptionally*.

You can ask the experimenter for message sheets and carbon paper in case you want to send a written message to more than one team member. The experimenter should also be asked to transmit a handwritten message, at which moment the written message is subjected to approval by the experimenter. You are notified if a written message has been approved and transmitted.

You can call the experimenter, for transmitting a message or for other help, through the teletype system. Simply address the following message to the experimenter: HELP.

D. Errors when using the message switching system.

1. If you are typing a nonformal message element (intentionally or by error) without having pressed ALTMODE first, your typing will be interrupted by the computer with the message:

NON-FORMAL

Only the *last* (corrected) message element has to be retyped.

2. You can erase the last message element you were (or are) typing by pressing RUB OUT. After you press RUB OUT, the computer will type out the last message element *that was accepted,* (i.e., the one you erased is excluded) from where you have to continue your message. (Do *not* retype the last accepted message element.)

If you want to erase more preceding message elements, you just repeat pressing "RUB OUT" as many times as wanted. Each time the last accepted message element will be typed out by the computer.

If you erase the first message element, the computer will type out: ***GO AHEAD*** and you can begin a complete new message. If you do not want to send a message at all any more or if you want to change the destination(s), you again press RUB OUT, thus erasing the complete message-heading. The computer will then type out:

MSG ATTEMPT CANCELLED

After this point you can only start a new message by pressing CARRIAGE RETURN. Examples of use of FSL are given under part G, below.

E. Formal Language Elements
    1. Verbs.   (You may also use the past tenses of these verbs.)

	Opinions:	Directions:	Computations:
be	think	decide	compute
been	suggest	instruct	add
am	predict	start	increase
is	propose	remain	decrease
are	recommend	hold	maximize
was	agree	retain	minimize
were	disagree	change	optimize
		continue	
		follow	
		repeat	
	Needs:	finish	
has		end	Relations:
have	need		
had	want		relate
	request		depend
shall	require	Functions:	cause
will			result
should		coordinate	see
would	Inflow/Outflow:	authorize	show
		invest	help
may	receive	borrow	meet
might	accept	sell	
	earn	set/production	General:
can	send	(= produce)	
could	provide	set/purchasing	do
	report	(= purchase)	make
			use
	Correction:	lease	set
		expand	
	correct		
	ignore		

2. Nouns

	Accounting		
firm	investment	operation	amount
product	borrow/ing	summer	size
A	interest	winter	number
B			
C	Market/ing	communication	level
D	demand	information	time
E	price	survey	trend
F	competition	data	period
	liquidation	graph	
	stockout	analysis	condition
return		formula	uncertainty
earn/ing/s	Production	relationship	facility
profit	labor	computation	appendix
loss	capacity	suggest/ion	
cash	inventory	predict/ion	
cost		instruct/ion	
	Purchasing	decision	
	raw material	proposal	
statement	order		
income			
position			

3. Prepositions, Suffixes, & Pronouns

about	so	what	I
above	such	when	you
after		where	he
	than	who	we
as	to	why	they
at	too		
because		ctd. (continued)	me
before	under	msg. (message)	him
below		Please	us
but		O.K.	them
by	with	accord/ing	
		regard/ing	my
for			your
from			his
			our

in	Suffixes:		their
of	d	?	President
on	ed	:	Mgr (manager)
out	es	(blank for spacing)	
	er		
per	ion	,	
	ing	.	
	ly		
	s		

4. Adjectives   ## 5. Miscellaneous

	financial		
	gross		
	net		
little	total	past	a
less	fixed	last	the
least	variable	present	it
much	average	now	some
many	marginal	next	all
more	optimal	future	this
most	linear		that
good	possible	there	
better	equal		
best	final		and
bad			or
worse	slight		
worst	strong		
	full		yes
new	sufficient		no
old	exact		not
right	near		
wrong	important		
high			
low	fully		
	very		
same			
other			

F. List of symbols. (All symbols refer to *one* decision period.)

Quantity	Value	Cost	
I Investment ($)	PI Return on investment ($ per $ invested)	CB Cost of borrowing (loan; $ per $ borrowed)	
B Borrowing ($) (loan)			
M Market sales, finished goods	P Price of finished goods sold on market	CM Cost of goods sold	
LQ Liquidation sales, finished goods	PLQ Liquidation price, finished goods		
LR Liquidation sales, raw materials	PLR Liquidation price, raw materials		
S Stockout finished goods		CS Cost of stockout	
Q Production		CQ Cost of production (total)	
K Plant capacity		CK Cost of plant capacity	
LA Labor hours		CLA Cost of labor (total)	V } Coefficients of labor
		CW Cost of labor wage (per hour)	W } production function
			$LA = V*Q + W*Q**2$
R Raw material purchased per order		CR Cost of purchasing (total)	
N Number of orders		CN Cost of ordering (fixed per order)	
RIA Average inventory, raw materials		CH Cost of holding inventory ($ per $ raw material value)	
RIE End inventory, raw materials		U Unit cost, raw material	
		C Total unit cost	
		CV Variable cost	
		CF Fixed cost	Z Profit
		CT Total cost	ZO Operating profit
			ZN Net profit
	MR Marginal return	MC Marginal cost	MZ Marginal profit

Note; The prefix E (expected) can be added to the above symbols, whenever appropriate, for example, EM = expected market sales, finished goods.

G. *Examples of Messages that Can Be Sent in* FSL.

1. Suppose you are the marketing manager (2) and you want to send a message to the president (1) and the production manager (4).

You type:	Comments	Message received will be:	Comments
CR	Carriage return required to start	Computer: FROM 2 TO 1, 2, 4 TIME 00:24	You are included in destinations
Computer: ***TO WHOM***		I suggest that price "A" be increased to $575.	
1, 4 ↑	Specify destinations end with deliminter		
Computer: ***GO AHEAD***			
I CR			
suggest CR			
that CR			
pride CR	Error		
Computer: ***NON-FORMAL**			
price CR			
A CR			
be CR			
increase CR			
d CR			
to CR			
$600 CR	Error not in FSL, so:		
Computer: **NON-FORMAL**			
@$600 CR	Use ALTMODE		
CR			
RUBOUT CR	You change your mind and you want $575 rather than $600. Two last elements have to be RUBBED OUT.		
Computer: $600			
RUBOUT CR			
Computer: to			
@$575 CR			
. CR			
↑	Delimiter required to send the message		

2. Suppose you are the production manager (4) and you want to ask the accounting manager (2) to do some calculations for you.

You type:	Comments	Message received will be	Comments
CR			
Computer: ***PLEASE WAIT***	Computer is busy	Computer: From 4 to 2,4	Msg. was sent one
CR	with other mes-sages. Try again.	TIME 0130	hour and 30 min after start
Computer: ***TO WHOM***		Please compute produc-	
2		tion cost F.	
Computer: ***GO AHEAD***		Use formula:	
Please CR		$CQ(F) = CK + CLA = CK + CW*(V*$	
compute CR		$Q + W*Q**2)$	
production CR			
cost CR			
F CR			
. CR			
use CR			
formula CR			
: CR			

$@CQ(F) = CK + CLA = CK + CW*(V*Q + W*Q**2)CR$
↑

Note: In most cases you will have to type only the first two or four characters of a message element, after which the computer types out the remaining part and also provides the carriage return. The product groups are designated by a letter between quotation marks. For example, "A" = product group A. Message elements listed as verbs can sometimes also be used as nouns. For example, "result." New words can sometimes be formed by combining message elements. For example, STOCK-OUT = STOCK OUT. Suffixes are used to form past tenses, plurals, new nouns, comparatives, and adverbs. For example:

change / d = changed   instruct / ion = instruction

repeat / ed = repeated   regard / ing = regarding

loss / es = losses   strong / ly = strongly

high / er = higher   decision / s = decisions

More suffixes can sometimes be used. For example:

$$
\left.\begin{array}{l}
\text{earn} \\
\text{ing} \\
\text{s}
\end{array}\right\} = \text{earnings}
\qquad
\left.\begin{array}{l}
\text{suggest} \\
\text{ion} \\
\text{s}
\end{array}\right\} = \text{suggestions}
$$

Final Note:

1. At the beginning of each period, you will receive the following message:

> FROM 0 TO 0 1 2 3 4 5 6 7 8 9   TIME _____
> ** START PERIOD
> __ (period number)
> SET TIME**

Upon receipt of this message, you should set your watch to the time indicated in the heading of the above message. You can start sending messages.

2. At the end of the message-sending part of the period, you will receive the following message:

> FROM 0 TO 0 1 2 3 4 5 6 7 8 9   TIME: _____
> ** END COMMUNICATIONS OF PERIOD
> __ (period number)
> NO MORE MSG.S**

Upon receipt of this message you should stop sending messages. You may only send your proposed decision to the chief executive if you did not do so before. During the remainder of the period the chief executive should prepare the final decisions for the period.

Appendix 2

FORMULATION AND SOLUTION OF THE SCENARIO PROBLEM IN AN ANALYTIC MODEL

A. MATHEMATICAL MODEL AND OPTIMAL SOLUTION

The following symbols are used in this appendix (all referring to the same decision period):

S = market sales price finished goods (*decision variable*)

x = quantity finished goods sold on market (demand)

U = cost per unit raw material

A = fixed order cost per order of raw material

F = fixed expenses (administrative and other)

Q = quantity produced (*decision variable*)

R = quantity of raw material purchased per order (*decision variable*)

N = number of orders (*decision variable*)

E = end inventory raw materials before liquidation

H = raw material inventory holding cost, given in dollars per season per dollar inventory investment (this is the opportunity cost)

T = stockout cost per unit for finished goods

W = liquidation sales price per unit for finished goods

V = liquidation sales price per unit for raw materials

K = cost of procurement of finished goods (production + purchase cost)

$\left.\begin{array}{c} r \\ s \end{array}\right\}$ = coefficients of the labor production function in dollars per unit produced

π = profit

$\left.\begin{array}{c} a \\ b \end{array}\right\}$ = coefficients of the demand function $x = -aS + b + \epsilon$

$\left.\begin{array}{r}d \\ e\end{array}\right\} =$ coefficients of the demand function $S = d - e\mu$. Hence $d = b/a$ and $e = 1/a$.

$\mu =$ expected demand.

The following symbols appear only with the numerical data:

$P =$ plant capacity. P is such that it does not form an effective constraint on the optimal solution, calculated without considering P.

$\left.\begin{array}{r}\bar{r} \\ \bar{s}\end{array}\right\} =$ coefficients of the labor production function in manhours per unit produced $\left.\begin{array}{r}\\ \\ \\ \end{array}\right\} \Rightarrow r = \bar{r} \cdot L$ and $s = \bar{s} \cdot L$

$L =$ wage rate

$\bar{H} =$ raw material inventory holding cost given in dollars per season per dollar inventory investment (direct charges only)

$i_1 =$ percent interest rate on money borrowed, if demanded

$i_2 =$ percent interest rate on money borrowed, if not demanded but required

$i_3 =$ percent interest rate on money invested (investments are to be held for at least 20 periods)

$H = H + i_3/100$, that is, the opportunity cost of carrying inventory includes the cost of lost investment.

Preceding remark: The instructions specify that the quantity purchased per order R should be equal for all orders within a season. Also it is stated that the production Q is evenly spread out over the season. So, if there is any remaining inventory of raw materials at the end of the season, E, this must have been gradually built up as illustrated in Figure A2.1. The average raw material inventory in any season is therefore $\frac{1}{2}(R + E)$.

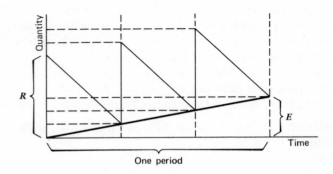

Figure A2.1

From regression analysis on the data given in Appendix 1, the demand relationship can be derived:

$$x = -aS + b + \epsilon, \text{ where } \epsilon \text{ is } N(0, \sigma^2) \tag{1}$$

$$\Rightarrow E(x) = \mu = -aS + b \text{ or:}$$

$$S = \frac{b}{a} - \frac{1}{a}\mu = d - e\mu \tag{2}$$

where a, b, d, and e are coefficients and $N(0, \sigma^2)$ is a normal distribution with mean 0 and variance σ^2. Hence x has a $N(\mu, \sigma^2)$ distribution $[= f(x)]$.

The expected profit function can be written as follows:

$$E(\pi) = \underbrace{S \int_0^Q x \cdot f(x)\, dx + W \int_0^Q (Q - x) \cdot f(x)\, dx}_{(E(\pi) \text{ if } Q \geqq x)}$$

$$+ \underbrace{SQ \int_Q^\infty f(x)\, dx - T \int_Q^\infty (x - Q) \cdot f(x)\, dx}_{(E(\pi) \text{ if } Q \leqq x)} - K(Q,R) \tag{3}$$

The first two terms in (3) state the expected profit in the case of liquidation sales (production above demand), the third and fourth term state the expected profit in the case of stockouts (production below demand). The last term in (3) represents the procurement costs and can be specified as follows:

$$K(Q,R) = N \cdot R \cdot U + N \cdot A + \frac{1}{2}(R + E)H \cdot U - V \cdot E$$
$$+ rQ + sQ^2 + F \tag{4}$$

Our task is to maximize $E(\pi)$ for S, Q, N, and R (the decision variables). Noting that $E = N \cdot R - Q$, and $N \cdot R \cdot U = Q \cdot U + (N \cdot R - Q) \cdot U$, we can rewrite (4) as

$$K(Q,R) = Q \cdot U + N \cdot A + \frac{1}{2} \cdot R \cdot H \cdot U + rQ + sQ^2$$
$$+ F + (U + \frac{1}{2}H \cdot U - V)(NR - Q) \tag{5}$$

Maximizing $E(\pi)$ with respect to N and R in (3) is equivalent to minimizing $K(Q,R)$ for N and R in (5). For any given Q we have $N \cdot R \geqq Q$ (if not, Q would be reduced to satisfy this relationship), so from (5) it is immediate that $N \cdot R = Q$ under conditions of optimization. Replacing

$N = Q/R$ in (5) and deleting the last term (which becomes zero), we get:

$$\bar{K}(Q,R) = Q \cdot U + \frac{Q}{R} \cdot A + \frac{1}{2} RHU + rQ + sQ^2 + F \qquad (6)$$

Minimization of $K(Q,R)$ with respect to R requires $\partial \bar{K}(Q,R)/\partial R = 0$[a]:

$$\frac{\partial \bar{K}(Q,R)}{\partial R} = -\frac{Q}{R^2} \cdot A + \frac{1}{2} \cdot H \cdot U = 0$$

So:

$$R^* = \sqrt{\frac{2 \cdot Q \cdot A}{H \cdot U}}, \qquad (7)$$

the well-known Wilson formula. Note that (7) only holds if $R^* \leqq Q^*$, since the scenario does not allow holding inventories beyond one period.

Substituting $R = R^* = \sqrt{2 \cdot Q \cdot A/(H \cdot U)}$ in (6) we get:

$$K(Q) = Q \cdot U + \sqrt{\frac{H \cdot U \cdot Q \cdot A}{2}} + \frac{1}{2}\sqrt{2 \cdot Q \cdot A \cdot H \cdot U}$$
$$+ rQ + sQ^2 + F \qquad (8)$$

or

$$K(Q) = Q \cdot U + \sqrt{2 \cdot Q \cdot A \cdot H \cdot U} + rQ + sQ^2 + F \qquad (9)$$

We now turn back to (3) and first write (3) in the following form (replace $K(Q,R)$ by $K(Q)$):

$$E(\pi) = (S - W)\mu - (S - W + T) \int_Q^\infty (x - Q) \cdot f(x) \, dx$$
$$+ W \cdot Q - K(Q) \qquad (10)$$

Using (2) and (9) we get the final equation for $E(\pi)$:

$$E(\pi) = (d - e\mu - W)\mu - (d - e\mu - W + T) \int_Q^\infty (x - Q) \cdot f(x) dx$$
$$+ WQ - [Q \cdot U + \sqrt{2 \cdot Q \cdot A \cdot H \cdot U} + rQ + sQ^2 + F] \qquad (11)$$

Maximization of $E(\pi)$ with respect to μ (instead of S) and Q requires $\partial E(\pi)/\partial Q = 0$ and $\partial E(\pi)/\partial \mu = 0$:

$$\frac{\partial E(\pi)}{\partial Q} = -(d - e\mu - W + T) \frac{\partial \left[\int_Q^\infty (x - Q) \cdot f(x) \, dx \right]}{\partial Q}$$
$$+ W - U - \left[U + \sqrt{\frac{A \cdot H \cdot U}{2Q}} + r + 2sQ \right] = 0 \qquad (12)$$

[a] Using $\bar{K}(Q,R)$ of (6) in (11) (see below) and differentiating $E(\pi)$ of (11) with respect to μ,Q, and R, respectively, leads to the same result.

Since:

$$\frac{\partial \left[\int_Q^\infty (x - Q) \cdot f(x)\, dx \right]}{\partial Q} = \frac{\partial \left[\int_Q^\infty x \cdot f(x)\, dx \right]}{\partial Q} - \frac{\partial \left[Q \int_Q^\infty f(x)\, dx \right]}{\partial Q}$$

$$= - Q \cdot f(Q) - [Q \cdot (-f(q)) + F(Q)] = - F(Q)^b \quad (13)$$

we can write for (12):

$$\frac{\partial E(\pi)}{\partial Q} = (d - e\mu - W + T) \cdot F(Q) + W$$

$$- \left[U + \sqrt{\frac{A \cdot H \cdot U}{2Q}} + r + 2sQ \right] = 0 \quad (14)$$

Similarly we set $\partial E(\pi)/\partial \mu = 0$:

$$\frac{\partial E(\pi)}{\partial \mu} = (d - 2e\mu - W) + e \int_Q^\infty (x - Q) \cdot f(x)\, dx$$

$$- (d - e\mu - W + T) \frac{\partial \left[\int_Q^\infty (x - Q) \cdot f(x)\, dx \right]}{\partial \mu} = 0 \quad (15)$$

Since $f(x)$ is $N(\mu, \sigma^2)$, we have[c]:

$$\int_Q^\infty (x - Q) \cdot f(x)\, dx = \frac{1}{\sigma} \int_Q^\infty (x - Q) \cdot \phi\left(\frac{x - \mu}{\sigma}\right) dx =$$

$$\left(\text{substituting } Z = \frac{x - \mu}{\sigma}\right)$$

$$= \int_{\frac{Q-\mu}{\sigma}}^\infty (\mu + \sigma \cdot Z - Q) \cdot \phi(Z)\, dZ = \sigma \int_{\frac{Q-\mu}{\sigma}}^\infty Z \cdot \phi(Z)\, dZ$$

$$- (Q - \mu) \int_{\frac{Q-\mu}{\sigma}}^\infty \phi(Z) \cdot dZ =$$

$$(\text{substituting } V = \tfrac{1}{2} Z^2):$$

$$= \int_{\frac{1}{2}\left(\frac{Q-\mu}{\sigma}\right)^2}^\infty 2 \frac{1}{\sqrt{2\pi}} e^{-V}\, dV - (Q - \mu)\Phi\left(\frac{Q - \mu}{\sigma}\right) =$$

$$= \frac{1}{\sqrt{2\pi}} e^{-\frac{1}{2}\left(\frac{Q-\mu}{\sigma}\right)^2} - (Q - \mu)\Phi\left(\frac{Q - \mu}{\sigma}\right) =$$

$$= \sigma\phi\left(\frac{Q - \mu}{\sigma}\right) - (Q - \mu)\Phi\left(\frac{Q - \mu}{\sigma}\right). \quad (16)$$

[b] $F(x)$ represents the complementary cumulative probability function of x.
[c] $\phi(x) = \tfrac{1}{2}\pi e^{-\frac{1}{2}x^2}$, that is, the standard normal distribution $N(0, 1)$.

The last partial derivative in (15) can be determined as follows [noting that $f(x)$ is $N(\mu, \sigma^2)$]:

$$\frac{\partial \left[\int_Q^\infty (x - Q) f(x)\, dx \right]}{\partial \mu} = \int_Q^\infty (x - Q) \cdot \left[\frac{\partial f(x)}{\partial \mu} \right] dx =$$

$$= \int_Q^\infty (x - Q) \cdot \left(\frac{x - \mu}{\sigma^2} \right) \cdot f(x)\, dx =$$

(substituting $x = \mu + z \cdot \sigma$)

$$= \int_{\frac{Q-\mu}{\sigma}}^\infty (\mu + Z \cdot \sigma - Q) \cdot \frac{Z}{\sigma} \cdot \phi(Z)\, dZ =$$

$$= \left(\frac{\mu - Q}{\sigma} \right) \int_{\frac{Q-\mu}{\sigma}}^\infty Z \cdot \phi(Z)\, dZ + \int_{\frac{Q-\mu}{\sigma}}^\infty Z^2 \cdot \phi(Z)\, dZ =$$

$$= \left(\frac{\mu - Q}{\sigma} \right) \cdot \phi \left(\frac{Q - \mu}{\sigma} \right) + \Phi \left(\frac{Q - \mu}{\sigma} \right) + \left(\frac{Q - \mu}{\sigma} \right) \cdot \phi \left(\frac{Q - \mu}{\sigma} \right)$$

$$= \Phi \left(\frac{Q - \mu}{\sigma} \right) = F(Q) \quad (17)$$

Using the findings of (16) and (17), we can write for (15):

$$\frac{\partial E(\pi)}{\partial \mu} = (d - 2e\mu - W) + e \left[\sigma\phi \left(\frac{Q - \mu}{\sigma} \right) - (Q - \mu)\Phi \left(\frac{Q - \mu}{\sigma} \right) \right]$$

$$- (d - e\mu - W + T) \cdot \Phi \left(\frac{Q - \mu}{\sigma} \right) = 0 \quad (18)$$

Realizing that $F(Q) = \Phi(Q - \mu/\sigma)$, we can derive from (14):

$$\Phi \left(\frac{Q - \mu}{\sigma} \right) = \frac{[U + \sqrt{(A \cdot H \cdot U/2Q)} + r + 2sQ] - W}{d - e\mu - W + T} \quad (19)$$

Substituting the expression for $\Phi \left(\dfrac{Q - \mu}{\sigma} \right)$ found in (19) into (18) gives:

$$(d - 2e\mu) + e \left[\sigma\phi \left(\frac{Q - \mu}{\sigma} \right) - (Q - \mu)\Phi \left(\frac{Q - \mu}{\sigma} \right) \right]$$

$$= U + \sqrt{\frac{A \cdot H \cdot U}{2Q}} + r + 2sQ \quad (20)$$

Finally we can rewrite (19) and (20), replacing $Q = \mu + z \cdot \sigma$, where $-\infty < z < \infty$:

$$\Phi(z)$$

$$= \frac{\{U + \sqrt{[A \cdot H \cdot U/2(\mu + z \cdot \sigma)]} + r + 2s(\mu + z \cdot \sigma) - W\}}{(d - e\mu - W + T)} \quad (21)$$

$$(d - 2e\mu) + e \cdot \sigma[\phi(z) - z\Phi(z)] = U + \sqrt{\frac{A \cdot H \cdot U}{2(\mu + z \cdot \sigma)}}$$
$$+ r + 2s(\mu + z \cdot \sigma) \quad (22)$$

Equation (22) represents the familiar marginal return = marginal cost condition for profit maximization. The second term of the equal sign left accounts for the probabilistic nature of demand and for the allowed disparity between expected units sold (μ) and units procured (Q). Equation (22) has many solution pairs (μ, Q), which can be found by choosing different values for z. Each value for z also leads to a solution pair (μ, Q) from equation (21). The optimal solution is found when the two solution pairs (μ, Q) from (21) and (22) are the same for some z. Figure A2.2 will clarify this.

Equations (21) and (22) need not always have a feasible solution. By a suitable choice of parameters feasibility can always be assured, however. Similarly our parameter setting is such that a feasible solution exists and that second-order conditions are satisfied. An iterative procedure was used to solve equations (21) and (22) for μ and z. Q^* can then be derived from $Q = \mu + z \cdot \sigma$ and R^* is computed from (7).

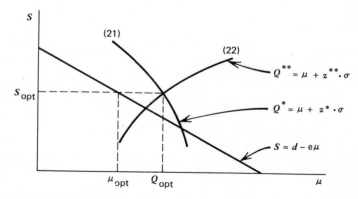

Figure A2.2 Equilibrium pairs (Q^*, μ) solving equation (21); equilibrium pairs (Q^{**}, μ) solving equation (22).

Note: In the deterministic cases the parameter setting will be such that $Q^* = \mu^*$, which requires that:

$$W < [(\text{Marginal cost} = \text{Marginal revenue})|_{Q=\mu}] < (S + T)$$

If the inequality on the left is violated, it is advantageous to increase S and thus reduce μ and to increase Q such that $Q^* > \mu^*$. Since $S \geqq$ marginal revenue, violation of the right-hand side is only possible if $T < 0$, that is, if there should exist a stockout bonus.

Table A2.1. Parameter Values for First 10 Periods

Parameter[d]	Product					
	A	B	C	D	E	F
d	900	40	300	750	75	400
e	9	.04	2	6	.01	5
$a = 1/e$	.111111	25.	.5	.16667	100	.2
$b = d/e$	100	1000	150	125	7500	80
SIGMA	8	0	30	0	200	5
$\bar{r}$	2.548	.54	7.69	3.48	1.112	7.62
$\bar{s}$	.15	.0002	.002	.02	.001	.002
T	—	8.00	31.00	15.00	3.20	102.00
W	40.00	15.00	70.00	100.00	—	118.00
V	40.00	12.00	15.00	90.00	15.00	20.00
U	110.00	14.00	38.00	97.50	51.00	80.00
A	121.00	24.50	368.60	3.00	72.25	5.00

P	Plant capacity per season:	1500 man hours (= plant-capacity at beginning of period 1)
L	Wage rate:	$5. = per man hour
$\bar{H}$	Raw material inventory holding cost (direct charges):	$.17 per season per dollar inventory investment per season
F	Fixed operating expenses:	$16,000.
	Interest rate on money borrowed,	
i_1	if demanded:	4% per season
i_2	if not demanded, but required:	5% per season
i_3	interest rate on investments:	3% per season

[d] The meaning of the product-related parameters is stated at the beginning of Appendix 2. Note that:

$r = \bar{r}L$

$s = \bar{s}L$

$H = \bar{H} + i_3/100 = \$.20$, that is, the opportunity cost of carrying inventory includes the cost of lost investment

B. NUMERICAL PROBLEMS

The parameter setting for the six products is given in Table A2.1. Products A, B, and C refer to the summer season, products D, E, and F to the winter season.

The values of the decision variables under the optimal solution are given in Table A2.2. Note that plant capacity is more than adequate for summer as well as the winter season.

Table A2.2. Optimal Decisions for First 10 Periods

Optimal Solution	Product					
	A	B	C	D	E	F
S^* (price)	540.00	28.80	190.00	438.00	67.50	259.92
μ^* (expected demand)	40.00	280.00	55.00	52.00	750.00	28.00
$Z^*[(Q^* - \mu^*)/\sigma]$	.50	0	1.4	0	−1.2	2.4
Q^* (production)	44.00	280.00	97.00	52.00	510.00	40.02
R^* (order size)	22.00	70.00	97.00	4.00	85.00	5.01
N^* (number of orders)	2	4	1	13	6	8
$E(\pi^*)$ (expected profit)	13,632	3.114	4,977	16,453	1,850	3,869
Labor hours required	403	167	765	239	826	308
Labor hours required per season	1,334 < P			1,373 < P		

Appendix 3

THE MONITOR PROGRAM[e]

The monitor program acted as a traffic-regulating device[f] for the communications between team members and also formed the means by which the controls, discussed in the text (see pp. 49–51), were exerted. The general logic of the program can best be explained by reviewing its main subroutines:

a. INITIATOR. This subroutine initiated the program after it had been read into core memory from tape. The teletype stations (codes of the participants in the experiment) were prepared for sending and receiving. An area in core memory was reserved for each station and contained all information pertinent to it. The first word (12 bits) in each station area was the STATUS word, which was the first word to be tested each time a station was serviced by the program. The content of the STATUS word directed the program to the proper subroutine. The STATUS word was set equal to 0000_8 (free to send and/or receive) by the INITIATOR. This subroutine also started a software clock, updated by an interrupt at one-second intervals. After the program had been initiated, the INITIATOR could be destroyed and its area used for additions to the vocabulary.

b. SWITCHYARD. This was the primary coordinating routine of the program. SWITCHYARD was continually checking on the flag of the 630 interface. If the flag was up, a station needed service, that is, a character was to be transmitted. SWITCHYARD found out which station needed service, and transferred control to the proper subroutine

[e] Programming assistance was received from Edward R. Berman, who wrote the monitor program called FOLIE (Formal Language Implementation Experiment) in PDP-5 assembly language. Included as part of FOLIE is a message-switching program written by Sypko W. Andreae, who also assisted in the early development phase of FOLIE. The program consists of 2005 statements and occupies 2700 words of the PDP-5's 4096 12-bit word magnetic-core memory.

[f] Interface between the PDP-5 and the subjects' teletypes is the 630 Data Communications System to which the teletypes are hooked up.

146

according to the contents of the STATUS word of that station. After service (i.e., sending or receiving and checking the character) the subroutine(s) would return control to SWITCHYARD.[g]

If no flag was up during one scanning cycle of all stations, SWITCH-YARD transferred control to the DISTRIBUTOR.

c. RX-SUB, the receiving subroutine, received a character that had been typed by a station. All checks discussed in the text (see pp. 50–51) were now applied. To illustrate we discuss the check on formal message elements.

The complete vocabulary of formal message elements was stored in the computer's memory. When the first two characters of a new message element had been received from a station, the initial letters of all message elements in the vocabulary starting with the same two characters were set aside and referred to as the list of "candidates." A similar match was made between the next two characters received and the corresponding characters of the candidates. The nonmatching candidates were dropped from the list. Continuing this procedure, the list would narrow down until only one candidate remained. The yet untyped characters of the remaining candidate were typed out by the program. If at any time during this procedure *no* candidate remained, it meant that the subject was typing a nonformal message element and the proper subroutines were invoked.

The remaining receiving subroutines took care of special situations:

1. SW0 received and checked the initiation of a new message.

2. SW2 received and checked the first two characters of each new message element (SW1 was a filter before the candidate routine, sending all ALTMODE, i.e., intentionally nonformal messages to a special subroutine).

3. NEWMSG received and checked a new message element to be added to the vocabulary (sender and destination should both be station 0, the experimenter).

d. DISTRIBUTOR came into action if none of the stations needed service at this time. This subroutine assured that a message was sent to all requested (and verified) destinations. A station could start a new message only after its last message had reached all its destinations, since

[g] Only one character is handled during one such cycle, which gives the system the appearance of simultaneously serving all stations needing service. Because of the speed of the computer compared to that of teletype typing/printing, a subject will have the impression of receiving uninterrupted service.

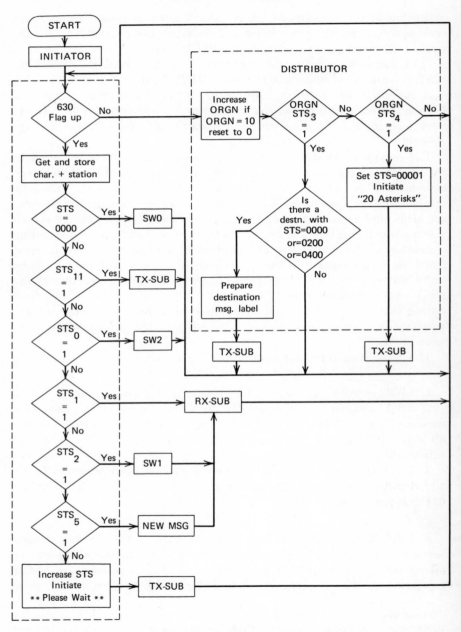

Figure A3.1 General flow-chart of monitor-program FOLIE.

only then could the station area—where each new message was received—be cleared. DISTRIBUTOR attempted to find (1) a station that had a message to send (station area was not clear) and (2) a destination free to receive that message and to which that message must be sent. A series of asterisks indicated to the sender that his message was delivered to all destinations. DISTRIBUTOR prepared the message label (sender, receiver, and time of sending) and then transferred control to TX-SUB, the transmitting subroutine.

e. TX-SUB, the transmitting subroutine, finally transmitted a message from the sender's station area to the teletype of a destination. After transmitting, TX-SUB transferred control back to SWITCHYARD.

Numerous special subroutines appeared in the program, but their discussion would not contribute further to an understanding of its operation. The flow chart[h] of Figure A3.1 summarizes the discussion of this section.

---

[h] The flow chart uses the following notation: STS = STATUS word; STS_i = ith bit of STATUS word (bits are numbered 0–11 from left to right); and ORGN = Origin, a variable that keeps track of the station being considered for receiving a message.

Appendix 4

DECISION FORM

The subject (President of the firm) was asked to fill out the following form at the end of each period:

FINAL DECISIONS FOR PERIOD _____

From: _____   Team: _____
To: UMPIRE   Date: _____

Product group   __   __   __
Prices ($)   __   __   __
Production (tons)   __   __   __
Number of orders   __   __   __
Order size (tons/order)   __   __   __
Borrowing ($ total)   __
Investment ($ this period)   __
Other expenses ($)   __

Appendix 5

DECISION RULES FOR MANAGERS

The managerial proposals for period t $(t = 3, \ldots 14)$ were computed by a subroutine of the program that computed the financial results of period $(t - 2)$. These computations were performed during period $(t - 1)$ so that the computer handouts and the new decision proposals were ready at the beginning of period t. The rationale behind the decision rules is given in the text (pp. 52–53). (*Note:* We define $0/0 = 0$ and $x/0 = +\infty$ if $x > 0$, $x/0 = -\infty$ if $x < 0$.)

DECISION RULES FOR THE ACCOUNTING MANAGER

$$\bar{I}_t = c_1(R_{t-2} - T_{t-2}) + c_2 \cdot A \qquad t = 3, \ldots 14$$

where:

$\bar{I}_t$ = proposed investment decision (if negative: borrowing decision) for period t.

I_t = actual investment (borrowing decision) for period t.

R_t = owners' equity (capital stock + retained earnings) up to and including period t.

T_t = total investments up to and including period t $\left(= \sum_{i=1}^{t} I_i\right)$

$\begin{aligned} A = \ &(1 - c_1) \cdot (R_{t-2} - T_{t-2}) \text{ if } (I_{t-2} - \bar{I}_{t-2}) \geqq 0 \\ &c_1(R_{t-2} - T_{t-2}) \qquad \text{if } (I_{t-2} - \bar{I}_{t-2}) < 0 \end{aligned}$

c_1, c_2 are coefficients. If $(R_{t-2} - T_{t-2}) \geqq 0$,

$c_1 = 0$ for $t = 3, 4$

$c_1 = .50$ for $t \geqq 5$

$\begin{aligned} c_2 = \ &[(I_{t-2} - \bar{I}_{t-2})/\bar{I}_{t-2}] \text{ if } -.75 \leqq [(I_{t-2} - \bar{I}_{t-2})/\bar{I}_{t-2}] \leqq .75 \\ = \ &.75 \qquad \text{if } [(I_{t-2} - \bar{I}_{t-2})/\bar{I}_{t-2}] > .75 \\ = \ &-.75 \qquad \text{if } [(I_{t-2} - \bar{I}_{t-2})/\bar{I}_{t-2}] < -.75 \end{aligned}$

If $(R_{t-2} - T_{t-2}) < 0$,

$$c_1 = 1$$
$$c_2 = 0$$

DECISION RULES FOR THE MARKETING MANAGER

$$\bar{S}_t = \bar{S}_{t-2} + c_3(S_{t-2} - \bar{S}_{t-2}) - c_4[(Q_{t-2} - E_{t-2})/a] - c_5[(Q_{t-2} - D_{t-2})/a]$$

where:

$\bar{S}_t$ = proposed price decision for period t.
S_t = actual price decision for period t.
Q_t = actual production for period t.
E_t = expected demand for period t.
  = $-aS_t + b$ (a, b are coefficients).
D_t = actual demand (including unsatisfied demand) for period t.
c_3, c_4, c_5 are coefficients.
c_3 = .25 for all t.

The values of the coefficients c_4 and c_5 depend on the absolute value of the deviation of the actual demand from the expected demand and on the period. The values of c_4 and c_5 are given in Table A5.1.

Table A5.1. Reaction Coefficients in Decision Rule for the Marketing Manager

Period	$\lvert Q_{t-2} - D_{t-2}\rvert < .25D_{t-2}$		$\lvert Q_{t-2} - D_{t-2}\rvert \geq .25D_{t-2}$	
	c_4	c_5	c_4	c_5
$t \leq 6$	.25	.45	.30	.54
$t > 6$	.70	.10	.84	.12

DECISION RULES FOR THE PRODUCTION MANAGER

$\bar{Q}_t$ is determined such that $r\bar{Q}_t + s\bar{Q}_t^2 = \bar{L}_t$

and:

$$\bar{L}_t = r(-a\bar{S}_t + b) + s(-a\bar{S}_t + b)^2$$
$$+ c_6[r[\{33 - (Q_{t-2} - D_{t-2})/D_{t-2}\} \cdot (K - \Sigma)]$$
$$+ s[\{33 - (Q_{t-2} - D_{t-2})/D_{t-2}\} \cdot (K - \Sigma)]^2]$$

where:

$\bar{Q}_t$ = proposed production decision for period t.

Q_t = actual production decision for period t.

$\bar{L}_t$ = production hours corresponding to $\bar{Q}_t$.

K = total production capacity (1500 manhours).

Σ = summation over the three products of the "basic" number of production hours allocated to each product

$$= \sum_{j=1}^{3} [r(-a\bar{S}_t + b) + s(-a\bar{S}_t + b)^2]_j, \text{ where } j \text{ refers to product } j.$$

The other symbols were defined before. $c_6 = 1$ if $(Q_{t-2} - D_{t-2}) < .25D_{t-2}$ and if the demand is stochastic. $c_6 = 0$ otherwise.

Note: If the sum of the production hours for the three products, each computed according to the above rule, exceeded the total available capacity, the production was proportionally reduced until the capacity constraint was just satisfied. The proposed price decision was adjusted accordingly, if necessary.

DECISION RULES FOR THE PURCHASING MANAGER

$$\bar{N}_t = \bar{N}_{t-2} + c_7(N_{t-2} - \bar{N}_{t-2}) + H_{t-2}/(c_8 \cdot B_{t-2})$$

where:

$\bar{N}_t$ = proposed number of orders for period t.

N_t = actual number of orders for period t.

H_t = actual inventory holding cost in period t.

B_t = actual order cost in period t.

Table A5.2. Decisions of Periods 1 and 2

	Period 1			Period 2		
Decision	Product					
	A	B	C	D	E	F
Price	350.	24.	150.	460.	70.	200.
Production	60.	350.	80.	40.	550.	40.
Purchasing orders	1	1	1	1	1	1
Investment: 0						
Borrowing: 0						

c_7, c_8 are coefficients

$$c_7 = .25$$

$$c_8 = 15 \ \text{ if } t \leqq 5$$

$$= \ 5 \ \text{ if } t > 5$$

The order size $\bar{V}_t$ is determined such that $\bar{V}_t \cdot \bar{N}_t = \bar{Q}_t$.

The decisions for the first two periods were arbitrarily determined at what seemed a reasonable level. The actual and proposed decisions were equal for these periods. They are summarized in Table A5.2.

SCENARIOS OF AUTONOMOUS MESSAGES SENT BY THE MANAGERS

Each confederate manager ("editor") was supplied with a minute-by-minute scenario of autonomous messages for each decision period. The layout of these scenarios was such that an editor could easily keep track of the developments requiring modifications of autonomous messages and initiation of induced messages in each of the four teams he was serving. The scenarios are presented here in a condensed format. The first column in each scenario refers to the decision period in which the message was sent, the second column to the time of sending (the communication time in each decision period was 20 min). Note that the messages are all in the formal language (see instructions, Appendix 1). The decision proposal, which was the final message of a period for each manager, is omitted in all cases.

1. SCENARIOS FOR ACCOUNTING MANAGER

Two scenarios existed for the accounting manager, one for the integral, the other for the explicit understanding approach. For ease of comparison between the two, a combined presentation of these scenarios is given below. If a message is sent under the integral understanding approach only, it is preceded by a G. If a message is sent under the explicit understanding approach only, it is preceded by a C. Messages that were sent under both approaches are not marked.

Period	Minute	Message
3	3	Instructions suggest that I do analysis of operations. I will do analysis on summer operations. O.K.?

Period	Minute	Message
	8	I propose no investments because uncertainty is too high, and no borrowing because cash is sufficient.
	15	I received demand formulas from marketing manager. Graphs will be sent.
4	4(G)	We should maximize profit and set marginal profit = 0 for all products.
	4(C)	We should maximize profit. Formula: $Z = (P - C)*M$. What is unit cost C? We should set marginal profit = 0. Formula: $MZ = MR - MC = 0$.
	9	I continue summer analysis. No time for winter analysis.
5	2(G)	I am computing total costs consisting of holding, order, labor, and material cost. Purchasing should equal production because liquidation price and inventory raw material is low.
	2(C)	Total cost formula: $CT = N*R*U + N*CN + .5*R*CH*U + (V*Q + W*Q**2)$. We should have: $N*R = Q$, because liquidation price end inventory raw material is low.
	7(G)	Marginal cost purchasing should be 0. The optimal decision for purchasing will follow from this computation.
	7(C)	Marginal cost purchasing should be 0: $MC(R) = .5*CH*U - Q*CN/R**2 = 0$. The optimal purchasing decision follows: $R = Rt[2*Q*CN/(CH*U)]$
	14	My computation shows purchasing should use formula: A: $R = Rt(11 * Q)$ B: $R = Rt(17.5 * Q)$ C: $R = Rt(48.5 * Q)$
6	1	Summer analysis. Because demand for B depends exactly on price, we can set production exactly equal to demand.
	1(C)	Profit is $Z = P*M - CT$. Total cost as before.
	11(G)	Summer analysis. Decision is optimal when marginal profit = 0. I computed optimal sale for B: $M = 280$. Other computations follow.
	11(C)	Summer analysis. Decision is optimal when marginal profit = 0. For B: $MZ(M) = D - 2*E*M - (U + .5*CH*U/Rt(17.5*M) + V + 2*W*M) = 0$ I computed optimal sale for B from this formula: $M = 280$. Other computations follow.

Period	Minute	Message
7	1(G)	Result of computation for B: $M = 280$. $P = \$28.80$. $Q = 280$. $R = 70$. $N = 4$ These are optimal decisions.
	1(C)	Result of computation for B: $M = 280$. $P = D - E*M = 40 - .04*280 = \$28.80$ $Q = M = 280$. $R = Rt(17.5*Q) = 70$. $N = Q/R = 4$ These are optimal decisions.
	4(G)	See graph for optimal decisions A and C. Computations follow.
	4(C)	See graph and formulas for optimal decisions A and C. Computations follow.
	16	Computation optimal decisions for product A: Price: \$540 Production: 44 tons Purchasing: 2 orders, 22 tons per order.
8	6	Can you compute optimal decisions for D or send me the formula? I do E and F.
	14	Computation optimal decisions E: Price: \$67.50 Production: 510 tons Purchasing: 6 orders, 85 tons per order. F: Price: \$259.90 Production: 40 tons Purchasing: 8 orders, 5 tons per order.
9	1	*If optimal decisions were followed in period 7:* I recommend we continue to make optimal decisions, because there are no changes. *If optimal decisions were not followed in period 7:* I recommend we make optimal decisions. I repeat: (optimal decisions A and B are repeated). Decisions are optimal, because there are no changes.
10	3	*If all decisions were optimal in period 8:* I recommend to continue to make optimal decisions. Profit will be maximal in long run. *If E and/or F were optimal, but not D in period 8:* Did you compute optimal decisions for D? *If no optimal decisions were made in period 8:* We should make optimal decisions. Computations are good, since there are no changes. Profit will be maximal in long run. I repeat: (optimal decisions E and F are repeated).

Period	Minute	Message
11	1	Survey results have changed. Shall I do new analysis?
	7	*If no answer to previous question:* What about new analysis?
	10	I am computing optimal decisions for A and B. Can you help with C?
	10(C)	The same formulas can be used as before with new values.
	18	New optimal decisions. A: Price: $332.50 Production: 34 tons Purchasing: 2 orders, 17 tons per order. B is unchanged: (optimal decisions are repeated)
12	2	I will compute new optimals E and F.
	2(C)	Same formulas can be used again with the new values.
	15	New optimal decisions. E: Price: $67.03 Production: 657 tons Purchasing: 7 orders, 93.86 tons per order. F: Price: $258.80 Production: 33 tons Purchasing: 7 orders, 4.72 tons per order.

2. SCENARIO FOR MARKETING MANAGER

Period	Minute	Message
3	4	Price B will be increased this period in order to decrease stockout cost.
	8	Purchasing manager should have more orders for B. His cost is: $CR = CN*N + .5*R*CH*U$
	15	I had graphs made on survey results. Graphs show that demand is related linearly with price. Formula: $P = D - E*EM$ for all products.
4	4	Stockout causes stockout cost and loss of sales. Production of E should be higher.
	9	I computed marginal return. Formula: $P = D - E*M$ and $P*M = D*M - E*M**2$ and so: $MR = D - 2*E*M.$
	12	Marginal return A: $MR = 900 - 18*M$ B: $MR = 40 - .08*M$ C: $MR = 300 - 4*M$ D: $MR = 750 - 12*M$ E: $MR = 75 - .02*M$ F: $MR = 400 - 10*M$

Period	Minute	Message
5	4	Production manager suggests to set production at capacity. I will set prices accordingly.

| | 8 | *If liquidation sale C in period 3:*
 Liquidation sale C result of decreased demand.
 If liquidation sale A or B, but not C in period 3:
 I will set price _____ a little lower in order to decrease liquidation sale.
 If no liquidation sales in period 3:
 Price will be increased in order to decrease stockout for product(s) _____ |

| 6 | 5 | *If profit in period 4 and no liquidation sale E:*
 I suggest decisions should remain the same. Decisions are near optimal.
 If profit in period 4 and liquidation sale E:
 Production manager should not set production of E too high because $PLQ = 0$ for E.
 If loss in period 4:
 Price _____ should be higher (lower) in order to decrease liquidation sale (stockout cost). |

| | 12 | I received cost formula:
 $CT = N*R*U + N*CN + .5*R*CH*U + V*Q + W*Q**2$
 and: $N*R = Q$ because we should not have end inventory raw materials. |

| 7 | 3 | *If period 5's decision(s) were changed by president and profit:*
 I agree with change price decision _____ in period 5. I propose to increase (decrease) price _____ somewhat this period.
 If period 5's decision(s) were changed by president and loss:
 Change of price decision(s) _____ period 5 was not good. Price(s) should be about _____
 No change of decision(s) by president and profit in period 5:
 Price decisions will remain about the same as in period 5.
 No change of decision(s) by president and loss in period 5:
 I will set price _____ higher (lower) in order to decrease loss. |

| | 11 | Accounting manager has good analysis, but if production is set at capacity because of fixed cost I should set prices accordingly. |

| 8 | 3 | *If profit in period 6:*
 Price decision(s) will be increased (decreased) to about _____ (or: remain the same).
 If loss in period 6:
 I propose somewhat higher (lower) prices for period 8 for _____ about _____. Profit can be made. |

| 9 | 3 | *If decisions were optimal in period 7:*
 I propose that price decisions remain the same. But if pro- |

Period	Minute	Message
		duction changes his decisions, I cannot set the same optimal prices.

No optimal decisions and proposed decisions changed by president in period 7:
I disagree with your change of my proposed decisions. I will propose higher (lower) price decisions for _____ this period.

10	6	*If proposed decisions were changed in period 8:* Why did you change my proposed decisions for _____ *If proposed decisions were not changed in period 8:* I will suggest somewhat higher (lower, same) prices this period at about _____
11	5	Regarding changed survey results. Same formula can be used and gives for A: $P = D - E*EM = 500 - 5*EM$ and marginal return is: MR $= 500 - 10*EM$ for A.
	8	No change for B, C, D, E, and F.
	10	Graphs will be sent.
12	4	No change in demand relationships for D, E, and F. I propose higher (lower, same) prices for _____ Do you want price _____ to be changed more?

3. SCENARIO FOR PRODUCTION MANAGER

Period	Minute	Message
3	4	Stockout was too high. Production was at capacity.
	10	Purchasing manager should have more orders. Purchasing should be just sufficient for production.
	14	I received graphs of survey results from accounting manager. We need trend of demand over time.
4	3	We should use graphs of demand. Production will be at capacity. Marketing manager should set prices such that liquidation sales and stockout are both = 0.
	13	I will propose higher production for E. We should not have stockout. Production will be _____
5	5	*If profit and full capacity production in period 3:* We made profit in period 3. Production should remain high. Can labor cost be decreased? *If profit and no full capacity production in period 3:* We should have production at capacity. Stockout costs are too high. Prices can be higher too.

Period	Minute	Message

If loss and full capacity production in period 3:
Loss in period 3 resulted from wrong prices. I suggest that prices should be at least (at most): _____ [all prices should be set 10% higher (lower) than period 3 if stockout (liquidation sale)].

10

If proposed decisions were left unchanged in period 3:
I suggest that we add other production. Profit (loss) cannot be increased (decreased) with present products.
If proposed decisions were changed in period 3:
I will propose decisions at about _____

6   4

If profit period 4 and losses before:
Financial statement shows that we can make profit. Demand has been too low for F. Should price F be decreased?
If profit period 4 and profit before:
Operations of firm are as good as optimal. Demand F may be increased by lower price.
If loss in period 4:
Demand F has been too low. Can be increased by lower price.
If stockout: I will increase production.

11

Production will remain at about capacity, if liquidation sale is not too high, because of fixed cost.

7   2

If profit and liquidation sales in period 5:
Price _____ should be lower. Will increase profit.
If profit and no liquidation sales in period 5:
Price _____ should be higher. Will increase profit.
If loss in period 5:
I suggest that you coordinate decisions of all managers. Loss will decrease.

11

I suggest decisions be coordinated. Prices should be _____ Production will be _____

17

I received decision proposals from accounting manager. (*Compare with values in foregoing message and:*) I suggest that price _____ should be higher (lower), and production _____ should be higher (lower). We should follow financial results better.

8   5

If proposed decisions period 6 were changed to optimal: Should we not set production at capacity because of fixed expenses? I think this agrees with financial reports.
If proposed decisions period 6 were changed, but not to optimal:
I disagree with change in production decisions in period 6. I propose production for period 8 to be _____

12

Can we add other products? This should increase profit with our fixed cost.

Period	Minute	Message
9	6	I suggest decisions continue to follow the changes in result of financial statements each period.
10	2	*If period 8 profit:* I suggest we continue as is. Maybe we can invest more. *If period 8 loss:* Loss in period 8 resulted from wrong prices. Price of _____ should be higher (lower).
	5	If we cannot decrease fixed expenses and cannot add another product we should set prices such that capacity production is possible.
11	7	I will set production of A lower because the demand for A is lower. Change of cost per order should not change production.
	13	Production will be about _____ Price of A should be decreased (increased) to about $375.
12	2	Liquidation price D and F decreased. Marketing manager should set prices such that liquidation sale will be = 0. Prices should be about _____
	9	Production of E will be such that stockout will be = 0, because cost of stockout increased. I will suggest production of E to be _____

4. SCENARIO FOR PURCHASING MANAGER

Period	Minute	Message
3	4	Purchasing decisions will be set equal to production decisions. I will make _____ orders for B.
	9	I suggest we make about same decisions as in period 1 for prices and production.
4	4	I will increase number of orders and decrease amount per order for all products.
	8	I suggest the following number of orders for this period _____ Purchasing will be sufficient for production and such that no end inventory will remain.
5	3	*If proposed decisions were changed in period 3:* Why did you change my proposed decisions of period 3? *If proposed decisions period 3 were left unchanged and change in period 5:* I propose increased number of orders to _____ *If proposed decisions period 3 were left unchanged and no change in period 5:* I propose to make same purchasing decisions.

Period	Minute	Message
6	5	*If proposed decisions were changed in period 4:* I will increase (decrease) the number of orders to _____ This should do it. *If proposed decisions were left unchanged in period 4:* Purchasing decisions are about right, now. I will set decisions at _____
	11	Analysis accounting manager is not sufficient, because production has too many changes in answer to changes of demand. I will set purchasing such that inventory holding cost is not higher than two times order cost.
7	5	*If proposed decisions were changed in period 5:* I will increase (decrease) purchasing of _____ to _____ *If proposed decisions were left unchanged in period 5:* I propose you coordinate decision proposals when you receive them at end of period. Communications are too bad.
	14	*If profit in period 5:* I suggest prices be decreased such that capacity can be used fully and all products can be sold. *If loss in period 5:* I suggest prices be increased (decreased). Production should be sufficient not to have stockout.
8	2	*If profit in period 6:* I suggest decisions remain the same. *If loss in period 6:* I do not follow analysis accounting manager. I think communication is more important.
9	3	*If decisions were optimal in period 7:* I agree with production manager. We should make a new product in order to use capacity fully. *If decisions were not optimal in period 7:* I suggest that present decisions are right. Uncertainty may cause loss sometimes, but following demand should give profit in long run.
	14	Purchasing decisions will remain the same from now on.
10	3	I will propose purchasing decisions as follows: _____
11	5	I will change number of orders for C to 3 orders, because fixed order cost has changed. I propose for other products: _____
	11	For how many future periods do we have to make decisions?
12	4	Changes for products D, E, and F will not change purchasing decisions.
	10	Decisions sent this period should again be good for all future periods, if there are no new changes.

Appendix 7

RESPONSE RULES GOVERNING
THE INDUCED MESSAGES
OF THE MANAGERS

Complementary to the confederate managers' scenarios were instructions that prescribed as explicitly as possible the kind of action that should be taken on incoming messages. Classification of an incoming message and determination of the response lagtime were discussed in the text (pp. 54–55). In general, the contents of the responses given by a manager were to be in line with his scenario and the decision proposals supplied to him at the beginning of each period. Deviation from the decision proposals was allowed only if the president gave complete explicit instructions to prepare another proposal. Responses could be incorporated in or added to a prepared scenario message or could lead to the modification or deletion of such a message. The confederate managers never actually communicated with each other through the teletype system, even though their scenarios and responses indicated that such communications took place. Only when a message from a president should affect the scenarios of other managers considerably did the receiver of the message inform those managers. (In most cases the president would send copies of his message to the other managers directly.) Extreme positions with respect to a president's opinions were to be evaded, but disagreement had to be expressed whenever the situation called for it. Explicit rules for creating a response were given to each manager period by period. A summary of these rules is given below.

1. *The Accounting Manager.* The accounting manager undertook a study of the summer operations even if the president did not confirm or explicitly approve the announcement of it. The information on the optimal solutions did not run ahead of the scenario presentation unless a president gave explicit instructions (by sending a formula) to compute the optimal solution. In periods 3–7 all responses had to reflect the manager's concentrated effort to find an optimal solution. As much information and help (in terms of requests for computation) as possible was given (the umpire assisted with computations). The distinction between the explicit-understanding and integral-understanding approach, as expressed in the scenario, was strictly carried through in the responses. That is, a response contained the same persuasive argument, but was always supported by its mathematical derivation under the explicit-understanding approach. Up to period 8, the accounting manager took an understanding view of the president's problems even if the president completely rejected the optimal proposals. In periods 8–10 the accounting manager pressed much harder for the adoption of his proposals and expressed his strong disagreement whenever he received a nonoptimal argument from a president. When the arguments of other managers were passed on by the president to the accounting manager, the latter responded by emphasizing his consideration of basic parameters as opposed to the other managers' interest in the financial reports. During the last two periods (11 and 12), the accounting manager emphasized how easily the changes of parameters were taken care of in his model, since none of the underlying relationships had changed.

2. The Marketing Manager. The marketing manager, like the accounting manager, approached the firm's problems analytically, but he did not take a systems approach. He restricted himself to his own function and took the actions of other managers, especially of the production manager, as given. His reactions to the accounting manager's proposals were always sympathetic, but he was never to go so far as to condemn the production manager's proposals. In particular he never took a firm stand against the production manager's argument of using full capacity because of fixed expenses. Questions on competition were handled by referring to the price–demand relationship. The marketing manager exhibited a Bayesian attitude with respect to the financial reports, but with a subjective tendency to take each new demand observation as coming from a sample distribution with near-zero variance (the survey data notwithstanding), which explains his proposals to raise prices when liquidation sales occurred and to lower prices when stockouts occurred in the before-last period. Nonintroduction of the optimal proposals was explained by pointing at the (nonoptimal) decisions of the production manager with which the accounting manager had to be consistent.

3. The Production Manager. The production manager was the strongly heuristically oriented member of the team. He disliked the use of formulas based on historical information and emphasized a dynamic approach to the problems of the firm. He disregarded the formulas of the accounting manager completely if these were sent to him by the president. He strongly opposed the optimal proposals, which required below-capacity production. A "safety margin" of production above expected demand was proposed by him to handle the uncertainty in demand. He was strongly opposed to production below expected demand, especially since there seemed ample capacity available for the current production lines. If full-capacity production led to extraordinary liquidation sales, the production manager would (temporarily) abandon the idea of full-capacity production, but he would bring it up again at a later point of time. The production manager expressed concern when problems of competition, expansion, communication, and organization were brought up. These extraneous factors were also invoked to discredit the accounting manager's proposals as too limited, too rigid, and not businesslike. The basic principle of setting marginal cost equal to marginal return was not contradicted, but the rigid formulation of, for example marginal revenue was. The production manager would supply any pieces of cost information he was asked for.

4. The Purchasing Manager. The purchasing manager, like the production manager, approached the firm's problems heuristically. He thus was the important last element that balanced the heuristic and analytic influences in the president's environment. The purchasing manager's arguments were in a way symmetric to those of the marketing manager, but now on the heuristic side. Thus the purchasing manager never directly opposed the accounting manager's proposals. Rather he pointed to the need for production to adapt to a constantly changing demand, which made using the accounting manager's formulas—even if they were good—an extreme nuisance. Instead the purchasing manager proposed to use as a rule of thumb that inventory holding cost should never exceed two times the total order cost. The purchasing manager also agreed with the production manager on using full capacity. He also was the one who brought up the problems of communication. He never sent formulas nor did he do a mathematical analysis of the firm's or his own functional problems. To the purchasing manager the problem of setting up a good communication system that would allow an immediate exchange of new information and a jointly consistent reaction to it was the most important problem with which the firm had to deal.

Appendix 8

ATLAS TEST

The ATLAS test was one of the three tests given to the subjects during the first experimental session and served to determine a subject's cognitive-style tendency.

ATLAS TEST—PART A

NAME:_____

Below you find a description of a decision situation based on an actual case involving a large American corporation. Although the situation has been simplified and the figures have been disguised, the essence of the problem remains the same. Read this description carefully and be sure to ask any questions that may arise. Then turn to the questionnaire (page 170) and answer the questions.

Atlas Manufacturing Company (A)

The Atlas Manufacturing Company is a well-known and highly regarded firm which produces and markets a special patented section of steel that was specifically designed for use as roof and floor joists (a joist is a parallel set of beams which hold up the planks of a floor or the laths of a roof or ceiling. They are used principally in nonresidential, hotel, and apartment construction). Atlas operates in the eastern and which serves the southern United States market. Currently, Atlas' midwestern regions and has recently opened a new facility in Atlanta which serves the southern United States market. Currently, Atlas' management is considering expanding into the west coast market and establishing a new plant, located in California but serving the 11 western states.

The crucial decision to be made at this point is that of determining

Table I

Demand in Tons per Month	Efficient Plant Size
2500 and greater	1
1600 up to 2500	2
750 up to 1600	3
475 up to 750	4
below 475	5

the size of the new plant. That is, how many joists should Atlas be able to produce and supply in a one-month period?

Currently there are five different plant designs under consideration which, according to engineering performance figures, operate most efficiently in different ranges of volume. Owing to these technological considerations, Atlas' management classifies sales volume into five classes corresponding to the five plant designs, as shown in Table I.

The central question, Atlas' management feels, thus becomes to estimate the demand for Atlas joists in the western region that may be expected. Management therefore requested the marketing research department to gather information deemed relevant for an estimation of the demand in the 11 western states. *A summary of the information* the department came up with is given below:

1. *The Atlas Manufacturing Company is currently operating in five market areas.* Data relevant to these five areas is presented in Table II.

2. *Total industry demand for joists* (per month) in the western region was derived from a survey of total construction activity in the 11 western states for the past 50 months. Table III gives the total joist tonnage which would have resulted *if all floor and roof areas had employed joist-type construction.* The second column shows the number of times each volume occurred.

3. *A prominent construction magazine* has estimated the market for open web joists for flooring and roof framing in the 11 western states construction at an average of 6600 tons per month for 1967 of which 3000 tons would represent the California market.

4. An independent study by *the California Roofers Association* estimates the California market for *roof joists alone* at 1200 tons per month.

5. *Atlas' vice-president of marketing* indicates that sales participation by the Atlas joists could amount to at least half the total market if supported by (*a*) a west coast point of fabrication, (*b*) a promotional program accentuating Atlas' strong reputation, and (*c*) Mercury Steel's,

Table II

Region Number (R)	Headquarters (HQ)	Atlas' Market Share[a] (MS)	Total Non-residential Construction (Billions of $) (C)	Time Atlas Has Been in Region (in Years) (T)	Atlas' Relative Size in Region[b] (S)
1	New York	.40	6	20	1
2	Philadelphia	.25	2	20	2
3	Chicago	.30	4	18	4
4	Minneapolis	.15	1	12	3
5	Atlanta	.08	2	1	4
Proposed Western region	In California region	?	5	0	1

[a] Market share = percentage of total roof and floor tonnage employing Atlas joists.
[b] Atlas' relative size in a region is given as an index on a scale of 1–5. A rating of 1 indicates that Atlas is the largest firm in the region; a rating of 5 that all competitors in the region are larger than Atlas.

the major west coast competitor, continuance of their existing production and marketing practices.

6. *The general sales manager*, after analyzing the characteristics of existing customers and users in the other regions and comparing them with conditions in the west, estimates Atlas' achievable sales at 3000 tons per month.

7. *Atlas outsells Mercury Steel*, a California firm and the only major

Table III

Total Joist-Tonnage	Times Occurring during 50 Months
32,500	1
20,000	2
12,000	6
9,000	9
5,700	4
4,500	20
2,500	5
1,200	2
500	1
	50

potential competitor in the 11 western states, in each of the five other regions.

8. *Sales by Mercury Steel* are believed to approximate 500 tons per month in the 11 western states at present. The floor and roof construction in this region which Mercury does not supply utilizes either wood timbers or steel beams.

9. *Joist construction* is considered to be a *highly promotional* technique in a very competitive field in which, on the west coast, wood timbers and steel beams are firmly entrenched.

After the subject had read the foregoing, he was asked to fill out a brief questionnaire:

ATLAS—First questionnaire: Please answer the following questions

NAME:

1. a) If you were in the position of Atlas management, what demand would you expect for Atlas' joists in the Western region?

b) What size plant would you build?

2. How did you arrive at the figures given in the first question? (Give *brief* explanation)

3. If you were allowed more time to tackle Atlas' problems, how would you arrive at a decision? (Assume that you can get no more data.)

Atlas Manufacturing Company (B)

The information provided by Atlas' marketing research department formed the basis for a long discussion of the new venture into the western region, but top management remained divided over the problem of the plant size. After this meeting, the president of Atlas decided to call upon two independent consultants for advice. The consultants, American Marketing Research Corporation and Allston Management Consultants, were provided the information given in part A above. They were told to come up with an explicit recommendation regarding the plant size to be built. A summary of the consultants' reports follows below (a highly simplified version!).

Please read these reports carefully. Then turn to the questionnaire after each report and answer the questions.

Report of the American Marketing Research Corporation. We recommend that Atlas should build the plant with a capacity of 750–1500 tons per month, plant number 3. This recommendation is based on a scientific analysis of the data as well as on the consultation of experts in the field of joist construction and west coast building.

It appeared to us that the most important parameter to be estimated at the outset was the market share or market penetration factor (the percentage of total roof and floor tonnage employing Atlas joists). One would expect the market share of a firm to increase somewhat linearly with increases in (*1*) the extent to which joists are used in construction and (*2*) the relative size of the firm. As a function of time, the market-share might be expected to increase rather rapidly in the beginning years and then to level off as the firm gets "situated in the market."

We decided to build a linear regression model to estimate market share from the three factors mentioned in the preceding paragraph.[a] We believed that, in the interest of simplicity, a linearity assumption for the variable "time" would be satisfactory for the estimate. Since data on the extent to which joists are used in construction are not directly available we used the level of nonresidential construction instead. (Other studies indicate that joist use in construction is generally dependent upon overall size of buildings being constructed. The level of nonresidential construction has proven to be a good indicator of this factor.)

This leads to the following linear regression model:

$$MS = a_0 + a_1C + a_2T + a_3S + e \qquad (1)$$

where:

MS = market share (fraction)
C = level of nonresidential construction (billions of \$ per year)
T = time in region (years)
S = relative size of the firm (index on scale 1–5).[b] The a_is are the regression coefficients to be fitted by least squares and e is the error term.[c]

The data for this model are given in information item (1) of part A. The solution to the model revealed that the regression coefficients (the a_i's) in equation (1) are statistically significant at the .40, .025, .025, and .25 level, respectively. The following estimates of the regression coefficients and (in parenthesis) the number of times each coefficient exceeds its

---

[a] A linear regression model establishes the relationship between *a variable to be explained* (in our case: market share) and the *explaining variables* (in our case: nonresidential construction, relative size of the firm, and time). The relationship established is *linear*, that is a change in any of the explaining variables leads to a *proportional* change of the explained variable.

[b] Note that the scale is inverted from the one given in part A. The bigger the firm, the higher its market share; that is, a_3 will be positive.

[c] The regression coefficient, or the proportionality factor, estimated by the "method of least squares" is the *most likely* value, given the data we have available, of the *true* relationship between explaining and explained variables.

standard error were obtained[a]:

$$a_0 = 0.00207 \qquad (0.365)$$

$$a_1 = 0.03553 \qquad (23.784)$$

$$a_2 = 0.00837 \qquad (15.982)$$

$$a_3 = 0.00418 \qquad (1.599)$$

The multiple correlation coefficient adjusted for one degree of freedom (we have five observations to estimate four coefficients, so d.f. = 5 −4 = 1) is[b]:

$$R^2 = .968354$$

Thus these coefficients can be considered the result of a "good fit" on the data.

Applying these coefficients to the corresponding variable values for the proposed western region market area [last row of information item (1) of part A] we get:

$$MS = -0.00207 + 0.03553(5) + 0.00837(0) + 0.00418(5)$$

$$= \quad 0.00207 + 0.17765 \quad\quad + 0.0 \quad\quad\quad + 0.02070$$

$$= \quad 0.19648 \text{ approximately equal to } 0.20$$

Accordingly, it is established that Atlas' participation in this market will be approximately 20%.

The expected demand can now be calculated using the data of information item (2) of part A as shown in Table I.

Our estimate of an expected demand of 1415 tons per month in the

---

[a] The standard error is a measure of how closely the data follow the proportional relationship as expressed by the regression coefficient. A standard error of 0 means a perfect relationship. Each region of values around the estimated regression coefficient can be expressed as a number of times (say n times) the standard error above or below the estimate. The larger n, the lower the probability, α, that the *true* regression coefficient does not lie within the region. The region *below the value zero* (if the regression coefficient is negative) or *above zero* (if the coefficient is positive) similarly corresponds to certain values for n and α, which are the values given in the text. For example, for a_3 we have $n = 1.599$ and $\alpha = .25$, that is, the probability that the true value for a_3 is *below* zero (which would mean an opposite relationship to the one we estimated) is is .25 or: "the estimated regression coefficient a_3 is statistically significant at the .25 level."

[b] The correlation coefficient, R^2, is a measure of the overall quality of the regression model. R^2 may vary from 0 (no explanation of the dependent variable by the model) to 1 (perfect explanation of the dependent variable by the model).

Table I

Total Joist Tonnage (1)	Market Share (2)	Atlas' Joist Tonnage (3) = (1) × (2)	Probability of Occurrence (4)	Atlas' Expected Demand (5) = (3) × (4)
32,500	.20	6,500	1/50	130
20,000	.20	4,000	2/50	160
12,000	.20	2,400	6/50	288
9,000	.20	1,800	9/50	324
5,700	.20	1,140	4/50	91.2
4,500	.20	900	20/50	360
2,500	.20	500	5/50	50
1,200	.20	240	2/50	9.6
500	.20	100	1/50	2
			1	1414.8

western region, together with a consideration of cost effects of idle capacity, the possibility of expanding facilities and/or overtime use of the facilities, led to our decision to recommend the building of plant number 3. (See also Table I of part A.)

It should be noted that this result is completely consistent with the construction magazine's estimate [see information item (3) of part A]. An average of 6600 tons per month with a .20 market share yields monthly sales for Atlas of 1320 tons, which is well within plant number 3's efficient production range.

Through the rigor introduced by the application of the linear regression model and through seeking the advice of people knowledgeable in the west coast joist market we were able to discover some of the underlying factors which influence Atlas' market share percentage. In this way we were able to demonstrate that the .20 factor is more representative of Atlas' potential market share than are those indicated by other estimates, such as found in information items (5) and (6) of part A. In particular, by employing the index of relative size factor (S) in the regression model, the influence of competitive activity, such as referred to in information items (7), (8), and (9) can be summarized quantitatively and weighed against the importance of other influencing factors.

Report of the Allston Management Consultants. It is our recommendation that plant number 2 be built, the plant that is most efficient when demand falls in the range of 1600 up to 2500 tons.

We reached this conclusion after a careful analysis of all relevant information. Our first step was to determine what market for joists in the 11 western states may be expected. Information items (2), (3), and (4) of part A deal with this question. The total potential demand can be estimated from information item (2) as a weighted average (see Table I):

Table I

Total Joist Tonnage (1)	Relative Frequency of Occurrence (2)	Expected Demand 3 = (1) × (2)
32,500	1/50	650
20,000	2/50	800
12,000	6/50	1,440
9,000	9/50	1,620
4,500	4/50	456
4,500	20/50	1,800
2,500	5/50	250
1,200	2/50	48
500	1/50	10
	1	7,074

Hence, if no serious demand shifts for joists occur in the western region, a total demand of 7074 tons monthly may be expected. We note that the magazine's estimate of the total demand in the 11 western states of 6600 tons per month [information item (3) of part A] comes reasonably close to the estimate of 7074 tons, which is based on historical data for the past 50 months. Moreover, the discrepancy of about 500 tons is easily explained from the fact that not all floor and roof areas *do* employ joist-type construction as was assumed in information item (2) of part A. The estimate of 7074 tons is therefore rather an estimate of the *potential* demand, in our view the more relevant figure when one considers a new settlement.

Given an estimate for the total expected demand in the western region we could determine—using Table I of part A—the most efficient plant size for every possible market share for Atlas. For example, if Atlas would be able to get 40% of the western joist market, its expected monthly demand would be .40 × 7074 = 2830 tons. Since plant number 2 is most efficient when the monthly demand is above 2500 tons (see Table I of part A), a market share of .40 corresponds to plant size number 1.

More interesting, we determined the *critical* market share values, that is, those values for Atlas' market-share at which a bigger plant size becomes efficient. For example, to determine the market share, say f, above which plant number 2 and below which plant number 3 is more efficient, we calculate:

$$f = \frac{1{,}600 \text{ (from Table I of part A)}}{7{,}074 \text{ (total estimated demand, see above)}} = .23$$

Using a monthly demand figure of 7074 tons and the information in Table I of part A, we calculated all critical market-share values (see Table II):

Table II

Efficient Plant Size (1)	Demand (Tons per Month) (2)	Critical Market Share (3) = (2)/7074
1	2500 and greater	.35 and greater
2	1600 up to 2500	.23 up to .35
3	750 up to 1600	.11 up to .23
4	475 up to 750	.07 up to .11
5	below 475	below .07

From Table II we can immediately read the most efficient plant size for any possible market share. For example, a market share of .27 requires a plant size number 2.

In which of these ranges is Atlas' market share most likely to fall? Before coming to a conclusion, we carefully evaluated the pros and cons for each relevant market-share range:

Looking at what happened in Atlanta [see information item (1) of part A], a low estimate of the market share in the western region, say, in the .07 up to .11 range seems appropriate. The Atlanta plant has been operating for one year now and has only obtained 8% of the market. It takes a long time to build up the vital contacts with contractors, architects, and builders that are necessary to secure a large market share. However, it should be noted immediately that Atlas will be the biggest firm in the western region, while in Atlanta it has three bigger competitors. Information item (1) of part A illustrates that Atlas does better and receives a larger market share in areas in which it has no bigger competitors. Moreover, as the construction magazine estimate confirms [see item (3) of part A], the western area is a big nonresidential market: Information item (1) gives a figure of $5 billion for total nonresidential construction. In both other areas with large nonresidential construction, Chicago ($4 billion) and New York ($6 billion), Atlas' market share is very high (30 and 40%, respectively).

Atlas will be a new company in the west coast market and as such must overcome severe obstacles in gaining acceptance by its customers. It will be hard for Atlas to do much outside of California for some time. This puts forth the California demand figures of 3000 and 1200 tons [items (3) and (4) of part A] as the more relevant ones. Much higher market shares than those given in Table II are required in this more restricted area in order to reach demands at which the different plant sizes become efficient. With the difficulties of penetrating the market and establishing a new operation in the face of competition, it would again seem that a smaller size plant should be chosen, even more so in view of the possibility of expanding the facilities at a later time.

We therefore tested the estimates of Atlas' vice president of marketing and those of the general sales manager against the opinions of some experts in the industry. General agreement was found that both estimates may be somewhat high, but feasible and certainly not merely induced by wishful thinking on the part of sales management. Hence, *even if* we assume—a too pessimistic assumption in our opinion—that Atlas' sales will be restricted to California initially, a market share of .50 (the vice president's estimate) would generate a demand of .50 × 3000 = 1400 tons per month, which by itself would already justify a plant of at least size number 3. Moreover, we should bear in mind that the estimates of the construction magazine as well as the one of the California Roofers Association were made *without the knowledge* that a major producer of steel joists would establish operations in the west.

Finally, we explored the possible reactions of Atlas' two competitors, Mercury Steel and the forest products industry. Mercury is a California-based firm and has been operating in the western area for some time. They still have been unable to exceed the 500-ton level, mainly because of the heavy competition from wood timbers and steel beams [see items (8) and (9) of part A]. The nation's largest timber stands are on the west coast. West coast builders are accustomed to using wood products and, furthermore, they are skilled in employing wooden beams.

Atlas' strong reputation and aggressive promotional techniques will primarily hurt the forest products and steel beams industry. A strong California market—Atlas' home base—as predicted by both the construction magazine and the California Roofers Association, will enable

Atlas to back up its promotion with fast deliveries to customers. Some concentration on this market area should give immediate results. Even a moderate initial success in the other 10 states, *together* about 60% of the western market, will provide a good support for the California operations. The 10-state area, moreover, holds obviously high promises for the future.

Mercury's reactions are likely to be mild for the simple reason that Mercury *initially* might very well benefit from Atlas' coming to the area. Mercury, being an established west coast producer, might temporarily be able to attract some of the new business being generated by Atlas' promotional campaign, while at the same time Atlas' cut in their sales may not yet be too alarming. Atlas' size and reputation, however [Atlas is much bigger than Mercury, see information item (1)], should soon drive Mercury effectively out of the market. Paradoxically, Mercury's expected initial attitude of waiting is likely to speed up this development.

Summarizing our analysis, we find that all arguments finally lead us to expect a demand of minimally 1500 tons. Even the most speculative part of our analysis—competitor's reactions—does nowhere indicate that our estimates should be revised downwardly. More likely the demand will be in the 2000–2500 range with *considerably higher* estimates for the future. Atlas should be prepared to cope with this demand *immediately*. Late deliveries, because of inadequate facilities, might prevent the operation from getting off the ground and will hurt Atlas' reputation permanently. In view of the possibility of expanding the facilities at a later time, we recommend building the plant with efficient capacity in the range of 1600 up to 2500 tons, plant number 2.

(*Note:* The following questionnaire was given two times, once after each report.)

ATLAS Report questionnaire Please answer the following questions:

1. a) After reading the foregoing report: If you were in the position of Atlas management, what demand would you expect for Atlas joists in the western region?
   b) What size plant would you build?
2. If the figures given in question 1 differ from your estimate given in answer to the same question after part A: Why?
3. Did you find the report helpful in coming to a decision about what demand can be expected for Atlas joists in the new Western region and what plant size should be built? In what way?

TURN TO NEXT PAGE.
DO NOT TURN BACK TO THIS PAGE.

NAME:

ATLAS final questionnaire: Please answer the following questions.
Check (✓) your answer.

	Am. Mkt. Res. Corp.	Allston Mgt. Cons.
1. Which report provided you with the best insight into the policy alternatives available to Atlas?		
2. a. Which report approaches, in your opinion, the problem in the best way?		
b. Do you see improvements for each report within the frame set by the consultant?		
3. If only one report were available, which report would you, as Atlas' president, prefer to receive?		

After reading both reports:

4. a. If you were in the position of Atlas management, what demand would you expect for Atlas' joists in the western region?

   b. What size plant would you build?

5. Comments (Use the back of this page, if necessary.)

Appendix 9

HAT TEST

The HAT test consisted of two behavior tests used during the first experimental session to establish a subject's cognitive-style tendency.

INSTRUCTIONS

Pitcher Test

The pitcher test consists of two parts, A and B. Both parts refer to the following problems:

You have one barrel filled with wine ($31\frac{1}{2}$ gal to a barrel). The only measures you have are two (empty) pitchers, whose capacities are stated in quarts. There are no marks on the pitchers, hence the *only* amount you are able to measure exactly with the pitcher is its capacity. The capacity of the pitchers is different for each question.

Your problem in each case is to measure a specific number of quarts, given the capacity of the pitchers. No wine may be spilled. Remember that you have no containers other than the two pitchers.

Examples:

Capacity, Pitcher 1	Capacity, Pitcher 2	Quarts Required
4	1	3

In stating your answer, you may use the following abbreviations:

$$B = \text{barrel}$$

$$P_1 = \text{pitcher 1}$$

$$P_2 = \text{pitcher 2}$$

The answer to the above question then becomes:

$$B \rightarrow P_1; \; P_1 \rightarrow P_2; \; 3 \text{ quarts left in } P_1$$

Note that the quarts required have to be measured *exactly*.

You should give detailed solutions (step by step, as in example) to the questions of part A. For the questions in part B, you have only to state if you would be able to solve the problem (yes or no).

You have 25 min to complete both parts A *and* B. (This is a suggested time limit.)

Part A

	Pitcher 1	Pitcher 2	Required
a	4	3	2
b	8	3	4
c	13	4	10

(Note: The original test form leaves room for answers on the same sheet.)

Part B

For the following questions you only have to state if you would or would not be able to measure the required amount of quarts.
(Answer with yes or no.)

	Pitcher 1	Pitcher 2	Required	Answer
a	16	4	6	
b	61	12	50	
c	29	9	24	
d	32	7	29	
e	25	6	20	
f	47	13	42	

Coin Test

The coin test again consists of two parts, A and B. Both parts refer to the following problem:

You have a number of similar coins, which are all except one of the same weight. The number of coins is different in each question. The one coin that differs in weight is *heavier* (in all cases), but can in no other way be distinguished from the others. The only weighing instrument you have is a balance.

Your problem in each case is to determine which coin is the heavier one, *given* a limited number of times that you may use the balance.

Example:

Number of Coins	Number of Times You May Weigh
4	2

In your answer you should clearly specify which coins you take to weigh each time. In example:

$$W_1: \quad 2\text{--}2$$

$$W_2: \quad \text{Take two heavier ones, } 1\text{--}1$$

Heavier one is the answer. Only the questions of part A should be answered in detail (step by step). For the questions in part B, you have only to state if you would be able to solve the problem (yes or no). You have 25 min to complete both parts A *and* B. (This is a suggested time-limit.)

Part A

	Number of Coins	Number of Times You May Weigh
a	7	2
b	10	2
c	16	3

(Note: The original test form leaves room for answers on the same sheet.)

Part B

For the following questions you have only to state if you would or would not be able to determine which coin is the heavier one, given the number of coins and the number of times you may weigh. (Answer with yes or no.)

	Number of Coins	Number of Times You May Weigh	Answer
a	23	3	
b	26	3	
c	30	3	
d	36	3	
e	48	4	
f	77	4	
g	79	5	
h	187	5	
i	220	5	

DO NOT TURN THIS PAGE UNTIL TOLD TO DO SO

LAST PAGE

After both tests had been completed, the subject was asked to fill out the following questionnaire:

Answer the following questions.

                                                   Pitchers   Coins

a. Have you done this type of problem before?
b. Do you like this type of problem?
c. How did you try to solve the problems?
    (Please describe as explicitly as possible the
    way you *actually* approached the problems on
    the foregoing pages.)

Appendix 10

ANALYTIC SOLUTIONS TO THE PITCHER AND COIN TESTS

This Appendix presents the analytic solutions to the two behavior tests of Appendix 9.

A. THE PITCHER TEST

Let:

$$P_1 = \text{larger of the two pitchers}$$
$$P_2 = \text{smaller of the two pitchers}$$
$$[P_1/P_2] = \text{fractional part of } P_1/P_2$$
$$x = \text{number of gallons required } (X \leqq P_1)$$

x can be measured exactly if it is an integer multiple of the largest common divisor of

$$P_2 \cdot \left[\frac{P_1}{P_2}\right] \text{ and } P_2 \cdot \left(1 - \left[\frac{P_1}{P_2}\right]\right)$$

B. THE COIN TEST

Let:

$$C = \text{number of coins}$$
$$x = \text{number of weighings allowed}$$

It is possible to detect the one heavier coin from C coins in maximally x weighings, if $C \leqq 3^x$.

Appendix 11

ADDITIONAL INFORMATION SENT TO THE SUBJECTS BY THE ACCOUNTING MANAGER

In addition to the teletype messages, the subjects received some graphs. A plot of the demand–price relationship with a statement of the mathematical formula was sent to *all* subjects after period 3 by the marketing manager (not reproduced in this appendix). A graph and formulas that explained the optimal solution were sent by the accounting manager in period 7. When the integral-understanding approach was used by the accounting manager, the subjects received only the graph (Figure A11.1). When the explicit-understanding approach was used, the subjects received the graph as well as the formulas (Figure A11.2).

Provided on request of accounting manager and sent to all managers
Demand is uncertain for products A and C. Production will therefore usually not be equal to market sales. We can distinguish two cases:

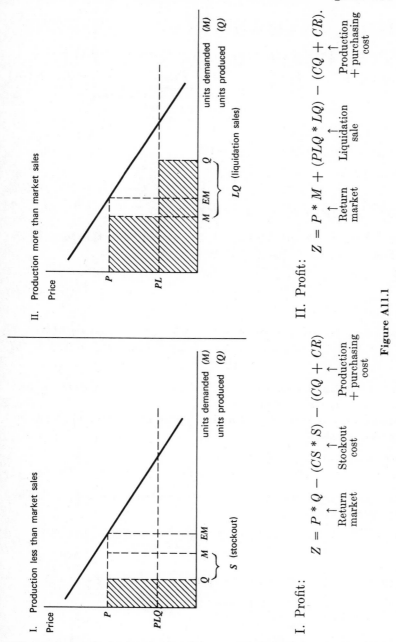

II. Profit:

$$Z = P * M + (PLQ * LQ) - (CQ + CR).$$

   ↑ Return market   ↑ Liquidation sale   ↑ Production + purchasing cost

I. Profit:

$$Z = P * Q - (CS * S) - (CQ + CR)$$

   ↑ Return market   ↑ Stockout cost   ↑ Production + purchasing cost

Figure A11.1

I am computing the optimal decisions for both cases by finding production and price combination for which the *marginal profit* is equal to zero.

Formulas used

The two cases mentioned can be combined into one formula:

I

$$Z = P * Q - (CS * S) - (CQ + CR)$$
$$= [PLQ * Q + (P - PLQ) * (M - S)] - (CS * S) - (CQ + CR)$$
$$= PLQ * Q + (P - PLQ) * M - \underbrace{(P - PLQ + CS) * S} - (CQ + CR)$$

only difference between
the two formulas.

II

$$Z = P * M + (PLQ * LQ) - (CQ + CR)$$
$$= [(P - PLQ) * M + PLQ * M]$$
$$+ PLQ * (Q - M) - (CQ + CR)$$
$$= PLQ * Q + (P - PLQ) * M - (CQ + CR)$$

Since $S = 0$ (no stockout) for formula II, we may add this term to the second formula without changing it. So we get:

Profit $Z = PLQ * Q + (P - PLQ) * M$
$$- (P - PLQ + CS) * S - (CQ + CR)$$

and:

Expected profit $EZ = PLQ * Q + (D - E * EM - PLQ) * EM$
$$- (D - E * EM - PLQ + CS) * ES - (CQ + CR)$$
$$(EM) \qquad\qquad\qquad\qquad (Q)$$

To calculate optimal decisions take derivatives with respect to price (or: exp. demand) and production.

Marginal profit with respect to EM (*given* production, i.e., when production decision is fixed):

$$MZ(EM) = (D - 2 * E * EM - PLQ)$$
$$- (D - E * EM - PLQ + CS) * XS + E * ES \quad (1)$$

Marginal profit with respect to Q (*given* expected demand, i.e., when price decision is fixed):

$$MZ(Q) = PLQ + (D - E * EM - PLQ + CS) * XS - M.C.(Q) \quad (2)$$

and:

$$MC(Q) = U + Rt[A * CH * U/(2 * Q)] + V + 2 * W * Q$$

Figure A11.2

Note: $f(X)$ = probability distribution of demand; $EM = \int_0^\infty X \cdot f(X)\,dX$;

$ES = \int_Q^\infty (X - Q) \cdot f(X)\,dX$ = expected stockout (normal distrib.)

XS = probability that demand exceeds production

$= \int_0^\infty f(X)\,dX$; Derivatives: $\partial ES/\partial EM = XS$ and $\partial ES/\partial Q$

$= -XS$

Solution of the simultaneous equations (1) and (2) for EM and Q will give optimal decisions. Computations follow.

Figure A11.2 (*Continued*)

Appendix 12

RANDOM NORMAL NUMBERS USED TO GENERATE THE ACTUAL DEMANDS FROM THE DEMAND DISTRIBUTIONS

The same sequence of random normal numbers (z) was used in all experiments to generate the actual demand (X) from the normal demand distribution with mean μ and variance σ, that is, $X = \mu + z \cdot \sigma$. The sequence of randomly drawn values of z is presented in Table A12.1.

Table A12.1. Random Normal Numbers Used in Experiment[a]

Product	Period						
	1–2	3–4	5–6	7–8	9–10	11–12	13–14
A	.10	1.05	.40	1.20	−.60	.45	−.20
C	.15	−.60	−.45	−1.90	1.30	−.10	−2.30
E	.95	.30	.20	−.55	−1.50	−1.10	−.55
F	−2.10	−1.20	−.50	1.90	−.50	−.45	−1.45

[a] Products B and D have a deterministic demand.

Appendix 13

PARAMETER CHANGES AND NEW OPTIMAL DECISIONS

The parameter setting remains unchanged during the first 10 periods of the experiment, that is, until five decisions for each product have been made. At the beginning of period 11 parameter changes are announced. The new parameter setting as well as the new optimal solution are given in Tables A13.1 and A13.2, respectively.

All other entries in Table A13.1 are the same as in Table A2.1 of Appendix 2. The new optimal decisions are presented in Table A13.2.

Table A13.1. Parameter Values from Period 11 On

Parameter	Product					
	A	B	C	D	E	F
d	500					
e	5					
$a = \dfrac{1}{e}$	.2					
$b = \dfrac{d}{e}$						
SIGMA						
$\bar{r}$					.5	
$\bar{s}$						
T						200.00
W				25	30	50.00
V						
U						
A			10			

Table A13.2. Optimal Decisions from Period 11 On

Optimal solution	Product					
	A	B	C	D	E	F
S^*	332.50	28.80	188.76	438.00	67.03	258.79
μ^*	33.50	280.00	55.62	52.00	797.00	28.00
Z^*	.05	0	1.55	0	$-.70$	.95
Q^*	33.90	280.00	102.12	52.00	657.00	33.00
R^*	16.95	70.00	17.02	4.00	93.86	4.72
N^*	2	4	6	13	7	7
$E(\pi^*)$	4,827	3,114	5,600	16,453	4,148	3,476
Labor hours required	259	167	806	235	760	254
Labor hours required per season	1232 $< K$			1249 $< K$		

Appendix 14

INSTRUCTIONS FOR THE MEETING

After period 12 (the last formal period) of the experiment a meeting was held between the accounting manager, the production manager, and the presidents (at most four presidents at a time). At the beginning of the meeting the experimenter revealed part of the experimental design by stating that the accounting and production managers had been instructed to act as such for four teams simultaneously. ("They received extra help to do this. To be able to maintain an informal discussion format the marketing and purchasing managers, who were different people for each team and whose main role was to complete their teams, have not been invited to the meeting.") The presidents were told that the "subjects" who were given the role of accounting and production manager had been chosen for their respective functions on the basis of the tests. We also told them that the accounting and production managers had been asked to explain, without being restricted by teletype communications or a formal language, how the firm ("identical for all teams") ought to be run. Each manager got 10 min to explain his basic position. The presidents were allowed to interrupt the explanations with questions, but were asked not to get into a discussion among themselves. If necessary, the managers would each get five minutes for rebuttal.

After his introduction the experimenter gave the word to one of the managers (in one-half of the cases first to the accounting manager, in the other half first to the production manager) and withdrew. The presentations of the two managers were rotated among three persons in order to prevent confounding the effect of presentation with the effect of persons giving the presentation.

An outline of the meeting scenarios for the two managers follows:

1. *Accounting Manager.* "My function was such that I really did not have much to do, except for some calculations (and even those I could have done by the experimenter, such as those graphs that were made). I got from the instructions already the impression that our firm's problem was very well-structured and since the instructions said something

about the accounting manager doing a study of the operations, I started to do some analysis. Actually I thought that we should all together have worked on this analysis. We would have had the results faster. For the time being, we could have set the decisions just as they were in periods 1 and 2 when we made a profit. I really hardly looked at the financial statements and worked all the time on the analysis of the summer-products 'A,' 'B' and 'C.' I felt that, as long as there was no announcement of any basic changes, we could not learn too much from the financial reports.

"The main problem I had to solve was to set up a profit-function. This function had to contain all elements talked about in the instructions: market revenue (price × demand), liquidation sale revenue, ordering cost, inventory holding cost, production-labor cost and stockout cost. The next thing I did was to determine for which values of price, production and purchasing this function reached its maximum. I left the fixed cost completely out of consideration, since the decisions can not change them and should therefore be independent of them. It actually happened that we should use somewhere between 1300 and 1400 hours of capacity (which is 1500 hours).

"As far as the individual products go, product 'B' was straightforward, because there we could set production exactly equal to demand, which we knew with certainty for every price. It then was a matter of expanding production of 'B' until the point that the cost of an extra unit became equal to the revenue from that unit. Products 'A' and 'C' were less obvious, since we did not have complete control over demand by setting our price. But there we found the linear relationship to exist between price and expected (average) demand. The actual demand could lie above or below the expected demand, but the larger the discrepancy the lower its probability of occurrence. However, it is no longer clear that production should equal the expected demand in this case: we should rather try to balance the expected cost of overproduction (production cost minus liquidation price times the probability that the production is higher than the actual demand) with the expected cost of underproduction (stockout cost times the probability that the production is lower than the actual demand).

"This is essentially the reasoning that I followed in setting up my equations. To solve them was not so hard, since I could give the formulas to the experimenter for calculation. I think, though, that we should have followed the resulting price, production and purchasing decisions *exactly*. The change after period 10 was really trivial in terms of the analysis, because the only thing that changed were the calculations and those we could have done by the Experimenter."

Second Explanation (Response to Production Manager). "I really think that you [production manager] are emphasizing too much the idea of full capacity production. Just *because* capacity means a fixed cost, it should not influence our decisions (except for the case that we would be operating at a loss, but that wasn't our case). It actually came out that we should *not* use full capacity (we should stay about 150–200 hours below capacity). (If the capacity-constraint had been effective, I would have had to redo my whole analysis.) I don't even think that we should use the overcapacity to produce more just to prevent stockouts. The costs of stockout were explicitly taken care of in my analysis, it does not make much sense to me to talk about losing business to competition if there is no information whatsoever that this happens *above* what is expressed by the demand functions. I also think that the analysis I did allowed a much faster and better-understood adaptation of the decisions than you would get by any other method."

2. *Production Manager.* "To me the central question became how we would be able to make best use of our production-capacity (1,500 hours). We should try to make full use of this capacity, because of its fixed cost. It does not make sense, on the other hand, to produce a product only to see it liquidated at a liquidation price of $0 (such as is the case for 'E'). My first idea was to introduce new products in order *to guarantee* full use of capacity. When this appeared to be impossible, I directed my attention to arrive at a good coordination with the marketing manager. He could manipulate the demand to a great extent by changing his prices. The demand graphs were extremely helpful to arrive at a coordination between our functions and I feel that we arrived at fairly good coordination toward the end, even though we sometimes had heavy losses.

"Our aim had to be, in my opinion, to produce as closely as possible to what could profitably be sold on the market. The financial reports were a good guide as to what adaptations had to be made. I thought it very important not to have stockouts, since this would cause a loss of good will and we might thus lose customers to competition. This would worsen the situation seriously for us, since it looked as if we have already too much production capacity. (I must say that I still don't know what kind of competition we had or if there was any.) The coordination with marketing was therefore very important as I said before. For instance, demand for 'C' was consistently below average during periods 3, 5, and 7 and the same thing happened for 'F' during periods 2, 4, and 6. Looking at the financial reports we saw this happening and could take some corrective action (at least that is what I proposed).

Thus we could sell at a market-price, what we otherwise would have had to sell at a (much lower) liquidation-price.

"I really think that the adaptive procedure that I proposed was the best way to get a good 'feel' of the market and I am sure that we would have become very good in adapting to all kinds of market changes that might occur just by keeping a close eye on those financial reports. Of course, it would take some more time when bigger changes occur like after period 10, but finally we would get back on the right track and we probably would be faster each time such changes occur."

Second Explanation (Response to Accounting Manager). "I felt that the procedure that I followed, and I think the marketing manager did, would lead us more surely to a good policy. I don't think we could afford to throw away the information we could get out of the financial statements as you (the accounting manager) seem to say. Those reports just gave us the chance to develop a market-feeling, which I think was our central problem. Moreover, I don't see how you would ever be able to capture all the aspects of this firm without really *doing* and that is what I and, I think, the other two managers (marketing and purchasing) did. I think that I got a much better idea about what is going on by making my decisions and adapting them if the reports indicated that this was necessary than by just *thinking* in some abstract way about all the firm's operations. For instance, one of your (accounting manager) conclusions was to produce 'E' below the expected demand. That certainly did not make much sense in view of the already available overcapacity we had, which allowed us to be prepared, at a very low cost, for any sudden increase in demand."

Appendix 15

QUESTIONNAIRES

Three questionnaires were used during the experiment. The first one was handed out after period 6, the second after period 12, and the last one after the final meeting between president(s) and the accounting and production managers.

QUESTIONNAIRE 1

Check ($\checkmark$) one answer for each question.   From: _____
                                                            Date: _____

1. Formal language

                                                            Yes   No
   a. Could you use the formal language to your own full satisfaction?
      If answer is no, to what extent did you feel inhibited by the required use of the formal language?
         strongly
         slightly
   b. Were you able to send the messages *essential* for effective performance?
   c. Would the firm's present performance be improved if you would not have to use the formal language, but you were still restricted to teletype communications only?
      If answer is yes, to what extent?
         strongly
         slightly
   d. Would the firm's present performance be improved if face-to-face meetings were allowed?

If answer is yes, to what extent?
strongly
slightly

2. Present performance of the firm

Yes   No

a. Do you find the present performance of the firm satisfactory?

b. Is further improvement of performance possible (under the given working conditions)? If answer is yes, how?

c. The instructions assign final responsibility for the firm's operations to the president. Should the president leave responsibility for individual decisions to his managers?

d. To what aspect of the operations did you pay most attention?

e. What are the firm's major problems at this point?

3. Performance of participants

How would you rate the performance of the participants with respect to:

	Pres.	Acct. Mgr.	Mark. Mgr.	Prod. Mgr.	Purch. Mgr.
a. Quality of communications (regarding *content*)					
Very good					
Good					
Medium					
Poor					
Very poor					
b. Quality of decision proposals					
Very good					
Good					
Medium					
Poor					
Very poor					

4. Comments:

QUESTIONNAIRE 2

Check (✓) one answer for each question. From: _____
Date: _____

1. Formal language

    Yes   No

   a. Did communications between team members improve during later periods?
   b. Would further improvement of communications lead to improvement of the firm's performance?
   —— if teletype communications, but not formal language, would be used.
   —— if face-to-face meeting were allowed
2. Present performance of the firm
   a. Do you find present performance of the firm satisfactory?
   b. Is further improvement of performance possible? (under the given working conditions)
   If answer is yes, how?
   c. To what aspects of the operations did you pay most attention?
   d. What are the firm's major problems at this point?
3. Performance of participants
   How would you rate the performance of the participants (since period 7) with respect to:

	Pres.	Acct. Mgr.	Mark. Mgr.	Prod. Mgr.	Purch. Mgr.
a. Quality of communications (regarding *content*)					
Very good					
Good					
Medium					
Poor					
Very poor					
b. Quality of decision proposals					
Very good					
Good					
Medium					
Poor					
Very poor					

4. Could you single out the
   team members to whose
   communication you paid
   extra attention? (or rank
   them? 1 = most, 5 = least)
5. Comments:

QUESTIONNAIRE 3

Check (√) your answers.   From: _____
                                                           Date: _____

	Acct. Mgr.	Prod. Mgr.

1. Was the face-to-face meeting beneficial to
   your understanding of the manager's view-
   point?
2. Rate the two presentations (1 and 2; 1 =
   preferred)
3. Do you agree with the manager's point of
   view?
4. Give your point of view on how the firm
   should operate:
5. Did you follow any team member's
   suggestions and/or decisions?

	Check if yes	Name manager

   a. to arrive at your decisions before
      the meeting
   b. to arrive at your decisions for
      period 13 and 14
   If you did *not* follow team member's suggestions, how did you arrive
   at your decisions?
6. Comments:

PROPOSAL-ADOPTION MEASURES D

The proposal-adoption measure D was defined in Section 3.8 as:

$$D_{jk} = \frac{1}{2} \sum_{\substack{i = \text{prod,} \\ \text{purch}}} \left[\text{Max.} \left\{ 1 - 10 \cdot \frac{|A_{ijk} - O_{ijk}|}{O_{ijk}}, \phi \right\} \right] \quad \text{if } |A - P|_i \geqq |O - P|_i$$
$$\text{for at least one } i$$
$$= 0 \qquad\qquad\qquad\qquad\qquad\quad \text{if } |A - P|_i < |O - P|_i$$
$$\text{for all } i$$

(The symbols are explained in the text, see p. 69.) The measure D was calculated for each product and each decision period. Its values are presented on the next two pages. The subjects are ordered according to the approach they received from the accounting manager and according to their classification on the basis of their opinion (ATLAS) and behavior (pitcher and coin) test results as illustrated in Figure A16.1.

Approach used by accounting manager	Subject's classification		Number of subjects in each category
	ATLAS-test	Pitcher + coin test	
Explicit understanding (code $A + C$)	Analytic	Analytic	4
		Heuristic	2
	Heuristic	Analytic	2
		Heuristic	9
Integral understanding (code B)	Analytic	Analytic	6
		Heuristic	3
	Heuristic	Analytic	3
		Heuristic	6

Figure A16.1

APPENDIX 16. PROPOSAL-ADOPTION-MEASURES D.

TEAM	A 3	5	7	9	11	13	B 3	5	7	9	11	13	C 3	5	7	9	11	13
AK	0.00	0.00	0.00	1.00	1.00	1.00	0.00	0.00	0.65	1.00	1.00	0.90	0.00	0.00	0.51	0.51	1.00	1.00
AL	0.00	0.02	0.00	0.07	0.83	1.00	0.29	0.15	0.51	0.95	0.31	0.95	0.00	0.00	0.00	0.15	3.51	1.00
CB	0.05	0.00	0.00	1.00	0.00	1.00	0.01	0.02	0.00	0.00	0.00	1.00	0.36	0.00	0.00	0.00	0.00	1.00
CE	0.17	0.31	0.00	1.00	0.00	0.41	0.75	0.65	0.55	0.99	0.65	1.00	0.00	0.00	0.00	0.51	0.00	0.00
CD	0.00	0.00	0.00	1.00	1.00	1.00	0.00	0.00	0.16	0.95	1.00	1.00	0.00	0.00	0.36	1.00	2.54	1.00
CH	0.00	0.02	0.00	0.00	0.00	1.00	0.00	0.00	0.00	0.00	0.00	1.00	0.00	0.00	0.00	0.00	0.00	1.00
AE	0.00	0.00	0.51	0.02	0.00	0.35	0.00	0.00	0.50	0.60	0.44	0.45	0.00	0.00	0.00	0.02	0.40	0.20
CK	0.00	0.00	0.00	0.00	0.00	1.00	0.00	0.00	0.00	0.02	0.00	1.00	0.00	0.00	0.00	0.00	0.00	0.00
AF	0.00	0.00	1.00	0.00	0.00	0.00	0.00	0.23	1.00	0.00	0.00	0.00	0.00	0.00	0.00	0.51	0.00	0.00
AG	0.00	0.00	0.00	0.00	0.00	0.00	0.00	0.00	0.00	0.00	0.00	0.00	0.00	0.36	0.27	0.00	0.00	0.00
AH	0.00	0.02	0.36	0.46	0.85	0.85	0.02	0.00	1.00	0.00	0.00	0.00	0.00	0.27	0.00	0.00	0.00	0.00
CC	0.00	0.00	0.17	1.00	1.00	1.00	0.02	0.00	0.93	0.85	0.95	1.00	0.02	0.00	0.00	0.00	0.38	1.00
CF	0.00	0.00	0.00	1.00	0.00	1.00	0.00	0.00	0.02	0.00	0.00	1.00	0.00	0.00	0.00	1.00	0.05	1.00
CG	0.00	0.00	0.00	0.00	0.71	0.00	0.00	0.00	0.00	0.02	0.00	0.30	0.00	0.00	0.00	0.00	0.00	1.00
CL	0.00	0.00	0.00	0.02	0.12	0.31	0.00	0.00	0.00	0.00	0.00	0.21	0.02	0.00	0.17	0.00	0.00	0.00
BB	0.00	0.02	1.00	0.51	1.00	1.00	0.00	0.00	1.00	1.00	1.00	1.00	0.00	0.00	1.00	0.00	0.56	0.56
BD	0.00	0.00	1.00	0.00	1.00	1.00	0.00	0.00	1.00	0.02	1.00	1.00	0.00	0.00	1.00	0.00	0.00	0.74
BU	0.05	0.59	0.71	0.95	0.00	0.00	0.01	0.02	0.99	0.45	1.00	0.76	0.00	0.36	0.02	0.00	1.00	1.00
BM	0.17	0.31	1.00	1.00	1.00	0.31	0.75	0.00	0.00	0.85	0.85	1.00	0.02	0.27	0.00	0.27	0.44	0.21
BR	0.00	0.00	0.00	1.00	1.00	1.00	0.02	0.00	1.00	1.00	1.00	1.00	0.00	0.00	1.00	1.00	0.64	1.00
BS	0.00	0.00	1.00	0.00	1.00	0.00	0.00	0.00	0.00	1.00	1.00	1.00	0.17	0.00	0.00	0.00	0.00	0.00
BA	0.00	0.00	0.00	1.00	0.00	1.00	0.00	0.00	0.00	0.00	0.00	0.00	0.00	0.00	1.00	0.00	0.00	1.00
BO	0.00	0.00	0.00	1.00	0.00	0.00	0.00	0.00	0.00	0.00	0.85	1.00	0.00	0.00	0.02	1.00	0.00	0.00
BP	0.00	0.00	0.00	0.00	0.00	0.00	0.00	0.00	0.00	0.00	0.00	0.00	0.00	0.00	1.00	1.00	0.00	0.00
BQ	0.00	0.02	1.00	1.00	0.00	1.00	0.00	0.00	1.00	1.00	0.00	1.00	0.00	0.00	1.00	0.00	0.64	1.00
BT	0.00	0.00	0.00	0.51	0.00	0.00	0.00	0.00	0.00	0.00	0.00	0.00	0.00	0.00	1.00	1.00	0.00	0.00
BU	0.00	0.02	0.00	1.00	1.00	1.00	0.02	0.00	0.07	1.00	1.00	1.00	0.17	0.00	0.00	1.00	0.64	1.00
BF	0.00	0.00	1.00	0.90	1.00	1.00	0.02	0.00	0.85	0.51	0.45	1.00	0.00	0.00	1.00	0.00	0.00	1.00
RG	0.02	0.00	1.00	1.00	1.00	1.00	0.00	0.00	1.00	0.95	0.95	0.95	0.00	0.00	1.00	0.00	0.16	0.16
BH	0.00	0.00	0.00	1.00	1.00	1.00	0.00	0.00	0.02	0.00	1.00	1.00	0.00	0.00	0.00	1.00	1.00	1.00
BK	0.00	0.00	0.00	1.00	1.00	0.00	0.00	0.00	0.00	1.00	1.00	1.00	0.02	0.00	0.02	1.00	1.00	1.00
BL	0.00	0.00	0.00	1.00	1.00	0.00	0.00	0.00	0.35	0.85	1.00	0.30	0.00	0.00	0.00	1.00	0.39	0.02
BN	0.00	0.00	1.00	1.00	0.00	0.00	0.00	0.00	1.00	1.00	1.00	1.00	0.00	0.17	1.00	1.00	0.69	0.00

APPENDIX 16. PROPOSAL-ADOPTION-MEASURES D.

D

TEAM	4	6	8	10	12	14
AK	0.00	0.00	0.00	0.00	0.00	1.00
AL	0.29	0.05	0.34	0.00	0.00	1.00
CB	0.64	0.00	0.00	0.00	0.00	1.00
CE	0.39	0.00	0.54	1.00	0.59	1.00
CD	0.05	0.00	0.00	0.88	0.83	1.00
CH	0.00	0.00	0.00	0.00	0.00	1.00
AE	0.00	0.10	0.00	0.00	0.00	0.35
CK	0.00	0.00	0.00	0.00	0.00	1.00
AF	0.00	0.00	0.00	0.74	0.00	0.00
AG	0.00	0.00	0.00	0.00	0.00	0.00
AH	0.23	0.67	0.00	0.99	0.00	0.31
CC	0.00	0.00	0.99	0.00	0.00	0.99
CF	0.00	0.00	0.00	0.00	0.00	1.00
CG	0.00	0.00	0.00	0.00	0.00	0.00
CU	0.00	0.00	0.00	0.00	0.00	0.00
CL	0.00	0.00	0.00	0.00	0.00	0.00
CM	0.00	0.00	0.00	0.00	0.00	0.29
BB	0.00	0.00	0.00	0.00	0.00	0.00
BD	0.00	0.00	0.00	1.00	0.00	0.00
BU	0.00	0.00	0.74	0.00	0.00	1.00
BM	0.84	0.83	0.39	0.79	0.93	0.53
BR	0.00	0.00	0.00	0.00	0.00	0.98
BS	0.00	0.00	0.00	1.00	0.93	0.95
BA	0.00	0.00	0.00	0.00	0.00	1.00
BD	0.00	0.00	0.00	1.00	0.00	0.00
BP	0.00	0.01	0.00	1.00	0.85	0.95
BQ	0.00	0.00	0.00	1.00	1.00	0.50
BT	0.00	0.00	0.00	0.00	0.00	0.00
BU	0.00	0.01	0.00	0.00	0.00	0.00
BF	0.00	0.00	0.00	1.00	0.00	0.50
BG	0.00	0.34	0.52	1.00	0.00	0.92
CH	0.00	0.75	0.00	0.94	0.00	0.88
BK	1.25	0.00	0.00	0.00	1.00	1.00
BL	0.20	0.00	0.00	0.00	0.00	0.00
BN	0.00	0.00	0.00	0.00	0.00	0.00

E

TEAM	4	6	8	10	12	14
AK	0.00	0.29	0.49	0.00	1.00	1.00
AL	0.00	0.00	0.31	0.00	1.00	1.00
CB	0.17	0.33	0.00	0.00	0.44	1.00
CE	0.44	0.00	0.93	0.69	0.44	0.49
CD	0.00	0.23	1.00	0.95	0.35	1.00
CH	0.31	0.00	0.36	0.00	0.00	0.55
AE	0.00	0.00	0.00	0.10	0.26	0.00
CK	0.00	0.00	0.36	0.46	1.00	1.00
AF	0.00	0.44	0.00	0.39	0.00	0.00
AG	0.00	0.43	0.00	0.00	0.00	0.00
AH	0.00	0.49	0.80	0.95	0.00	0.16
CC	0.00	0.00	0.95	0.95	0.95	1.00
CF	0.00	0.00	0.00	1.00	1.00	1.00
CG	0.00	0.00	0.00	0.45	1.00	1.00
CU	0.00	0.49	0.00	0.00	1.00	1.00
CL	0.00	0.30	0.31	0.41	0.89	0.79
CM	0.30	0.30	0.31	0.41	0.89	0.79
BB	0.00	0.74	0.78	0.00	0.00	0.00
BD	0.00	0.04	0.00	0.00	0.44	0.00
BU	0.00	0.44	0.02	1.00	1.00	0.29
BM	0.00	0.00	1.00	0.00	0.00	1.00
BR	0.00	0.00	0.00	0.00	0.50	0.50
BS	0.00	0.00	0.00	1.00	0.95	0.95
BA	0.00	0.00	1.00	0.00	1.00	1.00
BD	0.00	0.03	0.00	0.00	0.00	0.00
BP	0.00	0.02	0.04	1.00	1.00	1.00
BQ	0.00	0.03	1.00	0.80	1.00	0.00
BT	0.00	0.44	0.00	1.00	1.00	1.00
BU	0.30	0.03	0.04	1.00	1.00	1.00
BF	0.00	0.03	1.00	0.80	1.00	0.00
BG	0.00	0.44	0.00	1.00	1.00	0.35
CH	0.00	0.44	0.00	1.00	1.00	0.34
BK	0.44	0.00	0.02	0.95	1.00	1.00
BL	0.00	0.00	0.02	0.04	1.00	1.00
BN	0.00	0.44	0.47	0.44	0.89	1.00

F

TEAM	4	5	8	10	12	14
AK	0.29	0.50	0.00	0.00	1.00	1.00
AL	0.00	0.00	0.00	0.00	0.49	0.49
CB	0.00	0.50	0.00	0.51	0.00	1.00
CE	0.49	0.00	0.51	0.51	0.00	0.22
CD	0.00	0.00	1.00	1.00	0.71	1.00
CH	0.00	0.00	0.00	0.00	0.00	1.00
AE	0.00	0.00	0.49	0.00	0.00	0.05
CK	0.00	0.00	0.01	0.00	1.00	1.00
AF	0.00	0.00	0.00	0.01	0.00	0.00
AG	0.00	0.00	0.00	0.00	0.22	0.23
AH	0.00	0.20	0.00	1.00	0.00	0.06
CC	0.00	0.26	0.51	0.51	0.00	0.00
CF	0.00	0.00	0.51	1.00	1.00	0.00
CG	0.10	0.00	0.51	1.00	1.00	1.00
CU	0.00	0.00	0.00	0.00	0.71	1.00
CL	0.00	0.00	0.00	0.00	0.00	0.35
CM	0.00	0.00	0.00	0.00	0.00	0.00
BB	0.00	0.00	0.00	0.00	0.00	0.00
BD	0.00	0.00	0.00	0.00	0.00	0.23
BU	0.00	0.20	0.22	1.00	0.00	0.00
BM	0.03	0.00	1.00	0.00	0.55	0.55
BR	0.00	0.00	0.00	0.00	1.00	1.00
BS	0.15	0.00	0.00	0.00	0.71	0.00
BA	0.00	0.00	0.00	0.71	0.71	0.00
BD	0.00	0.47	0.98	0.00	0.49	1.00
BP	0.03	0.00	0.93	1.00	0.84	0.65
BQ	0.00	0.00	1.00	0.71	0.71	0.00
BT	0.00	0.00	0.93	0.43	0.43	0.51
BU	0.00	0.43	0.93	0.51	0.34	0.00
BF	0.00	0.00	0.00	0.71	0.71	0.00
BG	0.00	0.00	0.00	0.43	0.49	0.51
CH	0.03	0.00	0.00	0.51	0.51	0.00
BK	0.03	0.00	0.22	1.00	1.00	0.00
BL	0.15	0.00	0.51	1.00	1.00	1.00
BN	0.00	0.43	0.51	0.00	1.00	0.99

REFERENCES

[1] James H. Batchelor, *OR, an Annotated Bibliography*. St. Louis University Press, St. Louis, Missouri. Vol. 1, 1959 and Vol. 2, 1962.

[2] Paul Stillson, "Implementation of Problems in OR," *Operations Research*, Vol. 11-1, Jan.-Feb., 1963, p. 141.

[3] The American Management Association. Management Report #10, Finance Division: "OR Reconsidered," 1958.

[4] Richard B. Oldaker, *A Survey of OR Organizations in Selected U.S. Corporations.* Unpublished Master's thesis, Graduate School of Business Administration, University of California, Berkeley, January, 1966.

[5] Albert H. Rubinstein, Michael Radnor, Norman R. Baker, David R. Heiman, and John B. McColly, "Some Organizational Factors Related to the Effectiveness of Management Science Groups in Industry," *Management Science*, Vol. 13, No. 8, April, 1967, pp. B508–B578. Further references can be found in this article.

[6] Charles C. Schumacher, and Barnard E. Smith, "A Sample Survey of Industrial Operations-Research Activities II," *Operations Research*, Vol. 13-6, Nov.-Dec., 1965, pp. 1023–1027.

[7] McKinsey and Co., Inc., "A Limited Survey of Industrial Progress in OR," 1962; Reproduced in Learner, R. N., *The Management of Improvement*. Reinhold Publishing Co., New York, 1965.

[8] Harold F. Smiddy, "Planning, Anticipating and Managing," Address to the Seventh Annual Symposium on Long-Range Planning, The Institute of Management Sciences, May 21–22, 1964.

[9] Efraim Turban, *Some Determinants of the Use of Mathematical Models in Plant Maintenance.* Unpublished Ph.D. Thesis, University of California, Berkeley, June, 1966.

[10] Russel L. Ackoff, (ed.), *Progress in Operations Research*. John Wiley and Sons, New York, 1961. Chapter 1, pp. 3–34.

[11] Philip M. Morse, "OR—What Is It?" Proceedings of the First Seminar in Operations Research. Case Institute of Technology, November 8–10, 1951.

[12] A. Weston, (ed.), "The Emerging Role of I.E.," A summary report of I.E. symposia sponsored by the A.I.I.E." *The Journal of Industrial Engineering*, Vol. 12-2, part 2, March-April, 1961, pp. S3–S10.

[13] Russel L. Ackoff, with the collaboration of Shiv K. Gupta and J. Sayer Minas, *Scientific Method: Optimizing Applied Research Decisions*. John Wiley and Sons, New York, 1962, p. 426.

[14] C. C. Hermann, and J. F. Magee, "Operations Research for Management," *Harvard Business Review*, Vol. 31-4, July-Aug., 1953, p. 111.

[15] C. W. Churchman, and A. H. Schainblatt, "The Researcher and the Manager: A Dialectic of Implementation," *Management Science* Vol. 11-4, February, 1965, pp. B69-B87.

[16] D. G. Malcolm, "On the Need for Improvement in Implementation of OR," *Management Science*, Vol. 11-4, February, 1965, pp. 48–58.

[17] A. W. Gouldner, "Engineering and Clinical Approaches to Consulting" in Bennis, W. G., K. D. Benne and R. Chin (eds.), *The Planning of Change*. Holt, Rinehart and Winston, New York, 1961, pp. 643–653.

[18] Robert N. Lerner, *The Management of Improvement*. Reinhold Publishing Co., New York, 1965.

[19] Daniel Katz, and Robert L. Kahn, *The Social Psychology of Organizations*. John Wiley and Sons, New York, 1966, p. 249.

[20] Preston P. Le Breton, *General Administration: Planning and Implementation*. Holt, Rinehart and Weston, New York, 1965. Chapter 10, pp. 200–219.

[21] Floyd C. Mann, and Franklin W. Neff, *Managing Major Change in Organizations*. Report of meetings held in April and May 1959 under sponsorship of the Foundation for Research on Human Behavior. Braun and Brumfield, Ann Arbor, Michigan, 1961, pp. 55–56.

[22] G. D. Creelman, and R. W. Wallen, "The Place of Psychology in Operations Research," *Operations Research*, Vol. 6-1, Jan.-Feb., 1958, p. 119.

[23] Amitai Etzioni, and Eva Etzioni (eds.), *Social Change*. Basic Books, Inc., New York, 1964.

[24] Kurt, Lewin, *Field Theory in Social Science*. Harper, New York, 1951.

[25] Morton Deutsch, "Field Theory in Social Psychology" in Lindzey, G. (ed.), *Handbook of Social Psychology*, Addison-Wesley Publishing Co., Inc., Reading, Mass., 3d printing, 1959, pp. 181–222.

[26] L. Festinger, *Theory of Cognitive Dissonance*. Row-Peterson, Evanston, Ill., 1957.

[27] Leon Festinger, and Elliot Aronson, "The Arousal and Reduction of Dissonance in Social Contexts," Cartwright, Dorwin and Alvin Zander (eds.), *Group Dynamics* (ref. 28), p. 215.

[28] Dorwin Cartwright, and Alvin Zander (eds.), *Group Dynamics*. Row, Peterson and Co., Evanston, Ill., 2nd ed., 1960.

[29] Carl I. Hovland, and Milton J. Rosenberg (eds.), *Attitude Organization and Change*. Yale Studies in Attitude and Communication, Vol. 3. Yale University Press, New Haven, 1960.

[30] Carl I. Hovland, (ed.), *The Order of Presentation in Persuasion*. Yale Studies in Attitude and Communication, Vol. 1. Yale University Press, New Haven, 1957.

[31] Carl I. Hovland, Irving L. Janis and Harold H. Kelley, *Communication and Persuasion*. Yale University Press, New Haven, 1953.

[32] E. D. Chapple, and L. R. Sayles, *The Measure of Management*. Macmillan, New York, 1961.

[33] R. F. Bales, *Interaction Process Analysis*. Addison-Wesley, Cambridge, Mass. 1950.

[34] Eliot D. Chapple, "Quantitative Analysis of Complex Organizational Systems," *Human Organization*, Vol. 21-2, 1962, pp. 67–87.

[35] Chris Argyris, *Organization and Innovation*. Richard D. Irwin, Inc. and the Dorsey Press. Homewood, Ill. 1965.

[36] Leonard R. Sayles, "The Change Process in Organizations: an Applied Anthropology Analysis," *Human Organization*, Vol. 21-2, 1962, pp. 67–87.

[37] L. P. Bradford, J. R. Gibb, and K. D. Benne, *T-Group Theory and Laboratory Method*. John Wiley and Sons, Inc., New York, 1964.

[38] Matthew B. Miles, "The Training Group" in: *The Planning of Change*. Warren G. Bennis, Kenneth D. Benne, Robert Chin (eds.). Holt, Rinehart and Winston, New York, 1961, p. 720.

[39] Harold H., Kelley, and John W. Thibaut, "Experimental Studies of Group Problem Solving and Process" in: *Handbook of Social Psychology*, G. Lindzey (ed.). Addison-Wesley Publishing Co., Inc., Reading, Mass., 3rd printing 1959, pp. 735–786.

[40] W. J. H. Sprott, *Human Groups*. (Penguin Books) Cox and Wyman, Ltd., London. 2nd printing 1962, pp. 106–160.

[41] Dorwin Cartwright, "Achieving Change in People: Some Applications of Group Dynamics Theory," *Human Relations*, Vol. 4-4, 1951, pp. 381–392.

[42] Kurt Lewin, *Resolving Social Conflicts*. Ed. by G. W. Lewin, Harper-Row, New York, 1948.

[43] F. Roethlisberger, and W. J. Dickson, *Management and the Worker*. Harvard University Press, Cambridge, Mass., 1939.

[44] Alfred J. Marrow, and John R. P. French, Jr., "Changing a Stereotype in Industry," *Journal of Social Issues*, Vol. 2-1, 1945, pp. 33-37.

[45] Paul R. Lawrence, "How to deal with resistance to change," Harvard Business Review, May-June, 1954.

[46] Lester Coch, and John R. P. French, Jr.: "Overcoming resistance to change, "Human Relations," Vol. 1, no. 4, 1948, 512.

[47] E. B. Bennett, "Discussion, Decision, Commitment, and Consensus in Group Decision," *Human Relations*, Vol. 8-3, 1955, pp. 251–273.

[48] S. E. Asch, "Effects of Group Pressure upon the Modification and Distribution of Judgments," in *Readings in Social Psychology*. T. M. Newcomb and E. L. Hartley (eds.). N.Y., Holt, 1952, pp. 174–183.

[49] George C. Homans, *The Human Group*. Harcourt, Brace and World, Inc., New York, 1950.

[50] George C. Homans, *Social Behavior: Its Elementary Forms*. Harcourt, Brace and World, Inc., New York, 1961, pp. 83–111.

[51] Floyd C. Mann, "Studying and Creating Change: A Means to Understanding Social Organization." Research in Industrial Human Relations, Industrial Relations Research Association, Publication No. 17, 1957.

[52] E. L. Trist, G. W. Higgin, H. Murray, and A. B. Pollock, *Organizational Choice*. Tavistock Publications, London, 1963.

[53] E. L. Trist, and K. W. Bamforth, "Some Social and Psychological Consequences of the Long-wall Method of Coal-getting," *Human Relations*, Vol. 4-1, 1951, pp. 3-38.

[54] A. K. Rice, *Productivity and Social Organization: The Ahmedabad Experiment*. Tavistock Publications, London, 1958.

[55] Everett M. Rogers, *Diffusion of Innovations*. The Free Press of Glencoe, New York, 1962.

[56] Peter M. Blau, "A Theory of Social Integration," *American Journal of Sociology*, 65, 1960, pp. 545–556.

[57] Victor H. Vroom, *Some Personality Determinants of the Effects of Participation*. Prentice-Hall, Inc., Englewood Cliffs, N.J., 1959.

[58] L. Festinger, S. Schachter, and K. Back, *Social Pressures in Informal Groups*. Harper, New York, 1950.

[59] Eli Ginzberg, and Ewing W. Reilley, *Effecting Change in Large Organizations*. Columbia University Press, 1957.

[60] Warren G. Bennis, *Changing Organizations*. McGraw-Hill Book Co., 1966, pp. 85–91.

[61] A. Vazsonyi, "OR in Production Control," *Operations Research*, Vol. 4-1, Feb. 1956, pp. 19–31.

[62] R. L. Ackoff, "Unsuccessful Case Studies and Why," *Operations Research*, Vol. 8-2, March-April, 1960, pp. 259–263.

[63] Foster Weldon, "Cargo Containerization in the West Coast-Hawaiian Trade," *Operations Research*, Vol. 6-5, 1958, pp. 649–670. Comments on this study in: Kuffel, Michael P., "Implementation of OR Solutions," unpublished Master's thesis, Graduate School of Business Administration, University of California, Berkeley, April, 1963.

[64] C. West Churchman, "Case Histories Five Years After—a Symposium," *Operations Research*, Vol. 8-2, March-April, 1960, pp. 254–259.

[65] Harry T. Hicks, "An Analysis of Southern Pacific's Boxcar Information System and the Causes of its Failure," unpublished Master's thesis, Graduate School of Business Administration, University of California, Berkeley, December, 1959.

[66] David W. Miller, and Martin K. Starr, *Executive Decisions and Operations Research*. Prentice-Hall, Inc., Englewood Cliffs, N.J., 1960, pp. 415–434.

[67] David H. Stimson, *Research and Implementation*. Internal Working Paper No. 27, Space Sciences Laboratory, University of California, Berkeley, May, 1965, p. 16.

[68] C. West Churchman, "Managerial Acceptance of Scientific Recommendations," *California Management Review*, Fall 1964.

[69] Philburn Ratoosh, and C. West Churchman, "Innovation in Group Behavior," Center for Research in Management Science, University of California, Berkeley. Working Paper No. 10, January, 1960.

[70] C. West Churchman, and Philburn Ratoosh, "Report on Further Implementation Experiments," Center for Research in Management Science, University of California, Berkeley. Working Paper No. 26, March, 1961.

[71] Juergen Mueller, "The Influence of Sociometric Status on the Implementation of Change," Master's thesis, University of California, Berkeley, 1965.

[72] C. W. Churchman, "On the Intercomparison of Utilities." Essay 15 in: "The Structure of Economic Science," Essays on Methodology, Sherman Roy Krupp (ed.). Prentice-Hall, Inc., Englewood-Cliffs, N.J., 1966, pp. 243–257.

[73] Richard M. Cyert, and James G. March, *A Behavioral Theory of the Firm*. Prentice-Hall, Inc., Englewood Cliffs, N.J., 1963.

[74] Alex Bavelas, and George Strauss, "Group Dynamics and Intergroup Relations," W. F. Whyte, Melville Dalton, *et al.*, *Money and Motivation*. Harper and Brothers, New York, 1955, pp. 90–96.

[75] Herbert C. Kelman, "Processes of Opinion Change," *Public Opinion Quarterly*, Vol. 25, 1961, pp. 57–78.

[76] Brice Ryan, and Neal C. Gross, *Acceptance and Diffusion of Hybrid Corn Seed in Two Iowa Communities*. Ames, Iowa Agricultural Experiment Station Research Bulletin 372, 1950.

[77] R. R. Blake, J. S. Mouton, L. B. Barnes, and L. E. Greiner, "Breakthrough in Organization Development," *Harvard Business Review*, Vol. 42, 1964, pp. 133–155.

[78] J. March, and H. Simon, *Organizations*. John Wiley and Sons, Inc., New York, 1958.

[79] William I. Spencer, Vice President, First National City Bank, New York, in an address, "Plandemonium: The Art and the Artifice," at the Planning Conference, Stanford Research Institute, San Francisco. Quotation from "Notable & Quotable," *Wall Street Journal*, Sept. 29, 1966.

[80] Leona E. Tyler, The Psychology of Human Differences, Appleton-Century-Crofts, Inc., N.Y., 1956, Chapter 9, pp. 221–244.

[81] Samuel Messick, and John Ross (eds.), Measurement in Personality and Cognition, Part III: Stylistic Consistencies in Cognition, pp. 171–215, John Wiley and Sons, Inc., N.Y., 1962.

[82] H. A. Witkin, H. B. Lewis, M. Hertzman, K. Machover, P. B. Meissner, and S. Wapner, Personality through Perception, Harper, N.Y., 1954.

[83] John Erwin Roy, and James G. Miller, "The Acquisition and Application of Information in the Problem-Solving Process: An Electronically Operated Logical Test," *Behavioral Science*, Vol. 2-4, Oct. 1957, pp. 291–300.

[84] B. K. Rome, and S. C. Rome, "Leviathan: An Experimental Study of Large Organizations with the Aid of Computers." Report TM-744 of the System Development Corporation, Santa Monica, California (this is one of a series of reports).

[85] A. D. Hoggatt, "Measuring the Cooperativeness of Behavior in Quantity Variation Duopoly Games," *Behavioral Science*, Vol. 12-2, March 1967, pp. 109–121.

[86] B. K. Rome, and S. C. Rome, "The Leviathan Technique for Effecting and Monitoring Live-Artificial Communications." Report FM-761 of the System Development Corporation, Santa Monica, California.

[87] Paul A. Hare, "Computer Simulation of Interaction in Small Groups," *Behavioral Science*, Vol. 6-4, July 1961, p. 261.

[88] Bert F. Green, Alice K. Wolf, Carol Chomsky, and Kenneth Laughery, "Baseball: An Automatic Question Answerer," *Computers and Thought*, E. A. Feigenbaum and J. Feldman (eds.), pp. 207–216.

[89] G. W. Allport, Attitudes: A Handbook of Social Psychology, C. Murchison (ed.), 1935, Worcester, Mass., Clark University Press, p. 798.

[90] Martin Gardner (ed.), Mathematical Puzzles of Sam Loyd, Parts I and II, Dover Publications, Inc., N.Y., 1960, I-52, p. 50, I-108, p. 106, and II-23, p. 7.

[91] A. Luchins, "Mechanization in Problem Solving: The Effect of Einstellung," Psychological Monograph 54, No. 248, 1942.

[92] Andrew C. Stedry, Budget Control and Cost Behavior, Prentice-Hall, Inc., Englewood Cliffs, N.J., 1960, p. 63.

[93] Harold Guetzkow, and Lloyd Jensen, "Research Activities on Simulated International Processes," *Background, Journal of the International Studies Association*, Feb. 1966, Vol. 9-4, pp. 267–271.

[94] Sidney Siegel, Nonparametric Statistics for the Behavioral Sciences, McGraw Hill, N.Y., 1956.

[95] Lee J. Cronbach, Essentials of Psychological Testing, 2nd ed., Harper and Brothers, N.Y., 1960, pp. 96–123.

[96] V. P. Bhapkar, "Some Nonparametric Tests for the Multivariate Several Sample Location Problem," Institute of Statistics Mimeo Series, No. 415, Univ. of North Carolina, Dec. 1964, p. 4.

[97] Rupert G. Miller, Simultaneous Statistical Inference, McGraw Hill Book Co., N.Y., 1966.

[98] Amnon Rapoport, "Variables Affecting Decisions in a Multistage Inventory Task," *Behavioral Science*, Vol. 12, 1967, pp. 194–204.

[99] Gordon W. Allport, "What Units Shall We Employ?" in Lindzey, Gardner (ed.), *Assessment of Human Motives*, Rinehart & Co., N.Y., 1958, pp. 239–258.

[100] B. E. Wynne, Sr., "A Pattern for Reporting Operations Research to the Business Executive," Address to the Seventh International Meeting of TIMS, New York City, Oct. 1960.

[101] E. Spranger, Types of Men (Trans. by P. J. W. Pigors), Niemyer, Niemyer, Halle, 1928.

[102] G. W. Allport, P. E. Vernon, and G. Lindzey, Study of Values (rev. ed.), Houghton, Boston, 1951.

[103] Jacob Marschak, "Actual Versus Consistent Decision Behavior," *Behavioral Science*, Vol. 9-2, April 1964, pp. 103–110.

[104] Henry A. Landsberger, "The Horizontal Dimension in Bureaucracy," *Administrative Science Quarterly*, Dec. 1961, pp. 299–332.

[105] Donald F. Heany, "Is TIMS Talking to Itself?" *Management Science*, Vol. 12-4, Dec. 1965, pp. B146–B155.

INDEX